Praise for Take Captive Every Thought

"*Take Captive Every Thought* is a comprehensive book on the spiritual, mental, emotional, and physical realities of spiritual warfare. Packed with Scripture, it is a roadmap for how Christians can successfully fight against the schemes of the enemy by pursuing Jesus and His Word. An incredible resource for teachers and those who enjoy studying the Bible." —J. Dewald, Associate Pastor

"*Take Captive Every Thought* is a gripping compendium of the earthly struggle of good versus evil, and the very real corresponding battle in the spiritual realm. Backed by accurate scriptural documentation, the reader learns a practical approach to blocking evil worldly and spiritual influences, to live a more Christ-like existence. You will enjoy this captivating read. 5 out of 5 stars." —Dr. G. Vahjen

"The last few months have been rough and filled with interruptions outside my control as well as all the people telling me what I should be doing regarding all the above. Naturally, I initially blamed myself for not having control of those issues, so the guilt was intense. Now that I'm working through this awesome book, I am hypersensitive to what the devil is doing (or trying to do). Women say awful things to themselves (mom guilt, business owner guilt, busy daughter of an elderly mother who needs more time, etc.). I fight those voices like any middle-aged, professional woman does, but now I'm realizing that the unusually harsh voice isn't mine, and the interruptions aren't all my fault. They emanate from our enemy, Satan. I have had a blast learning from Jeff Rowe and feel lighter, yet I also feel heavily and confidently armed for battle." —J. D., Business Owner and Parent

"I was privileged to serve as a confidante and content editor as Jeff was writing Take Captive Every Thought. I know Jeff to be a strong Christian leader of great character and wisdom. He's been blessed with a powerful and "on-point" message from God that will benefit any Christian struggling to understand the depths of spiritual warfare and attain victory in their walk with the Lord. The completed work is something every Christian should read." —T. Massey

"Take Captive Every Thought is a must read in today's troubled times and directly confronts a vital subject that is often avoided or overlooked by the Church. This deep dive into spiritual warfare is a real wakeup call vividly describing the very real battle we are all in whether we realize or not. The book lays out the biblical basis for spiritual warfare as part of the eternal struggle between good and evil. In addition, our role in this struggle is made clear by showing why we have no choice but to participate in the struggle. Written in an easy-to-read style without overly complicated language, the book also incorporates scripture where appropriate to support the case being made by the author. In addition, the scripture is included in the text, so the reader doesn't have to constantly switch between the book and a bible to look up a scriptural reference. Reading Take Captive Every Thought is one of the best ways to ensure you and those you love are fully aware of Satan's plan to bring down God's Eternal Kingdom and the role you can and must play in that struggle."—J. Irwin

"Take Captive Every Thought is a well written book discussing the reality of Spiritual Warfare, a reality not often addressed in Christian literature. For the writer to have been able to write this work, when, as he states early in the writing, he is not formally trained with no seminary experience, makes it obvious that the Holy Spirit has worked through him in this writing. I too am just an untrained follower of Jesus Christ and I whole heartedly recommend this book to all who want to deepen their understanding of this vitally important subject." —R. Morton

"If you are curious about how the powers of darkness are working to kill, steal, and destroy the sanctity of our families, churches, communities, and our country, "Take Captive Every Thought" is a comprehensive and easy to read Bible study about how the enemy is successfully waging war against us, and the very souls of the ones we love. More importantly we learn from God's Word how to arm ourselves to defend and win the battle. Each scripture referenced is included with the commentary so there is never any doubt about God's directions and his desire to help us win. If you are a new Christian, or a trained leader in your church, you will find help and reassurance within these pages." —A. Deitz

"WOW, I am awestruck by what I'm reading and annoyed that this has never been taught to me before in such a direct way. I was baptized at age sixteen, and I have needed this insightful, clearcut, liberating information since then. It's scary to recognize when the devil is trying to hurt you or pull you away from God's intentions, but now having that awareness is empowering. Every Christian should read this book, but my prayer is that non-Christians find it as well. THANK YOU, Jeff Rowe, for listening to God and following all those hints to write this book! Your timing, in my life, was PERFECT." —J. C. Dyer, Christian Author

"Take Captive Every Thought explains the role Satan takes to not only deceive us but also to rob us of the peace and joy we can find in Christ. An excellent book giving the Christian insight and understanding of how important it is to be aware and sensitive to how one should stand against the devil's attacks. A must read!" —D. Eastham

"Whether you are a new believer of the Christian faith or you have been a believer your entire life, this divinely inspired book will equip you to face the daily onslaught of the attacks from the "evil" one - Satan himself." —J. Burke

Take Captive Every Thought

A Layman's Victory
Over the Realities of Spiritual Warfare

Jeff A. Rowe

Cover design by Bob Gurgul, bob@e4dcreate.com
Author website: www.takeeverythoughtcaptive.com
Follow on Facebook @takeeverythoughtcaptive

Paperback ISBNs 978-1-958533-15-4, 978-1-958533-17-8
Hardcover ISBNs 978-1-958533-16-1, 978-1-958533-18-5

Library of Congress Control Number: 2022923105

Printed in the United States of America

Take Captive Every Thought

A Layman's Victory
Over the Realities of Spiritual Warfare

Preface

I was thirty-four years old when I accepted Jesus Christ as my personal Lord and Savior. This book is the result of a process God started that moment. Following in the footsteps of believers worldwide, I read and was fascinated by all the stories in the Bible, especially since God called on ordinary people to carry out His extraordinary plans. I just never imagined I would be one of those people.

After ten years of dedicated research, it took me five years to write, edit, and publish this manuscript. The result is a well-documented Bible study on spiritual warfare, but little did I know that writing the book would be the easy part. You see, I know I am a somebody in God's eyes, but what I discovered in trying to advance God's agenda is that I was a nobody in most publishers' eyes. After all, I am not famous, this is my first book, and the topic is not mainstream Christian fare. Additionally, I did not have a detailed plan for how to sell the first 5,000 copies.

Regardless, this book is an attempt to share a message inspired by the Holy Spirit and desperately needed by Christians of every denomination and at any level of maturity. With faith and gratitude to God, and despite being a "nobody" in the publishing world, I persevered so that God's message could be delivered *through* me and *for* you. If you long for a deeper understanding of the spiritual battle for your soul, then I trust you will benefit from this much needed lifestyle training.

I walked through numerous trials as I matured in my faith, and I discovered that encountering challenges is typical for those whom God has called into His service. In the Bible, the story of King David certainly attests to this truth. While God consistently refers to the king as a "man after my own heart," there was no shortage of obstacles for David to overcome before or after he was appointed as ruler over the nation of Israel.

The story of King David is a fascinating narrative, one that concludes with David passing the baton of leadership to his son Solomon. Before the end of his reign, David's deep desire was to build a temple worthy of God's presence as represented in the Ark of the Covenant. However, God forbade David from building the temple. Instead, He chose David's son Solomon to follow in David's footsteps as king and be responsible for the project.

As the story continues, we are given insight to the extreme detail of the plans David passed down to his son, including the exact dimensions of the temple, all the surrounding rooms, the storehouses for the holy items, and the weight of all the gold and silver needed for the temple's ornaments. In reading the saga of King David, you may or may not remember these verses.

> Then David gave his son Solomon the plans for the portico of the temple, its buildings, its storerooms, its upper parts, its inner rooms, and the place of atonement. [12] He gave him the plans of all that the Spirit had put in his mind. (1 Chronicles 28:11-12[a]) (NIV)

The significance of Verse 12 is the proclamation that all God had revealed in David's mind was inspired by the Holy Spirit. I can tell you with all humility, and before we venture any further, that the entire scope and depth of this book has been an inspiration by the Holy Spirit. It was God who developed this rare interest in spiritual warfare within me, and as I continued to read the Bible, I began to catalog Scripture verses that had anything to do with the topic. Years later, with almost eight full pages of Old and New Testament Scripture and a basic outline of the pathway to spiritual victory, God began to encourage me to write about the subject.

Like Moses, I resisted at first and offered many excuses for why "I" couldn't do it. Over time, I would occasionally grant the idea casual consideration, but I continued to oppose God's prompting. After sidestepping the issue for as long as He would allow, I was given a rather obvious nudge to begin this journey (more about that later). To me, His was a clear directive. God was not interested in my ability or my spiritual intellect. He was interested in my availability. I would not be writing this material, He would. I just needed to say yes, sit down at my computer, and start the process. God would do the rest!

> *But the Advocate, the Holy Spirit, whom the Father will send in my name, will teach you all things and will remind you of everything I have said to you.* (John 14:26)

Just as Verse 12 from 1 Chronicles records God's governance in the life of King David, the verse above applies to this project. Now that the book is finished, I must tell you it has been an amazing journey to experience God working through me. I hope that the information shared in this study will be helpful, but trust me, the process of weaving eight pages of individual Scripture verses into a coherent and valid thesis is something only God could have accomplished. Without any previous experience as a writer or author, I trust the inspiration of the Holy Spirit will be self-evident as you progress through the chapters.

In the Bible, as you near the end of Chapter 28 in 1 Chronicles, David records the following in Verse 19. "All this, I have in writing as a result of the LORD's hand on me, and he enabled me to understand all the details of the plan." Like King David, I too am humbled that God had enabled me to understand all the details of His plan, and equally grateful for all He has revealed through this completed study.

Inspired by the Holy Spirit.
Penned by His faithful servant.

To God be the glory!

Acknowledgements

First and foremost, I give all praise and honor and glory to Almighty God, to Jesus Christ, my personal Lord and Savior, and to the unique inspiration of the Holy Spirit. This project was divinely inspired from start to finish, and I take no credit other than answering the call to obediently follow God's prompting.

Secondly, this project could not have been completed without the encouragement, patience, and prayer support of my wife, Delena Kay (DeeDee). For more than five years, she gave me the freedom to retire to my home office right after dinner each night as well as valuable weekend time to work on this project. She was my sounding board and proofreader as each chapter was completed. She prayed diligently for me as Satan repeatedly tried to dissuade this effort. She even managed the audio-visual equipment during our trial run at teaching this study. I am forever grateful for her love and support and thank God for her devotion to her faith and for living out the example of a Proverbs 31 wife.

My thanks to Dr. Mike Watson (currently Disciple Life Pastor at Hillcrest Baptist Church in Enterprise, Alabama). While at First Baptist Concord in Knoxville, Tennessee, Mike was gracious enough to review my notes, discuss my thesis, and then encourage me to begin writing. Mike also took the time to serve as initial editor upon completion of the first two chapters and was instrumental in making sure the material was biblically accurate, setting the standard for the rest of the book.

Upon Mike's departure, I enlisted the help of several other proofreaders. These were men and women I knew to be steadfast in their faith, mature in their understanding of the Bible, and therefore I trusted them to provide honest feedback regarding my desire to maintain biblical accuracy throughout the project.

- Jerry and Linda Johnson
- Tom and Vanessa Massey
- Dr. Glen Vahjen

My sincere gratitude to Jamie Dewald (Associate Pastor at First Baptist Concord), Jeff Irwin, and Don Cook. These dear friends took the time to read the completed first draft in its entirety and offer their help with copy editing and content suggestions.

I'm also grateful to the pastoral staff at First Baptist Concord for extending the invitation to lead multiple Bible studies based on the information provided in this book. It was an honor to be asked, and those who attended provided encouragement that the material was indeed something that could benefit all Christians.

The book cover was created by Bob Gurgul. Bob and I have known each other since we were five years old. He is a talented graphic artist and college professor. He was my first and only choice for this project, and I was thrilled when he agreed to work with us. The cover design speaks for itself.

Finally, I need to thank Jody Dyer, the entrepreneur behind Crippled Beagle Publishing. She was willing to take a risk on this first-time author and coached us to a remarkable finished product.

My heartfelt appreciation to these wonderful brothers and sisters in Christ.

Table of Contents

Chapter 1: What Have I Been Missing?

At 6:00 AM, long before the sun would rise that winter morning, I sat, quietly, all alone in my home office. I remember thinking, *Why isn't this working? What have I been missing?* While still a baby Christian, I had been sincere in practicing my faith, reading the Bible, and pursuing my relationship with God, but my life seemed to be spiraling in the wrong direction. My business was faltering, my finances were in distress, and my home was in turmoil. I stood at a critical crossroad early in my Christian journey. I questioned, *Do I take the road of least resistance and return to running my own life, or do I dig deeper to unlock the promises of my salvation?*

My desire to learn and grow in the Lord was genuine, but all the aspects of my life that I hoped would and expected to improve once I accepted Christ continued to unravel. So, the questions kept coming. *Why does this walk with God seem so mysterious at times? Isn't there a* Cliffs Notes *version to understanding God's truth and garnering His blessings? What will it take to turn the corner and improve my circumstances?*

In reality, the answers I sought had been right in front of me the whole time. Jesus promises us in the Bible; "Ask and it will be given to you; seek and you will find; knock and the door will be opened to you. For everyone who asks receives; the one who seeks finds; and to the one who knocks, the door will be opened" (Matthew 7:7-8). I decided to take Him at his word and made the decision to be more consistent in searching the Bible for answers.

What I discovered turned out to be a major turning point in my life. The experience transformed a former pathway to frustration and eventual defeat into an unexpected revelation. **I had been focused on only half the story!** Oddly enough, not until I uncovered what the Bible taught about evil, (its source, its tactics, and its agenda), could I genuinely pursue a victorious Christian lifestyle. For me, unveiling the complete truth and application of Scripture was supported by probing and understanding the depths of spiritual warfare. I now believe this to be true for all God's children.

If you identify as a Christian, of any denomination, and in any location around the globe, this may be one of the most important books you will ever read (other than the Bible). I know that is a bold statement considering the volumes of Christian literature available for those eager to advance in their faith. However, the topic of spiritual warfare is arguably the most neglected subject on Christian bookshelves today, and in my opinion, also lacks the proper merit from the pulpit.

Note: *If you identify with another world faith or as an agnostic or atheist, the principles outlined in this book still apply to you. Spiritual warfare is like gravity. It exists whether you choose to believe in it or not, and it will affect the outcome of your life.*

For my Christian brothers and sisters, if you have not done so before, ask yourself this question; when is the last time you heard a sermon series on spiritual warfare? I accepted Jesus Christ as my personal Lord and Savior at the age of thirty-four, and at the writing of this book, have been faithfully attending church under the Southern Baptist banner for twenty-eight years. My answer to that question is that I can't remember a single time this topic has been given appropriate acknowledgment from the pulpit. Has it been mentioned? Yes, but never taught in depth. What this book will address is the multitude of problems spiritual warfare creates for the bride of Christ (the church), of which you are a member.

You see, the Bible is a compilation of exciting history, intense stories, and marvelous truth woven around one eternal conflict: **good vs. evil**. Christians are often well trained in God's righteousness (the good); however, our enlistment in God's army places us at enmity with an unseen but real adversary, Satan (the source of all evil). This evil presents itself in the second chapter of Genesis and remains prevalent to the twentieth chapter of Revelation. I John 3:8 tells us, "The reason the Son of God appeared was to destroy the devil's work," yet few Christians know how Satan attacks, how to engage the enemy in battle, or how to ultimately win the war.

If you read your Bible (and that is a big *if* for many Christians) there is perhaps no stronger reference to this opposing spiritual kingdom than in Ephesians Chapter 6. Verse 10 starts a section titled "The Armor of God," and the subsequent verses serve as key reference points in understanding our spiritual battles.

> *Finally, be strong in the Lord and in his mighty power. Put on the full armor of God, so that you can take your stand against the devil's schemes. **For our struggle is not against flesh and blood, but against the rulers, against the authorities, against the powers of this dark world and against the spiritual forces of evil in the heavenly realms.*** (Ephesians 6:10-12)

Even though this message was written centuries ago by the apostle Paul to an infant church body, the same is true for us and the world we live in. Many of us as new believers, including me, are not only ignorant of this spiritual battle taking place all around us but also that it affects all of humanity. The full maturity necessary to see and understand the things that Paul knew to be true takes time and deep spiritual discernment. However, the importance of Paul's message in Ephesians is just as vital to us and our world today as it was to the church in Ephesus. Consider for a minute this reference from the *Layman's Bible Commentary Set.*

There is a tendency in modern society to dismiss evil spirits as incompatible with a scientific and sophisticated view of reality. Consequently, the devil has become the subject of jokes and cartoons rather than given serious consideration. Even among many evangelical Christians there is a reluctance to express belief in Satan as a personal being. However, the Bible is very clear about the reality of evil spirits and weaves that teaching into the sum and substance of its doctrine.

If one is to dismiss such biblical teachings about the devil, is it not also necessary to do the same for all teachings about the spiritual realm? If there is no devil, why should we believe there are angels? And if we rule out the devil and angels, why should we think there is a heaven or hell?

If we question the teachings of Jesus about Satan, do we also question the other things he taught? And how do we explain the foolishness, empty pride, cruelty, and selfishness of human beings that exceed anything else found in the animal kingdom? Like it or not, what the Bible says about Satan is important to a complete understanding of human and spiritual reality. [1]

Stop for a minute and read that last sentence again. The entire purpose of this study is an attempt to offer a "complete understanding of human ___and___ spiritual reality" by describing our plight and exposing the enemy's battle plan. You see, most people consider themselves physical beings searching for some kind of spiritual pragmatism, while the minority doesn't believe in the spiritual facet of life at all. The truth is, God created us as body, soul (mind), and spirit. ("Now may the God of peace Himself sanctify you completely; and may your whole spirit, soul, and body be preserved blameless at the coming of our Lord Jesus Christ" 1 Thessalonians 5:23.)

You are a spirit, living in a body, that has a soul. Your body is the physical manifestation of God's creation, your earth suit. It interacts with the material world through your five senses. Your spirit interacts with God and the spiritual realm through its own set of "senses," things like prayer, faith, hope, and worship. The soul gives your body life and vitality. It functions as the command center and is responsible for inspiration, perception, memory, emotions, and your will (all functions of the mind). The soul is the realm of decision and where your free will is exercised. **It is the line of communication from the spiritual realm to the physical realm and can only act on the influence received through the Spirit or through the body.** As a result, the soul of a believer can choose to walk in the Spirit or walk in the flesh. In a stubborn heart possessed by those without influence from the Holy Spirit, the soul is where Satan operates by making his appeal to the affections, desires, and emotions of mankind.

It is our spirit that is trapped in this temporal environment while waiting to return to our ultimate and eternal spiritual home (heaven or hell). Why is it so vitally important that we understand this battle for our souls (our minds)? Let me try to explain the challenge we Christians face by using an analogy. Since sports touch so many lives around the globe in one way or another, I will use a sports analogy. Imagine, as a gifted and aspiring athlete, you have been selected by your favorite professional sports team. In your first training camp they teach you the history of the organization, they boast about their winning culture, they introduce you to the coaches and top team players, and they highlight their patriarchs' retired jerseys. In preparation for league competition, they explain every aspect of the playbook and attend to your physical and emotional training.

Sounds good so far, doesn't it? But wait. What if minimal attention is given to studying the opposing teams or there is a complete lack of focus on your fiercest division rival? What if you never watch any game film, never study other teams' top players, and know nothing of the opposition's culture? How many competitive encounters do you think you would win? How long would you persevere if you quickly developed a losing record? More importantly, would your personal or team performance have any lasting influence on your intended audience? Are you beginning to understand the challenge?

I taught a Bible study based on the spiritual warfare material in this book. A retired defense lawyer attended. As the class began, I asked him what the outcome for his client might be if, in preparation for the trial, his legal team was denied access to the evidence gathered by the prosecuting attorneys. Without hesitation, he replied, "We'd get killed in the courtroom" (meaning they would lose the case badly). The same premise holds true in practically every profession and almost every aspect of our lives, including our walks as Christians.

If we lay claim to that title, we need to know both sides of the equation. We can't expect to win, we can't expect to walk daily in victory, and we can't expect to be the light of Christ to a lost and dying world if we know and understand only one half of what the Bible teaches. Returning to the sports analogy, we cannot play or win a game without knowing the rules that govern the game. Similarly, though the spiritual battle for our souls is not a game, we cannot expect to be victorious in our Christian walks if we remain unaware of our primary opposition. So often, I've observed Christians try to live Godly lives and churches try to carry out God's calling to positive influences and light to their communities, only to be defeated by a basic ignorance of Satan's schemes.

This study was written to break down the walls of ignorance and bring to light the full truth of the gospel message. It is centered on the pursuit of living a Christian lifestyle that is fruitful and brings glory to our Heavenly Father. That is a simply stated, generic goal, but as the apostle Paul illustrated in his writings, and as many of you have probably experienced, it is not easy! The material in this book is written with every intention of sharing God's truth in the pursuit of that goal.

As you begin this journey, I think it is only appropriate to tell you that the motivation for writing this material was born years ago. First, I was motivated by my frustration as a baby Christian with unrealistic expectations of how my life might change after accepting Jesus Christ as my Savior and inviting God to walk alongside me. Secondly, the frustration of observing so many Christians fall short of the life that God intends for them (some with miserable consequences) assured me something was missing in their Christian walks.

As a new Christian, I was encouraged by everything I was learning about Jesus, but it wasn't until much later, as I matured in my faith, that I discovered there was an enemy determined to undermine all that God intended for me. I did not realize it then, but my enlistment in God's army had immediately placed me at enmity with Satan and his legion of fallen angels (referenced in Scripture as demons). Before we venture further, allow me to share a little more of my background.

I grew up in Milwaukee, Wisconsin, and was the youngest of three sons. We were the typical middle-class, suburban family at that time, and I was blessed with the most wonderful childhood I could have imagined. My father worked thirty-six years for one company and retired with a pension. My mother did not start working until I was in first grade. By then, my grandmother had retired, and she lived with us full time. My mother eventually retired with a pension after twenty years of working part time with the phone company.

Both of my parents were heavily involved in the Catholic church, and from an early age, I attended mass every Sunday. In fact, my earliest memories were of an all-Latin mass. I even served as an altar boy in the church for several years. Perhaps it was because of my age and/or immaturity, but I never really gained any spiritual insight or depth of conviction about my faith, even after attending Catholic school through the eighth grade.

By age fourteen, I had fallen away from the church and stopped attending except on holidays. (You know, a "CEO Christian"—Christmas and Easter Only.) For the next twenty years, religion was a topic I purposely avoided. In fact, for most of those years, I was a practicing agnostic. I learned to rely on myself, and I developed a quiet confidence in running my own life. I was a proud, self-made man.

By the grace of God, I survived my ignorance and gained my salvation when I was thirty-four. A Baptist pastor, Dr. Joe Ford, became my spiritual mentor and one of my best friends. I recall his simple advice to buy a New International Version of the Bible, start reading in the New Testament, and join him for church on Sundays.

I took his advice, and once I started reading, the words came alive in my heart. I quickly developed a sincere hunger and a deep fascination for God's Word. At first, I was upset that no one had ever directed me to these simple yet powerful truths before. But once the truth was revealed to me, I wanted desperately to learn more and couldn't wait for Sunday mornings, when "Dr. Joe" would make the stories of the Bible come to life and apply them to my everyday circumstances.

I say all that to make this simple point. For the last twenty-eight years, I've done nothing special except strive to be consistent. I am not formally trained in any denomination of the church, I have not attended seminary, and I do not have a master's degree or doctorate in theology. I've just been reading my Bible, attending church on Sundays, and enjoying Christian literature (fiction, nonfiction, self-help, etc.). In that time, I have attended only three Baptist churches and am blessed to have been mentored by distinguished men of God who provided sound biblical teaching from the pulpit.

That may not be the background you expect for such a weighty topic, but it is the exact reason this study is so unique. I am no different than most of the people reading this book. Through consistent studying, and during a time of intense personal struggle (during which I lost my business of twelve years due to an economic downturn, suffered through an unwanted divorce from my wife, and subsequently became separated from my two daughters), the Holy Spirit opened my eyes to a common struggle among all Christians—the struggle with spiritual warfare.

You see, having been a "self-made" man, full of pride, and always able to handle any problem that was thrown at me, I was now broken and left without any answers as to why my life had fallen apart. I was desperately in need of transformation and hopeful that my newfound salvation would begin a rapid improvement of the mess I had created.

What I didn't fully understand at the time was that my unseen adversary, Satan, was not about to let me forget all that I had lost or how my newfound faith had seemingly let me down. It was as if I could hear him say, "God isn't real. If He loved you, why is all this happening to you? You don't need Him; you can fix this yourself."

As much as God had revealed to me, I was still a baby Christian. I often tell people that at this point I had two options; I could dive into a bottle, or dive into the Bible. By the grace of God, I chose the latter. Not fully understanding that I was on the front line of a spiritual battle, I was still determined to let God win in my life. I had read enough to know that He was real, and that the truth would set me free.

Somehow, I think God recognized my determination, and step by step, He began to broaden my understanding of Satan's schemes, his methods, and his goals. More importantly, God, through his Holy Spirit, began to show me in His Word how to not only fight the battle but also ultimately win the war. In my quest for victory, I studied God's Word and read numerous books pertaining to spiritual warfare that confirm the information shared in this study. So far, nothing that I have read has been formatted in the way God revealed His truth to me. And it is that truth that God has directed me to share with you.

Before we embark on this journey, some readers might ask this fundamental question. Who is Satan? What we know from Scripture is that Satan is a created being, an angel who at one time rebelled against his Creator, Almighty God. Many Christian scholars believe Ezekiel 28:11-19 is a dual prophecy describing both the king of Tyre as well as Satan himself. While there is some debate over this reference, these verses seem to point out that Satan was the model of perfection, full of wisdom, perfect in beauty, and blameless from the day he was created until the day that selfish pride was found in him. We see a similar reference from the prophet Isaiah.

> How you have fallen from heaven, morning star, son of the dawn! You have been cast down to the earth, you who once laid low the nations! 13 You said in your heart, "I will ascend to the heavens; I will raise my throne above the stars of God; I will sit enthroned on the mount of assembly, on the utmost heights of Mount Zaphon. 14 I will ascend above the tops of the clouds; I will make myself like the Most High. (Isaiah 14:12-14)

Once again, there is some debate over this reference; however, notice the phrase "I will" is repeated five times, revealing Satan's pride, arrogance, and desire to exalt himself higher than God. It was this sin of pride that separated him from perfect fellowship with his Creator and resulted in being cast out of heaven. Since then, God has allowed Satan to claim spiritual dominion over this world, and Satan falsely considers himself as the dominant authority of this earthly realm.

Most of the world is not aware of the fact that they are under the influence of the "evil one" (Matthew 6:13). Satan taps into our inherent pride and adamic nature, causing us to focus on ourselves and our own greatness rather than on God. His goal is for mankind to be so sure of their human abilities that it precludes all need for God, and this has affected every aspect of humanity. Fast forward to today. Satan has not changed. He still wants to be greater than God, and his aim is to bring everything and everyone under his influence.

As I studied the Bible and subsequent literature on this real-life battle between good and evil, I was amazed at how accurately it defined my personal struggle at the time. Of equal interest was the dilemma it represented to Christians at large. The excerpt below comes from *Rules of Engagement* by Derek Prince. This text is directed specifically at Christians and will serve as one of the foundations for this study. In Chapter 18, "Principles of Spiritual Protection," he writes the following.

> *When we are born again as Christians into the Kingdom of God, we discover that we are caught up in a war with an opposing spiritual kingdom—the kingdom of Satan. In this we have no option. Because the kingdom to which we belong is at war, we are part of the war. We discover, too, that we have various kinds of enemies, but the most powerful and the most formidable is a kingdom of rebellious angels in the heavenly places, under the rule of God's archenemy, Satan.* [3]

I will reference Dr. Prince and this same paragraph later in our study and for a different purpose; however, for now I would like to focus on that first sentence: "When we are born again as Christians into the Kingdom of God, <u>we discover</u> that we are caught up in a war with an opposing spiritual kingdom—the kingdom of Satan." Now, it may just be my interpretation, but the word structure indicates that the knowledge of this opposing kingdom and our involvement in spiritual warfare becomes immediately apparent to a new Christian. (Read it again.)

This raised an interesting question for me. When is it, exactly, that *we discover* our involvement in this battle? More directly, can you remember a time when you were formally trained in the subject matter? Who is this enemy? How does he attack? What do we do about him? Without that knowledge, I believe most Christians, regardless of denomination, are left to discover this reality on their own, if they ever discover it at all. Let me explain.

Learning about God and building a personal relationship with Him is a maturing process, and as long as we are in these earthly bodies, we will never know all there is to know about God, his Son Jesus Christ, and his Holy Spirit. We all start out as baby Christians, and our first introduction is to Jesus. The primary emphasis is most often found in the following verses:

- *For God so loved the world that he gave his only begotten Son, that whosoever believeth in him should not perish, but have everlasting life. (John 3:16)*
- *Jesus died on the cross for our salvation. (Romans 5:8)*
- *Jesus is the Way, the Truth, and the Life. (John 14:6)*
- *No one comes to the Father except through Jesus. (John 14:6)*
- *Jesus intercedes on our behalf before the Father. (Hebrews 7:24-25)*

For a new Christian, this basic knowledge of Jesus is a lot to process, much less comprehend and apply to life. Faith in Jesus Christ is the cornerstone of Christianity, and the church is correct in focusing our attention on Him, initially and continually. But here is the challenge for Christians at all levels of maturity. God initiated your salvation, and as such, He has a plan for your life. However, Satan is immediately and continually aware of your decision to accept and follow Jesus Christ as your Savior, and he has an opposing agenda for you.

I have certainly benefited from the wisdom of Dr. Prince, but perhaps a more accurate first sentence would read, "When we are born again as Christians into the Kingdom of God, **we are immediately** caught up in a war with an opposing spiritual kingdom—the kingdom of Satan—**whether we realize it or not.**" Do you see the problem? Satan doesn't wait on the battlefield until you finish your basic training! He immediately begins to attack, and without the proper instruction, we are unaware of where the attack is coming from, who is attacking us, and how to defend ourselves.

I refer once more to Dr. Prince, who stated, "**In this we have no option.** Because the kingdom to which we belong is at war, we are part of the war [immediately]." Remember, my frustration was born out of unrealistic expectations of how my life would change after accepting Jesus Christ as my Savior. With the best of intentions, the church was teaching me all about Jesus, the piece of the puzzle that had been missing in my life for twenty years.

It all sounded wonderful. I expected rapid improvement in my life. After all, Jesus was now on my side. What no one told me, and what I did not realize until much later, is that for every step forward I took with Jesus, Satan was knocking me two steps backward. It seemed as though I was fighting against a constant but invisible headwind that kept me from realizing any significant change in my circumstances. With God's help and a personal determination to press on, I survived long enough to discover what was happening to me.

Unfortunately, many Christians are dissuaded when the enemy attacks, especially in the early stages of their transformation. They do not realize that they have stepped into a spiritual battle and that they are under attack. As a result, they lose out on the best God has in store for them, or worse, many walk away and never return, unaware that they are allowing Satan to win the battle.

This study is intended to clearly disseminate the truth about spiritual warfare and to provide Christians (at any level of maturity) the wisdom, discernment, and determination necessary to defeat the enemy and allow God's plan to prevail in their lives. I do not claim to be an expert on the subject, but I do engage in the battle each day with a new perspective, and throughout this study I will do my best to share what the Holy Spirit has revealed to me about living a victorious Christian lifestyle. Perhaps we would all be wise to emulate the model laid out for us by the apostle Paul.

> Not that I have already obtained all this, or have already arrived at my goal, but I press on to take hold of that for which Christ Jesus took hold of me. Brothers and sisters, I do not consider myself yet to have taken hold of it. But one thing I do: Forgetting what is behind and straining toward what is ahead, I press on toward the goal to win the prize for which God has called me heavenward in Christ Jesus. (Philippians 3:12-14) (NIV)

While attending Oak Hill Baptist Church in Lawrenceville, GA, our pastor and my dear friend, Dr. Joe Ford, would preach the same sermon each year during the Memorial Day weekend. He used a military analogy to remind believers of their permanent standing in God's kingdom. He would tell the story of a military recruit stepping off the bus and lining up shoulder to shoulder with the other recruits, just outside the boot camp barracks.

The company commander would inspect and briefly test the resolve of these green recruits and then ask them to raise their right hands in preparation to take the oath to defend their country above all else. As their hands went up, each repeated the oath, phrase by phrase, as instructed by the commander. Upon completion, and after their hands returned to their sides, the commander affirmed that they were now permanent members of the U. S. military and would be afforded all the benefits of serving in the armed forces.

Then Dr. Joe would make this point. If, after taking the military oath, that recruit was hit by a bus and killed while crossing the road on his way to the barracks, he would be awarded the same consideration as any military veteran. He had not served the first day as a soldier, but his decision and personal profession of allegiance to protect and defend the constitution of the United States of America had secured the honor of a military funeral.

Your personal decision to accept Jesus Christ as your Savior and then public profession of faith through believer's baptism is much like the story above. Having followed that biblical path to salvation, you are now a permanent member of God's family and however well you serve, there is a place reserved for you in the kingdom of heaven. The benefits are many, but the war still has to be fought. Let me reassure you that God is on your side. He wants you to win and has provided His personal training manual to prepare you for victorious service. So, join me, and let us press on together.

Before entering any topic of biblical study, I believe it is important to establish the proper foundation. **First**, we need to make sure our theology is correct. In his book, *The Disappearance of God*, R. Albert Mohler, Jr. describes three levels of theological priorities facing

Christians today. We will focus on the first level as part of the introduction to this study.

Mohler states, "First level theological issues would include those doctrines most central and essential to the Christian faith. Included among these most crucial doctrines would be doctrines such as the Trinity, the full deity and humanity of Jesus Christ, justification by faith, and the authority of Scripture."

1. *The early church clarified and codified its understanding of the one true and living God by affirming the full deity of the Father, the Son, and the Holy Spirit—while insisting that the Bible reveals one God in three persons.*

2. *Christianity stands or falls on the affirmation that Jesus Christ is fully man and fully God. The church affirmed that both the full deity and full humanity of Jesus Christ are necessary to the Christian faith. The essential truths of the incarnation include the death, burial, and bodily resurrection of the Lord Jesus Christ.*

3. *The doctrine of justification by faith must also be included among these first-order truths. Without this doctrine, we are left with a denial of the Gospel itself, and salvation is transformed into some structure of human righteousness.*

4. *The truthfulness and authority of the Holy Scriptures must also rank as a first-order doctrine, for without an affirmation of the Bible as the very Word of God, we are left without any adequate authority for distinguishing truth from error.*

Mohler concludes by saying; "These first-order doctrines represent the most fundamental truths of the Christian faith, and a denial of these doctrines represent nothing less than an eventual denial of Christianity itself."

Second, there are several references in the Bible that speak to the concept of spiritual maturity. As Christians, we all mature at a different pace and there are many areas of our daily Christian life that require guidance from the Holy Spirit to bring us closer to Christ. These areas of growth include personal relationships (family, friends, others), personal responsibility and behavior, finances, etc. In his letter to the Corinthians, while Paul is addressing unrest in the New Testament church (over leadership preferences), he says the following.

> *Brothers and sisters, I could not address you as people who live by the Spirit but as people who are still worldly— mere infants in Christ. I gave you milk, not solid food, for you were not yet ready for it. Indeed, you are still not ready. (1 Corinthians 3:1-2)*

This concept is again addressed in Hebrews.

> *In fact, though by this time you ought to be teachers, you need someone to teach you the elementary truths of God's Word all over again. You need milk, not solid food! Anyone who lives on milk, being still an infant, is not acquainted with the teaching about righteousness. But solid food is for the mature, who by constant use have trained themselves to distinguish **good from evil**.* (Hebrews 5:12-14)

I bring this up because we will be chewing on some solid spiritual food. However, we will start with the basics and work at a pace that I believe all should be able to follow. I would like to make one more

31

important point. As you read this study, you will recognize that I have quoted a considerable volume of Scripture. This was done with dual purpose.

My intent is to share God's Word with you, not my interpretation of His word. Second, so many Christian books reference Scripture in parenthesis and leave it up to you to find the corresponding verses in the Bible. I have included almost all the verses I reference for ease of studying. You may still want to have your Bible available to cross reference, but with few exceptions, you will not have to search for the relevant verses. I hope and trust your investment will prove beneficial in strengthening your walk with the Lord.

1. *Layman's Bible Commentary Set, Vol. 11—Galatians through Philemon* (Uhrichsville: Barbour Publishing, 2008) 69
2. Derek Prince, *Rules of Engagement* (Grand Rapids: Chosen Books, 2016), 148
3. R. Albert Mohler Jr., *The Disappearance of God* (Colorado Springs: Multnomah Books, 2009), 3-5

Chapter 2: Take Captive Every Thought

The primary concept of this study was really birthed out of two main Scripture verses. The first is found in the book of Galatians. The apostle Paul starts his letter to the church in Galatia by saying the following in Chapter 1, Verses 6-7.

> I am astonished that you are so quickly deserting the one who called you to live in the grace of Christ and are turning to a different gospel - which is really no gospel at all. Evidently some people are throwing you into confusion and are trying to pervert the gospel of Christ.

Paul is chastising members of the church because they are abandoning the truth of the Gospel and returning to the Jewish Law for sanctification. In Chapter 3, Verses 1-3, he states,

> You foolish Galatians! Who has bewitched you? Before your **very** eyes Jesus Christ was clearly portrayed as crucified. I would like to learn just one thing from you: Did you receive the Spirit by the works of the law, or by believing what you heard (the Gospel)? Are you so foolish? After beginning by means of the Spirit, are you now trying to finish by means of the flesh?

As Paul continues to explain the obvious differences between the law and the promise of salvation through Jesus Christ, he makes this statement in Chapter 5, Verses 7-8. This caught my attention.

> You were running a good race. Who cut in on you to keep you from obeying the truth? That kind of **persuasion** does not come from the one who calls you.

Throughout his letter, Paul is repeatedly and emphatically telling the Galatians that Christ has set them free. They are a new creation, filled with the Spirit of God, partaking in God's promise to Abraham, and heirs according to that promise. So, who was it that stepped in and kept them from obeying the truth?

The word "persuasion" (or influence) caught my attention and troubled me. A focus on the word "persuasion" (or influence) is crucial to understanding Paul's message. It was Christ who had transformed them, but who was persuading them to walk away from that truth? If you read the book of Galatians, the obvious answer would be other members of their community. But as we explore further, I believe the real answer will become apparent.

The second set of Scripture verses that caught my attention can be found in 2 Corinthians, Chapter 10. This is mostly a letter of encouragement from Paul to the Corinthians. However, in Chapter 10, Paul is found defending his ministry and warning the church as he states the following in Verses 2-5:

> I beg you that when I come, I may not have to be as bold as I expect to be toward some people who think that we live by the standards of this world. For though we live in the world, we do not wage war as the world does. The weapons we fight with are not the weapons of the world. On the contrary, they have divine power to demolish strongholds. We demolish arguments and every pretension that sets itself up against the knowledge of God, **and we take captive every thought to make it obedient to Christ.**

These verses will serve as the foundational principle for this entire study, and they are a direct reference to the earlier quote from Dr. Prince, affirming the fact that we are engaged in a war. However, it also becomes apparent that we are not fighting with flesh and blood opponents, nor are we fighting with "weapons of the world."

THIS IS A SPIRITUAL BATTLE! We are engaged in Spiritual Warfare! As I studied these verses and visualized the traditional worldly weapons of war, it struck me as odd that the greatest discipline we can develop to demolish every argument that sets itself up against the knowledge of God is to "take captive every thought to make it obedient to Christ." Now, with the spiritual foundation in place, it is time to explore what I call The Engineering of Lifestyle! We will use the graphic below to illustrate the early stages of this biblical principle.

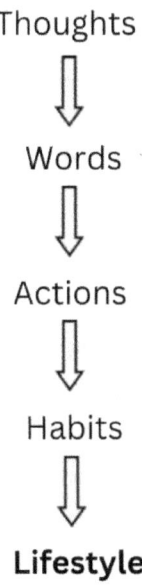

Thoughts

⇓

Words

⇓

Actions

⇓

Habits

⇓

Lifestyle

As you look at this simple diagram, it may appear quite elementary. In fact, it may look rather secular, like something you would find in a self-help book. You would be right. While I had immersed myself in reading the Bible, I was also reading a good number of secular books for encouragement as well.

Former Green Bay Packers coach and legend, Vince Lombardi, famously said the following:

> *Winning is a habit. Watch your thoughts, they become your beliefs. Watch your beliefs, they become your words. Watch your words, they become your actions. Watch your actions, they become your habits. Watch your habits, they become your character.*

There are many others who attest to the same premise and in similar quotes; however, in the secular world none venture to offer a suggestion of where your governing thoughts originate. It is only in God's Word that this question is addressed and clearly defined. Let me make an important point here. It is obvious by my introduction that I am offering a much-needed premise to believers of the Christian faith, but again, the reality is that this premise holds true for all of humanity, whether you profess to be a Christian or not.

I assume that by your selection and attentive reading of this book that we are alike in attempting to live a God-honoring lifestyle. May I also assume that you are sincere about maturing in your walk with Jesus Christ? If the answer is yes, then (like me) you have almost certainly discovered that trying to live a Christian lifestyle can be difficult, confusing, and even frustrating at times.

The good news is you are not alone. We all struggle with sin. This is probably best illustrated by Paul's words in Romans, Chapter 7, Verses 15-20, where he describes his struggle with sin.

> *I do not understand what I do. For what I want to do I do not do, but what I hate I do. And if I do what I do not want to do, I agree that the law is good. As it is, it is no longer I myself who do it, but it is sin living in me. For I know that good itself does not dwell in me, that is, in my sinful nature For I have the desire to do what is good, but I cannot carry*

it out. For I do not do the good I want to do, but the evil I do not want to do—this I keep on doing. Now if I do what I do not want to do, it is no longer I who do it, but it is sin living in me that does it.

The obvious question becomes; how does sin live in me? Let us take a closer look at our diagram from bottom to top.

Our lifestyle (Christian or secular) is created by our habits. You have probably heard the saying, "We are all creatures of habit." That is true. Our lifestyle is created by the things we do habitually, whether consciously or subconsciously.

Our habits are created by our actions. Research claims that any action done consistently for a period of 21 days will become a habit. Those things that we do repeatedly tend to become habits in our lives.

Our actions are created by our words. Some people have a hard time with this one, but let me ask you a simple question to help illustrate. Where will you have dinner tonight? Some have promised a spouse or family member that they will be home right after work. Some may have confirmed a late snack at a local restaurant. Those actions were spoken into existence. I am sure you could find some contradictions, but most significant activity in our lives is preceded by our words.

Our words are created by our thoughts. This is our natural neurological process for communication. What is conceived in the mind is communicated to others through our words. We have all experienced something popping out of our mouths without much thought behind it, but for the most part, we are usually deliberate in thinking things through before we speak.

As simple as it seems, this diagram will serve as a main reference point for our study on spiritual warfare. But if this simple diagram holds true, then the real question becomes, **where do our thoughts**

come from? Where does the "persuasion" that Paul mentioned to the Galatians emanate from? What is this weapon that has the power to demolish strongholds? Why are we encouraged to "take captive every thought to make it obedient to Christ?" As we look for answers to those questions, adding to the diagram will help to reveal God's truth.

In 1979, Dr. Francis Martin, Pastor of Family Life Christian Fellowship in Lafayette, Louisiana, published a brief but powerful, ninety-page book titled *Hung by the Tongue*. In Chapter 1, he states the following.

> *There are three sources from which we receive thoughts. First, thoughts come from your five senses. A second source from which a thought can come is the devil. We know this because the Scripture supports it. (John 13:2—* The devil put the thought of betrayal into Judas' heart). *Third, God can also put thoughts into your heart and mind by His Holy Spirit. God speaks to you through your spirit and your spirit speaks to your mind.* [1]

We will reference multiple Scripture verses to illustrate Dr. Martin's last two points, but visually it looks like this.

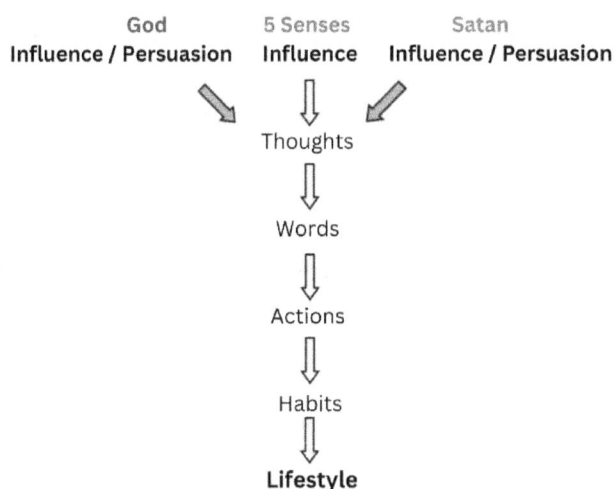

As you look at the expanded diagram, you will quickly notice that there are only three things that can influence our thoughts. The center of the outline is self-explanatory. Our five senses play a major part in our thought processes.

- Food that tastes good
- Flowers that smell good
- Music that is pleasing to the ear
- A beautiful sunset that is pleasing to the eyes and elicits pleasant thoughts
- A soft blanket that is fun to hold and rub against your hand

The examples of worldly influence could go on for quite some time. Important inclusions would be literature, movies, concerts, etc. All the things that are perceived by our senses can and do have an influence on our thought patterns. I will talk about the importance of some of these areas later in the study, but for now, the critical areas of spiritual influence will take prominence.

What Dr. Martin proposed, and what I believe our study of Scripture will reveal, is that there are only two other entities that can influence the thoughts that govern your life: God and Satan. To begin the discussion, I have selected two Scripture verses that illustrate this premise.

> *He who forms the mountains, creates the wind, **and reveals his thoughts to a man**, he who turns the dawn to darkness, and treads the high places of the earth—the Lord God Almighty is his name.* (Amos 4:13)

The same God that created the heavens and the earth created us. In Genesis 1:26, we learn, "Then God said, Let us make man in our image..." Before sin entered the world, He gave authority to Adam and Eve to rule over all of creation in continual and unhindered fellowship with Him—with one condition. "You are free to eat from any tree in the garden; but you must not eat from the tree of the knowledge of good and evil, for when you eat from it you will certainly die." (Genesis 2:16-17) However, in the second mention of evil in the Bible, Satan (disguised as a serpent) places this contrary thought in the mind of Eve (Genesis 3:1). "Did God really say, 'You must not eat from any tree in the garden?'"

Written thousands of years later, Paul's previously referenced warning to the Galatians could have easily been offered to Eve. "Who cut in on you to keep you from obeying the truth? That kind of **persuasion** does not come from the one who calls you." As you will see throughout this study, the slight and purposeful misrepresentation of God's Word is a common tactic used by the enemy and the subsequent fall of man has placed us all under the 'Adamic' or sin nature.

We can, however, be encouraged, because before sin entered the world, God rendered full provision for His only Son to serve as a sacrifice for our sins (1 Peter 1:20). Upon your salvation through

Jesus Christ, God-has promised you eternal life and an inheritance to the kingdom of heaven. And while you are still on this earth, He has given you His Word (the Bible) as a love letter, an instruction manual, <u>and as a battle plan</u>.

God loves you unconditionally and has a specific purpose for you as noted in Romans 8:28! "And we know that in all things God works for the good of those who love him, who have been called according to his purpose." In coming chapters, I will address how to fully appropriate this promise in your life. But in contrast, there is an enemy with a complete opposite and adverse purpose for your life.

> *As for you, you were dead in your transgressions and sins, in which you used to live when you followed the ways of this world and of the ruler of the kingdom of the air, the spirit who is now at work in those who are disobedient. All of us also lived among them at one time, gratifying the cravings of our sinful nature and following its desires and* ***thoughts****.* (Ephesians 2:1-3)

Let me take a step back at this point and reference one of the crucial doctrines referenced by Albert Mohler; "The truthfulness and authority of the Holy Scriptures must also rank as a first-order doctrine, for without an affirmation of the Bible as the very Word of God, we are left without any adequate authority for distinguishing truth from error."

Some Christians have a difficult time with the concept of Satan as referenced in the Bible. Often, he is misunderstood and casually dismissed in statements like; "the devil made me do it." However, if the Bible is the unerring Word of God (and it is), and Satan is referenced from Genesis to Revelation, then the devil exists! **This reality is vital to the application of this study.** Consider just the few verses referenced below.

Satan rose up against Israel and incited David to take a census of Israel. (1 Chronicles 21:1)

For we wanted to come to you—certainly, I, Paul, did, again and again - but Satan blocked our way. (1 Thessalonians 2:18)

(Jesus speaking to Saul) "I am sending you to open their eyes and turn them from darkness to light, and from the power of Satan to God, so that they may receive forgiveness of sins and a place among those who are sanctified by faith in me." (Acts 26:16-18)

Then Satan entered Judas, called Iscariot, one of the Twelve. And Judas went to the chief priests and the officers of the temple guard and discussed with them how he might betray Jesus. (Luke 22:3-4)

Throughout Scripture, Satan is represented as the antithesis to God, leading the whole world astray (not just Christians).

The great dragon was hurled down—that ancient serpent called the devil, or Satan, who leads the whole world astray. He was hurled to the earth, and his angels with him. (Revelation 12:9)

As stated earlier, we know that Satan is a created being, who at one time rebelled against God. He was expelled from heaven and allowed to rule this earthly kingdom for a period of time. We know that time is limited, and that God is victorious in the end. However, while Satan is allowed to roam this earth and the heavens, there is a real spiritual battle taking place, and we are involved in this spiritual warfare. (Reference Revelation, Chapter 12)

Now when we think of warfare, the image of a battlefield naturally comes to mind. We picture troops, tanks and artillery spread out over a large geographic area, perhaps with air support flying overhead. But as we review the original diagram, **our battleground is only six inches wide.** It is the space between our ears. Our mind is the battlefield, and this is where our spiritual battle will be won or lost!

> *Put on the full armor of God so that you can take your stand against the devil's schemes. For our struggle is not against flesh and blood, but against the rulers, against the authorities, against the powers of this dark world and against the spiritual forces of evil in the heavenly realms.* (Ephesians 6:11-12)

Not only does this verse confirm that we are in a war, it becomes obvious that our warfare is not with other human beings, but with the devil and his demons. The 'schemes' of the enemy are deliberate and well thought out plans to defeat us. It is a strategy of deceit and deception formulated from the "father of lies." With that understanding, I would strongly suggest that we, as Christians, need to begin immediately and then continually to think about what we are thinking about. That my friends, is the entire purpose of this study!

With the cornerstone in place, it is time to expand our diagram a little further to illustrate the nature of this battle for our minds and thoughts. I ask that you first focus on the left side of the diagram. Upon expanding the diagram, notice first that both "influence" and "persuasion" have been amended to include "agenda" and/or "motive."

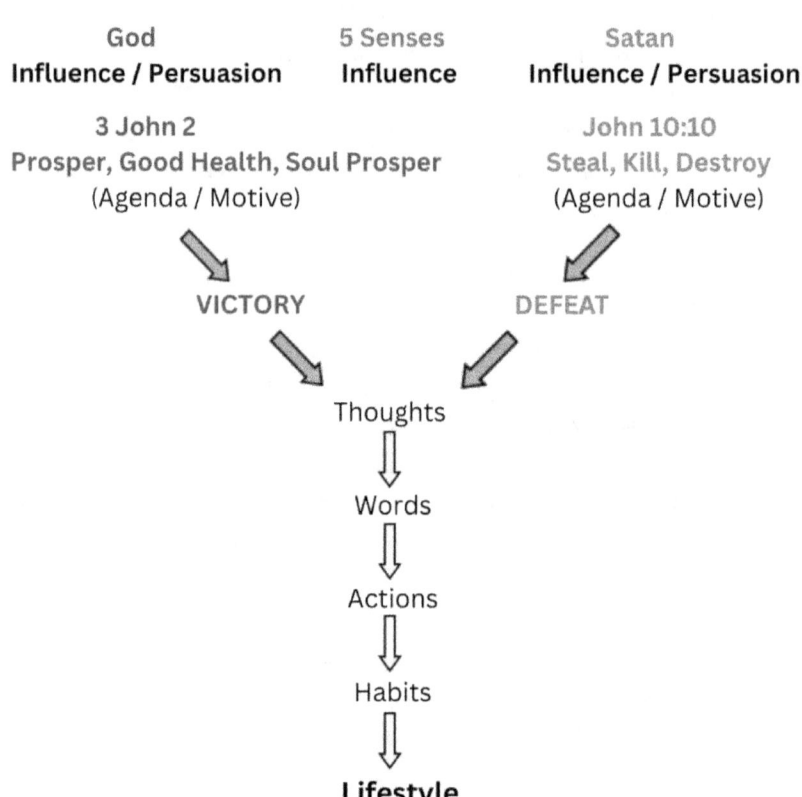

God
Influence / Persuasion

5 Senses
Influence

Satan
Influence / Persuasion

3 John 2
Prosper, Good Health, Soul Prosper
(Agenda / Motive)

John 10:10
Steal, Kill, Destroy
(Agenda / Motive)

VICTORY

DEFEAT

Thoughts
⇓
Words
⇓
Actions
⇓
Habits
⇓
Lifestyle

As referenced earlier in Romans 8:28, God has a purpose for your life. As your loving Creator and Heavenly Father, that purpose is designed for good. Specifically, it is designed for three main objectives.

1. **To bring glory to God (Father, Son, and Holy Spirit)**
   Now this is eternal life: that they know you, the only true God, and Jesus Christ, whom you have sent. I have brought you glory on earth by finishing the work you gave me to do. (John 17:3-4)

2. **To enjoy an intimate fellowship with God (temporally and eternally)**
   You have searched me, LORD, and you know me. You know when I sit and when I rise; you perceive my thoughts from afar. For you created my inmost being; you knit me together in my mother's womb. I praise you because I am fearfully and wonderfully made. Search me, God, and know my heart; test me and know my anxious thoughts. See if there is any offensive way in me and lead me in the way everlasting. (Psalm 139)

3. **To share the Gospel with others while on this earth (The Great Commission)**
   He said to them, "Go into all the world and preach the gospel to all creation." (Mark 16:15)

At risk of redefining your interpretation of God, allow me to make a bold statement and subsequently defend my understanding of Scripture with the best defense available—additional Scripture. **God wants you to be victorious in this battle!** That is His agenda and motive for you.

His winning message is confirmed throughout the Bible and clearly illustrated in the select Scripture verses to follow. We will begin with, 3 John 2, as it is perhaps the most clear and concise summary of God's intent for His beloved.

> *Beloved, I pray that you may prosper in all things and be in health, just as your soul prospers.* (3 John 2 NKJV)

In his third letter, John opens with the above greeting to his dear friend, Gaius ("whom I love in the truth"). While this is clearly a letter written from one friend to another, I believe this can also be interpreted as God's general motive for all His beloved in Christ (whom He also loves in the truth).

To illustrate this point, we are reminded in 2 Timothy 3:16-17, "All Scripture is God-breathed and is useful for teaching, rebuking, correcting, and training in righteousness, so that the servant of God may be thoroughly equipped for every good work."

In the spirit of teaching and training, it is important to review two other interpretations of 3 John 2.

> *Beloved, I wish above all things that thou mayest prosper and be in health, even as thy soul prospereth.* (KJV)

> *Dear friend, I pray that you may enjoy good health and that all may go well with you, even as your soul is getting along well.* (NIV)

So, considering a combination of the above, may we conclude that God's agenda for you, above all things, is that you may prosper in all things (that bring honor and glory to Him), and be in (enjoy) good health, even as your soul prospers? If you have never been able to appropriate that for your life, please pay close attention to what the Bible tells us. Before we go any further, there are important considerations when referencing 3 John 2.

1. If this comes across as being a bit self-centered, think about it this way; if you are or intend to be a parent someday, would your agenda for your children be any different?

2. When people first read this verse, there is a tendency to focus only on financial prosperity, but please hear me, I am not in any way promoting a health, wealth, and prosperity gospel. Yes, finances are included, but God intends for you to prosper in all areas of your life that bring honor and glory to Him (ministry, marriage, parenting, profession, etc.). Note—trusting God with your finances in the form of tithing and other ministry support affirms your faith in His promises and in so doing, honors Him. It is also one of the most tangible ways to experience God's blessings in your life. For reference, see Malachi 3:6-12.

3. Do not confuse this promise of blessing with a "works for salvation" proposition. You are saved by grace, not by works. However, God's Word is complete with a desire to bless those who honor him. As Christians, our "works" should be done as a *result* of our faith in Jesus Christ.

If we can agree on the points above, then to best understand this verse, we first need to focus on the importance of the comma ('comma' *even as your soul prospers.)* You see, your soul prosperity is a prerequisite for the other desires that God outlines for you in this verse. This is a vitally important point which we will address later in the study, but for now, suffice it to say that feeding your soul (daily Bible study, fervent prayer, regular church attendance, and Christian fellowship) will open the channel of blessing in your life.

Spiritual maturity affords greater responsibility as well as greater opportunity to serve. Why wouldn't God bless someone more willing and capable of serving and bringing honor to Him? Not only do these verses and those below confirm God's desire to bless His people, but in each instance, they also support the prerequisite for blessing which is soul prosperity and obedience (see bold print below).

> Blessed is the one who does not walk in step with the wicked or stand in the way that sinners take or sit in the company of mockers, **² but whose delight is in the law of the LORD, and who meditates on his law day and night.** ³ That person is like a tree planted by streams of water, which yields its fruit in season and whose leaf does not wither—<u>whatever they do prospers</u>. (Psalm 1:1-3)

> I the Lord search the heart and examine the mind, <u>to reward a man</u> **according to his conduct,** according to what his deeds deserve. (Jeremiah 17:10)

> But blessed is the one who trusts in the LORD, **whose confidence is in him.** They will be like a tree planted by the water that sends out its roots by the stream. (Jeremiah 17:7-8)

For additional support of this premise, we review God's conversation with the Israelites in the book of Deuteronomy, as well as His promise to Joshua.

> **Walk in all the way that the Lord your God has commanded you,** so that you may live and prosper and prolong your days in the land that you will possess. (Deuteronomy 5:33)

*Observe the 10 Commandments (Verse 1 summary). ...so that you, your children, and their children after them may fear the Lord your God as long as you live **by keeping all His decrees and commands that I give you**, and so that you may enjoy long life. Hear O Israel, and be careful to obey so that it may go well with you and that you may increase greatly in a land flowing with milk and honey, just as the Lord, the God of your fathers, promised you. (Deuteronomy 6:2-3)*

***Be careful to obey all the law my servant Moses gave you**; do not turn from it to the right or to the left, that you may be successful wherever you go. Keep this Book of the Law always on your lips; meditate on it day and night, so that you may be careful to do everything written in it. Then you will be prosperous and successful. (Joshua 1:7-8)*

Okay, now that God's agenda has been confirmed for you, let me emphasize a few other verses related to His influence on your thoughts. These are in addition to Amos 4:13 (mentioned previously).

*This is the covenant I will make with the house of Israel after that time, declares the Lord, **I will put my law in their minds** and write it on their hearts. I will be their God and they will be my people. (Jeremiah 31:33)*

*How long will you who are simple love your simple ways? How long will mockers delight in mockery and fools hate knowledge? Repent at my rebuke! **Then I will pour out my thoughts to you**, I will make known to you my teachings. (Proverbs 1:22-23)*

*How precious (or concerning) to me are your **thoughts**, O God. How vast is the sum of them! Were I to count them,* *they would outnumber the grains of sand.* (Psalm 139:17-18)

These next verses are interesting, as they reference God's ability to influence us even while we are sleeping. Since God does not sleep, He is able to speak to us twenty-four hours a day and may choose to influence us in a dream.

> *For God does speak—now one way, now another—though man may not perceive it. **In a dream**, in a vision of the night, when deep sleep falls on men as they slumber in their beds, He may speak in their ears and terrify them with warnings, to turn man from his wrongdoing and keep him from pride, to preserve his soul from the pit, his life from perishing by the sword.* (Job 33:29)

> *...he (God) said, "Listen to my words: When a prophet of the Lord is among you, I reveal myself to him in visions, **I speak to him in dreams**."* (Numbers 12:6)

> ***One night the Lord spoke to Paul in a vision**: "Do not be afraid; keep on speaking, do not be silent. [10] For I am with you, and no one is going to attack and harm you, because I have many people in this city."* (Acts 18:9)

NOTE: There is no reference in Scripture to any spiritual being sleeping. In fact, Revelation 12:10 states, "For the accuser of our brothers and sisters (the devil—Verse 12), who accuses them before our God day and night, has been hurled down." So beware, for Satan also has the ability to influence your thoughts twenty-four hours a day.

At this point, is there any doubt that God wants you to WIN? According to these Scripture references, God can and does influence your thoughts. Moreover, His motive and/or agenda for your life is victory through a passionate, determined, and intimate relationship with Him ("I will be their God and they will be my people.") (Jeremiah 31:33). Is there any reason why you would not pursue God's victorious plan for your life?

Sometimes, it helps me to picture it this way. I envision God the Father, Jesus, and the Holy Spirit as my coaches, along with all the angels and saints as cheerleaders on the sidelines. They are waving pom-poms. They are yelling encouragement, "You can do it! You're a winner! Keep going! Don't give up!" Listen to your coaches!

God is there telling me:
- I knew you before the beginning of time (Jeremiah 1:5); "Before I formed you in the womb, I knew you."
- I created you (Psalm 139:13); "You knit me together in my mother's womb."
- I have a plan for your life (Jeremiah 29:11); "For I know the plans I have for you," declares the LORD, "plans to prosper you and not to harm you, plans to give you hope and a future."
- I am working as your advocate (Romans 8:28); "And we know that in all things God works for the good of those who love him, who have been called according to his purpose."
- Stick with me, I've got your back (Psalm 23); "The LORD is my shepherd; I shall not want. He leads me in the paths of righteousness, for His name's sake."
- There are still others that need to know this truth (Matthew 28:19); "Therefore go and make disciples of all nations...."

Okay—so that may be a bit fanciful; however, the point remains the same. There is nothing but positive intent in God's agenda for you! **God desires victory for you in this battle**.

What agreement is there between the temple of God and idols? For we are the temple of the living God.

51

As God has said: "I will live with them and walk among them, and I will be their God, and they will be my people." (2 Corinthians 6:16)

Ah, but be careful my brothers and sisters in Christ, for there is one who has a complete and opposite agenda for you. As we will discover, Satan's method of influence is the same, but his intent is pure evil, as now represented in the right side of our diagram.

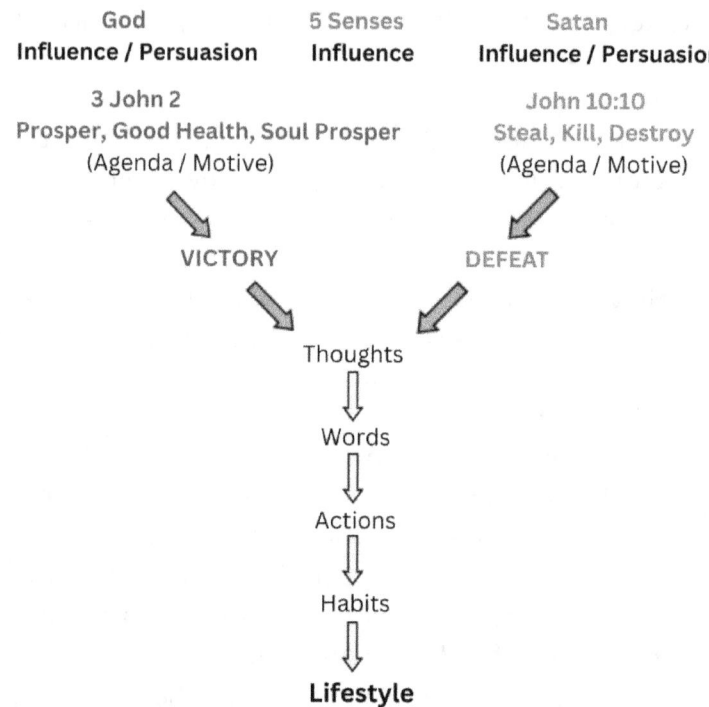

To help us understand the right side of the diagram, I want us to first draw our attention to the words of Jesus in the Gospel of John. By the time we arrive at the tenth chapter, the Pharisees have accused Jesus of being demon possessed multiple times. As he addresses the Pharisees again in Chapter 10, Jesus is teaching the parable of a shepherd and his flock.

*Very truly I tell you Pharisees, anyone who does not enter the sheep pen by the gate, but climbs in by some other way, **is a thief and a robber**. The one who enters by the gate is the shepherd of the sheep.* (John 10:1-2)

Then, in Verses 7-11, Jesus says this.

*Very truly I tell you, I am the gate for the sheep. All who have come before me are thieves and robbers, but the sheep have not listened to them. I am the gate; whoever enters through me will be saved. They will come in and go out, and find pasture. **The thief comes only to steal and kill and destroy**; I have come that they may have life, and have it to the full. I am the good shepherd.* (John 10:7-11)

In his commentary, James Hastings states the following regarding Verses 7-11:

Jesus is the Shepherd of the sheep. The Pharisees and Sadducees are the thieves. Jesus comes to give; they come to steal. Jesus comes to give life; they come to take life away. Jesus comes to give life in abundance; they come to destroy it altogether. The Pharisees and Sadducees of today are the enemies of Christ, be they who they may. They are the world, the flesh, the devil. The sheep are those for whom the choice is waiting (choose ye this day). We are the sheep of someone's pasture - His or the Devil's. We may follow Him to receive, to receive life, to receive life in abundance. We may follow Satan to lose, to lose life, to lose it utterly! [2]

In this story, it is quite consistent to identify the "thief" Jesus is referring to as Satan. This is referenced and (I believe) confirmed in two other parables told by Jesus.

First, The Parable of the Weeds, found in Matthew, Chapter 13:

*Jesus told them another parable: "The kingdom of heaven is like a man who sowed good seed in his field. But while everyone was sleeping, his **enemy** came and sowed weeds among the wheat, and went away. When the wheat sprouted and formed heads, then the weeds also appeared. The owner's servants came to him and said, 'Sir, didn't you sow good seed in your field? Where then did the weeds come from?' **'An enemy did this,'** he replied."* (Matthew 13:24-28)

Later, when Jesus was alone with the disciples, they asked him to explain the parable, and he said this.

*His disciples came to him and said, "Explain to us the parable of the weeds in the field." He answered, "The one who sowed the good seed is the Son of Man. The field is the world, and the good seed stands for the people of the kingdom. The weeds are the people of the evil one, **and the enemy who sows them is the devil**."* (Matthew 13:36-39)

Second, The Parable of the Sower found in Mark, Chapter 4. (Also referenced in Matthew, Chapter 13 and Luke, Chapter 8.)

Listen! A farmer went out to sow his seed. As he was scattering the seed, some fell along the path, and the birds came and ate it up. Some fell on rocky places, where it did not have much soil. It sprang up quickly, because the soil was shallow. But when the sun came up, the plants were scorched, and they withered because they had no root. Other seed fell among thorns, which grew up and choked the plants, so that they did not bear grain. Still other seed fell on good soil. It came up, grew and produced a crop, some multiplying thirty, some sixty, some a hundred times. (Mark 4:3-8)

Later, when Jesus was alone with the disciples, they asked him to explain the parable, and he said this.

*The secret of the kingdom of God has been given to you. "Don't you understand this parable? How then will you understand any parable? The farmer sows the word. Some people are like seed along the path, where the word is sown. As soon as they hear it, **Satan comes and takes away the word that was sown in them**.* (Mark 4:11 and 13-15) (He steals it!)

I want to bring attention to two important points here.

1. **The field the seeds are sown in is your mind!** The various soils mentioned in this parable represent human hearts and their receptiveness to the Gospel. However, before the Word can take temporary or permanent residence in your heart, it is first processed in the mind.

   In the parable of the soils, we see that one of the ways that Satan battles against the Gospel is by stealing it before it has a chance to take root. ("As soon as they hear it...."). The farmer (God) sows the Word (of God) in your thought life. But as soon as they (we) hear it, Satan comes to STEAL the Word from them (us). How does he do that? He attacks our thoughts to deceive us.

   Why is my language not clear to you? Because you are unable to hear what I say. You belong to your father, the devil, and you want to carry out your father's desires. He was a murderer from the beginning, not holding to the truth, for there is no truth in him. When

*he lies, he speaks his native language, for he is a liar
and the father of lies.* (John 8:43-44)

2. If you line up the words *steal, kill,* and *destroy* directly underneath the words *prosper, good health,* and *soul prosper,* you will quickly notice that they are exact opposites directly opposed to one another.

God wants you to **prosper** in his righteousness.
Satan comes only to **steal** that prosperity

God wants you to enjoy **good health.**
Satan comes only to **kill.**

God wants your **soul to prosper.**
Satan comes only to **destroy** your soul.

Remember the words of Jesus? "I have come that they may have life and have it to the full. I am the good shepherd." Contrast that with the following:

*Be self-controlled and alert. Your enemy the devil prowls
around like a roaring lion looking for someone to **devour**.*
(1 Peter 5:8) (Other definitions include demolish, destroy, etc.)

*As for you, you were dead in your transgressions and sins, in
which you used to live when you followed the ways of this
world and of the ruler of the kingdom of the air, the spirit who
is now at work in those who are disobedient. All of us also lived
among them at one time, gratifying the cravings of our
flesh and following its desires and thoughts. Like the rest, we
were by nature deserving of wrath.* (Ephesians 2:1-3)

As we continue, I believe it is important to examine each of these contrasts in greater depth.

God wants you to **prosper** (in his righteousness). "The thief comes only to **steal**..."

> *For we are God's handiwork, created in Christ Jesus to do good works, which God prepared in advance for us to do.* (Ephesians 2:10)

What is it exactly that Satan is trying to steal from you? First and foremost, the personal and intimate relationship that God intends to have with each one of us. Through deliberate lies and deceit, Satan's mission is to steal your fellowship with God, your praise, your worship, your witness, your discipleship, your joy, your time, and your identity in Christ Jesus. The list could go on and on, but I think you get the idea. God wants victory for you. Satan wants your identity in Christ defeated.

Please note that I mentioned your "identity in Christ" and not your salvation. While Satan may cause you to doubt your salvation, once you have accepted Jesus Christ as your Savior, that is the one thing Satan cannot steal from you. However, he will plant the seeds of doubt in your mind as long as you allow him to. For those who are not saved, nor have the indwelling of the Holy Spirit, Satan will attempt to blind them from the truth of the Gospel for as long as he can (as noted in the verses below).

- *The god of this age has blinded the minds of unbelievers, so that they cannot see the light of the gospel that displays the glory of Christ, who is the image of God.* (2 Corinthians 4:4)

- *The person without the Spirit does not accept the things that come from the Spirit of God but considers them foolishness and cannot understand them because they are discerned only through the Spirit.* (1 Corinthians 2:14)

- *For the message of the cross is foolishness to those who are perishing, but to us who are being saved it is the power of God.* (1 Corinthians 1:18) (Notice the word *perishing*!)

Perhaps the clearest example of Satan's harmful and ruinous persuasion can be found in the story of Ananias and Sapphira in Acts, Chapter 5.

*Now a man named Ananias, together with his wife Sapphira, also sold a piece of property. With his wife's full knowledge, he kept back part of the money for himself, but brought the rest and put it at the apostles' feet. Then Peter said, "Ananias, **how is it that Satan has so filled your heart** that you have lied to the Holy Spirit and have kept for yourself some of the money you received for the land?*

*Didn't it belong to you before it was sold? And after it was sold, wasn't the money at your disposal? **What made you think of doing such a thing?** You have not lied just to human beings but to God.*

When Ananias heard this, he fell down and died. And great fear seized all who heard what had happened. Then some young men came forward, wrapped up his body, and carried him out and buried him. About three hours later his wife came in, not knowing what had happened. Peter asked her, "Tell me, is this the price you and Ananias got for the land?" "Yes," she said, "that is the price." Peter said to her, "How could you conspire to test the Spirit of the Lord? Listen! The feet of the men who buried your husband are at the door, and they will carry you out also." At that moment she fell down at his feet and died. Then the young men came in and, finding her dead, carried her out and buried her beside her husband.

There is much to unpack and discuss in this passage of Scripture. Notice first that Peter knew exactly who and in what form the influence came from. Ananias and Sapphira were under spiritual attack! It does not require deep discernment to recognize that Satan is using the same tactic here that he used in the Garden of Eden, twisting the truth just enough to cause doubt in their minds about God's purpose for them. Genesis 3:1 reminds us, "Did God really say you must not eat from any tree in the garden?"

It is the same deception! You can almost hear Satan saying to Ananias and Sapphira, "Did God really say you should give *all* the money from the sale of your property to the disciples?" Satan planted the seed of doubt in their thoughts, and it most definitely altered their lifestyle. Look again at James 1:14-16.

...but each one is tempted when, by his own evil desire, he is dragged away and enticed. Then, after desire has conceived, it gives birth to sin: and sin, when it is full grown, gives birth to death. Don't be deceived my dear brothers.

When you review the story in Genesis, God eventually confronts Eve and says, "What is it you have done?" And Eve answered, "The serpent deceived me, and I ate." We all know the consequence of that one act of disobedience.

As you read the story of Ananias and Sapphira, they lost their lives by allowing Satan to influence their thoughts. The entirety of God's plan is not fully revealed in this story, and the consequence for their sin is dramatic, but the premise of this study is clearly demonstrated. Satan wants you defeated.

But I am afraid that just as Eve was deceived by the serpent's cunning, your minds may somehow be led astray from your sincere and pure devotion to Christ. (2 Corinthians 11:3)

God wants you to enjoy **good health**. "The thief comes only to steal and **kill**…"

As we explore this topic, it is only appropriate to offer a clear understanding of John's intent as he wrote to his good friend Gaius as well as the broader message provided to all generations through this Scripture passage. In the original Greek language, the word used for health is, ὑγιής, ἐς, which translated in the English alphabet is hugiés (pronounced 'hoog-ee-ace'). It means to be well in body and sound in doctrine. Therefore, it has both a physical and spiritual relevance to our lives. Maintaining a strong, healthy body is important to God, but it is not God's first objective for His children, godliness holds that priority. (Remember the prerequisite; "even as your soul prospers.")

8 For physical training is of some value, but godliness has value for all things, holding promise for both the present life and the life to come. 9 This is a trustworthy saying that deserves full acceptance.

16 Watch your life and doctrine closely. Persevere in them, because if you do, you will save both yourself and your hearers. (1 Timothy 4:8-9, 16)

Referring once again to the commentary from, James Hastings, he suggests, "Life and death are the great words of Scripture, and their meaning must be watched. 'Death' on the lips of Jesus is not physical, but spiritual. Spiritual life is correspondence with Him who is a spirit; it is trust, it is truth."

However, in the same paragraph, Hastings adds this: "Every antagonist of God - the world, the flesh, the devil - seeks to break our fellowship with God."[3]

While most commentaries will agree that the reference to "kill" in John 10:10 refers to a spiritual death, Hastings brings forward two antagonists of God that are not spiritual: the world and the flesh. I would suggest that our 'flesh' can be influenced by the world and/or Satan to negatively affect our health, thus creating the potential to break down our fellowship with God or hinder God's purpose for our lives.

So, the first question is, what does God consider good physical health? This is an extremely difficult topic to address, and I must admit, not that well defined in Scripture. However, we are given some references to consider.

- Leviticus Chapter 11 and Deuteronomy Chapter 14 both deal with clean and unclean food. The Lord describes the food that the Israelites are not to eat as 'unclean' or 'detestable.' We know by modern standards that these foods, without the proper storage and preparation methods available to us today, would have harbored dangerous bacteria, disease, or parasites that could have been harmful to their health.
- Ephesians 5:18 – "Do not get drunk on wine, which leads to debauchery. Instead, be filled with the Spirit."
- Proverbs 20:1 – "Wine is a mocker and beer a brawler; whoever is led astray by them is not wise."
- Proverbs 23:19-21 – "Listen, my son, and be wise, and set your heart on the right path: Do not join those who drink too much wine or gorge themselves on meat, for drunkards and gluttons become poor, and drowsiness clothes them in rags."

When it comes to physical health, individual definitions of the term *healthy* vary greatly, from simply maintaining an FDA approved body mass index to being physically fit for competition. Others might base this on the process of consumption (i. e., junk food vs. health food). Still others may see a determination to overcome a disability as a function of good physical and mental health.

Invariably, the question of disability, birth defects, crippling injury, or the like will come up. For example, we may ask, "If God wants us to be in good health, why does he allow these things to happen?" I will be the first to admit that I do not have an answer for those questions. God's Word tells us that there are simply some things he will not reveal to us. (Please notice the promise in this verse as well.)

> *The secret things belong to the LORD our God, but the things revealed belong to us and to our children forever, that we may follow all the words of this law.* (Deuteronomy 29:29)

However, if we remember the original meaning in the Greek saying, 'well in body and sound in doctrine,' it may help us to understand how some with what we would consider disabilities are able to look beyond those temporal limitations and still lead lives that bring glory to God and inspire others who face the same challenges. In most cases, where the determination of the heart and soul overcomes a physical or mental limitation, it is the direct inspiration of the Holy Spirit, and/or the influence of a spirit-filled mentor, that allows sound doctrine to inspire victory over defeat.

For the purpose of this study, I would suggest that good health is eliminating any physical and/or spiritual influence that would hamper or prevent you from accomplishing God's purpose for your life. Based on that definition, I feel a primary focus on the topic of substance abuse and addiction is warranted. For as I study Scripture and observe life in general, I believe these are primary tools of Satan to obstruct God's will for individuals and perhaps end their lives prior to a powerful witness and harvest, or a transformed life through salvation.

When speaking of addiction, I think most people would agree that it has the potential to completely derail an individual, or worse, end someone's life. Within this category, we can include alcohol, drugs, tobacco, gambling, pornography, and yes, food. As a disclaimer, I want to admit that addiction is difficult for me to understand.

Don't get me wrong, I drank alcohol recklessly from high school into my early thirties and experimented with drugs during that same timeframe, but by the grace of God, there was never a bad behavior that I was not able to walk away from. I was blessed to avoid terrible consequences. At the time, the behavior seemed fun, and the thing to do with either friends or family, but it never grabbed hold of me likes it does for some.

As we consider the worldly consequence of addiction and how it affects someone's health, there is also a spiritual corollary as presented in the context of our diagram. Remember this comment from James Hastings. "Every antagonist of God - the world, the flesh, the devil - seeks to break our fellowship with God." We know that God wants us to win, and that He has a plan and a purpose for our life. This plan includes our salvation and subsequent walk with God while we inhabit this (healthy or unhealthy) earth suit.

> *In love, He predestined us for adoption to sonship through Jesus Christ, in accordance with his pleasure and will.* (Ephesians 1:5)

I believe substance abuse and addiction are Satan's antagonists used to deliberately break our fellowship with God and the plans He has for us. Throughout the Bible we are warned about Satan's schemes, which can include his direct influence or that of those individuals (the world) doing his bidding (more about that in the next chapter). Ephesians 6:11 references this specifically; "Put on the full armor of God, so that you can take your stand against the devil's schemes."

When it comes to physical well-being, I would suggest that one of Satan's schemes is a patient, long term approach to destroying your health.

I think we could all agree that without a previous history of substance abuse or addiction, no one wakes up in the morning and says, "I'm going to..."

- drink a fifth of vodka today
- snort so much cocaine that I can't think straight
- smoke two packs of cigarettes today
- eat so much junk food that I make myself miserable

Remember our earlier point: The 'schemes' of the enemy are deliberate and well-thought-out plans to defeat us. It is a strategy of deceit and deception formulated from the "father of lies." **You see, all these things begin with a single thought**, perhaps start innocently, but when allowed to progress, have the potential to negatively affect your health or eventually kill you!

So, if you consider these abuses as part of Satan's schemes, the obvious questions become, "What is his agenda?" and "What is his goal regarding our health?" As we consider some of the negative possibilities, it will help with context if I first point out another positive aspect of God's agenda for you. God is abundantly patient and will allow the temporary stain of sin and imperfection as He pursues us.

> *The Lord is not slow in keeping his promise, as some understand slowness. Instead, he is patient with you, not wanting anyone to perish, but everyone to come to repentance. (2 Peter 3:9)*

Suppose any one of the abuses mentioned above has the potential to take ten years off your life. What if God's patient plan included your salvation during that ten-year period? Now, Satan has no way of knowing that, but he does know that his odds of preventing your eternal destiny increase with each day that your health decreases.

What if God's plan for you included a dynamic ministry and plentiful harvest during that ten-year period? How many others might miss their eternal destiny if you are not healthy enough to share the Gospel with them, and by God's grace, lead them to salvation? What if you missed the opportunity to witness to the next great evangelist, who in turn, would lead thousands to know Jesus as their Savior? I am sure there are others who could site similar examples of missed opportunity, but I hope the point is worth considering. Look again at the verse below.

> ...but each one is tempted when, by his own evil desire, he is dragged away and enticed. Then, after desire has conceived, it gives birth to sin: and sin, when it is full grown, gives birth to death. Don't be deceived my dear brothers. (James 1:14-16)

Let me make two more important points here.

1. As you review the diagram again, most people, when caught in a lifestyle that is troubling, will attempt to attack the problem by changing their habits. However, most lifestyle changes cannot be accomplished by simply changing your habits because you are not addressing the root of the problem. You must address the thought process that initiated and now feeds the bad behavior.

    Have you ever experienced or heard of people who could not break free of alcoholism, drug addiction, etc., until they accepted Jesus Christ in their life thus changing their thought process? For some, it breaks the chains immediately. For others, it is a process. But in either case, it is a matter of allowing God to influence your thoughts!

2. Please consider 1 Corinthians 6:19-20: "Do you not know that your bodies are temples of the Holy Spirit, who is in you, whom you have received from God? You are not your own; you were bought at a price. Therefore, honor God with your bodies." Now, I know this verse was written in reference to sexual immorality, however, remembering that your body is God's temple might prove beneficial in caring for and protecting your health as well.

To help make my point, the first several chapters of 2 Chronicles go into great detail describing the opulence of God's temple in Jerusalem (built by Solomon). It was built to bring glory and honor to the only high God, the God of Israel. However, God allowed that temple of stone, fine timber, precious metal, and expensive jewels to be destroyed because he had another plan. **You were that plan!** God desires to live within you not some fancy building. "Don't you know that you yourselves are God's temple and that God's Spirit dwells in your midst?" (1 Corinthians 3:16)

If you claim Jesus Christ as your Savior, then your body is now God's temple, and his Holy Spirit dwells in you. Might attending to your health also be a way to honor God with your body?

God wants your **soul to prosper**. "The thief comes only to steal and kill and **destroy**."

Dear friends, I urge you, as aliens and strangers in the world, to abstain from sinful desires (thoughts), **which war against your soul.** (1 Peter 2:11) (Bold added for emphasis.)

As we consider this final contrast, I believe once again that there are both temporal and eternal applications. As mentioned previously, for those who are not saved, nor have the indwelling of the Holy Spirit, Satan will attempt to blind them from the truth of the Gospel for as long as he can. Remember 1 Corinthians 1:18: "For the message of the cross is foolishness to those who are perishing, but to us who are being saved it is the power of God."

If you reference the word *perishing* in a thesaurus, you will come across several frightening synonyms including *hopeless*, and *doomed to failure*. Satan would like nothing better than to keep those who are not yet saved, blinded to the truth of the Gospel, effectively destroying their opportunity for eternal salvation. However, the message of the cross *is* the power of God! And the power of God, if sought, if cherished, if applied, will bring about soul prosperity both in this life and eternally.

For the purpose of this study, we are going to take a closer look at Satan's schemes to prevent your soul from prospering while pursuing a Christian lifestyle. Please notice that Peter warns to "abstain from sinful desires, which *war* against your soul." Can there be any doubt that we are engaged in spiritual warfare?

When we accept Jesus Christ as our Savior and are then granted salvation by God's saving grace, we are not called into religion. We are called into relationship. I don't know that there is any clearer demonstration of this than the consistent, hardened hearts of the Sadducees and Pharisees during Jesus' ministry on this earth. They were firmly grounded in religion (religious law) but missed the offer of relationship right in front of them. You may remember the trick question asked of Jesus by one of the Pharisees (an expert in the law).

"Teacher, which is the greatest commandment in the Law?"
Jesus replied: "Love the Lord your God with all your heart and

with all your soul and with all your mind. This is the first and greatest commandment." (Matthew 22:36-38)

Don't you see? We are called into relationship! And this is not meant to be a casual acquaintance. Note that the question is not; 'which is the greatest suggestion.' We are commanded to LOVE the Lord our God. Well then, if that is the case, the obvious question becomes, how do you build a relationship with someone? The simple answer is—you spend time with them. Scripture is incredibly clear in explaining how your soul may prosper while walking on this earth.

Soul Prosperity = Relationship with God

Soul Prosperity = Time spent deepening that relationship with God

Throughout the Scriptures, God has given us clear direction as to the importance of this task. Shortly after creating the 10 commandments, God gave this instruction to the Israelites.

Fix these words of mine in your hearts and minds; tie them as symbols on your hands and bind them on your foreheads. Teach them to your children, talking about them when you sit at home and when you walk along the road, when you lie down and when you get up. Write them on the doorframes of your houses and on your gates. (Deuteronomy 11:18-20)

In Hebrews 3:1, the author writes this; "Therefore, holy brothers and sisters, who share in the heavenly calling, fix your thoughts on Jesus, whom we acknowledge as our apostle and high priest."

It is not a secret that to build a relationship with someone, you need to spend time with them. Think about how you developed the relationship with your spouse or your best friend. It took time, didn't it? It required developing a personal interest in them, understanding what made them tick, and eventually placing their interests above your own.

Building a relationship with God is no different. However, might I suggest that it should be your first priority? Notice in Matthew 22:38 that Jesus says, "This is the <u>first</u> and <u>greatest</u> commandment." In the following verse, Jesus says; "And the second is like it: "Love your neighbor as yourself.""

Okay, now that we have defined soul prosperity as a personal relationship with God (Father, Son, and Holy Spirit), and to develop that relationship requires time spent with God, the next question becomes, "How do we spend time with God?" Be careful. The answer has two parts.

Part One: While church attendance and Christian fellowship play important roles in your spiritual maturity, nothing will grow your relationship with God more intimately than studying God's Word. Remember, we are called into a personal relationship with our Lord and Savior. Personal Bible study allows God to speak to you directly. He knows you better than anyone else. He knows your dreams, goals, and aspirations. He knows your fears, struggles, and weaknesses. He wants to speak with you through his Living Word!

During His earthly ministry, Jesus often taught in parables. I thought a parable that I discovered many years ago might be appropriate. As a father was preparing to go off to war, he wrote a series of letters, sealed them, and asked his wife to follow these instructions should he not return. As our infant son reaches kindergarten, please open the first letter. I want him to know how much I love him, miss him, and want the best for him. It will also outline the important principles that guide my life, my faith, my character, and hopefully will plant the seed for him to do the same.

Have him open the second letter as he enters middle school. Children can be cruel to each other, but I want him to know that no matter what anyone else says, there is a father that loves him unconditionally. He can rest in that truth and find his identity in my love for him.

Have him open the third letter when he enters high school. It will explain the transition to maturity and how to live a life of character. How to treat others with the same respect that he desires. How to treat a young lady as if she were a treasure and not an object to take advantage of. How to stay calm in difficult situations and rise above the pettiness of others, but if needed, how to defend your dignity and your faith in God.

In similar fashion, he provided letters with instruction for marriage, for rearing children, for proper work ethic when employed, for how to grow in continued reverence for the Lord and how to lead his family in the same way. In between those letters, and while able, he would share stories of victories and struggles during war, of those that fought alongside him, and sometimes the names of personal friends and their losses or triumphs.

There is a point to this parable. When I share in conversation with someone about their faith, I often ask people these two questions. When you want to talk with God, what do you do? Most answer immediately, "I pray." That is good. When God wants to talk to you, what does He do? This is when I get the 'deer-in-the-headlights' look. People hesitate; however, the answer is simple. He writes you letters and short stories! Of course, God is not limited in how he may communicate with you, but I have found that His most common form of communication is through His Word (the letters and stories He wrote *to you* thousands of years ago). Have you ever opened your Bible, started reading, and found the Scripture right in front of you has immediate application to a situation you or a loved one is dealing with that day? That is not a coincidence!

There is one more important consideration regarding personal Bible study. Remember the verses in the gospel of Mark as Jesus explains the parable of the sower?

> *The secret of the kingdom of God has been given to you. Don't you understand this parable? How then will you understand any parable? The farmer sows the word.* (Mark 4:11 and 13-15)

The secret of the kingdom of God has been given to you in God's Word. Do you need any more reason to spend time studying the Bible? Of course, I am not suggesting that you will ever understand all of God's plans, however, there are many secrets that He is willing to reveal to you if you will only take the time to discover them. And that is a perfect lead-in to our second point.

Part Two: Remember the question, "How do you spend time with God?" The second part of the answer has to do with your commitment level to studying God's Word. Are you casual and inconsistent in this effort, or have you developed an intentional and consistent habit of searching for truth in the Bible?

As Christians, we mature at individual paces. I believe God reveals truth to us according to his timing; however, the responsibility to pursue that knowledge is ours. God has given us free will. If we refer to the parable of the sower once again, Jesus said this of the seed sown in good soil.

> *Still other seed fell on good soil. It came up, grew and produced a crop, some multiplying thirty, some sixty, some a hundred times.* (Mark 4:8)

A farmer does not plant a seed one time, then walk away from it and expect it to mature into a healthy plant. He waters it, nurtures it, clears the weeds away from it, prunes it, and then enjoys the harvest. Your relationship with Jesus Christ is no different. The seed of salvation has been planted in you. What are you doing to nurture that seed into a prospering soul? And have you considered the potential harvest from your commitment to pursue a personal relationship with God?

As I stated in my introduction, once I opened the Bible, the truth began to jump off the page at me. I marveled at the revelations and their application to my life; however, I was not consistent in reading the Bible. I was attending church on a regular basis and hung on every word the pastor shared from the pulpit. I even participated in many of the church's activities and social events. My corporate worship was improving weekly, but developing my personal relationship with Jesus had not yet become a priority.

Like most baby Christians, my intentions were good, but personal Bible study was something that I would attend to if I had any spare time. I was like Paul in Romans 7:18[b]: "For I have the desire to do what is good, but I cannot carry it out." I had many friends, including my pastor, who were encouraging me in this area, but I felt like I was making sufficient progress in my Christian walk without this as a priority. Fortunately, through a brother in Christ, God gave me a little nudge (more like a significant shove) to remedy my ignorance. I received "A Letter from a Friend."

Before I share the contents of this letter, I want to point back to a particular sermon series that the senior pastor shared with our church early in his tenure at First Baptist Concord. The sermon series was titled "No Lonely Souls" and was intended to heighten our awareness of the many individuals who walk into a crowded church (with many Christians surrounding them) but feel lonely and out of place because no one has taken the time to connect with them.

I was fortunate to be leading a Bible study class during the series, and our curriculum followed the sermon series. I asked our class an interesting question. Can Jesus be lonely? After a brief discussion,

I shared the letter that had been given to me years earlier. This letter changed my casual and inconsistent attitude to personal Bible study into an intentional, daily fellowship with my Lord and Savior. I hope it will touch your heart the way it did mine.

A Letter from a Friend

Dear friend,

I just had to send you a note to tell you how much I love you and care about you. I saw you yesterday as you were talking with your friends. I waited all day hoping you would want to talk with me also.

And as evening drew near, I gave you a sunset to close your day and a cool breeze to rest you. And I waited, but you never came. It hurt me, but I still love you, because I'm your friend. I saw you fall asleep last night, and I longed to touch your brow. So, I spilled moonlight on your pillow and on your face. Again, I waited, wanting to rush down so we could talk. I have so many gifts for you. But you awakened late the next day and rushed off to work. My tears were in the rain.

Today you looked so sad and so all alone. It makes my heart ache because I understand. My friends let me down and hurt me so many times. But I love you. Oh, if you would only listen. I really love you.

I try to tell you in the blue sky and the quiet grass. I whisper it in the leaves on the trees and breathe it in the color of the flowers. I shout it to you in the mountain streams and give the birds love songs to sing. I clothe you with warm sunshine and perfume the air with nature's scent. My love for you is deeper than the ocean and bigger than the biggest want or need in your heart. If only you knew how much I wanted to help you.

73

I want you to meet my Father. He wants to help you too. My Father's that way you know. Just call me. I have so much to share with you. But I won't hassle you. I'll wait because I love you!

Your friend,

Jesus

If the key to building a relationship is spending time with that person, then it was imperative that I begin to dedicate time to building my relationship with Jesus. I tried several different options, but for me, I found that setting aside thirty to forty-five minutes first thing in the morning worked best for me. My mind is clearest when I am showered, dressed, and ready to take on the day. The house is quiet and free from distractions, and I can focus on God's Word and spend time in prayer, sharing my thoughts, hopes, concerns, joys, and intercessory prayers with my Lord and Savior, Jesus Christ.

Of course, for all this to prove beneficial, there is one caveat; it is important to actually apply all of God's truth to your life. Consider James 1:22.

Do not merely listen to the word, and so deceive yourselves. Do what it says. (James 1:22)

In Chapters 12 and 13 of John's gospel, Jesus had already predicted His death and identified the one who would betray him (Judas Iscariot). He then tells his disciples that he will not be with them much longer and that where He is going, they cannot follow (John 13:33, 36). What appears next in Chapter 14 is a marvelous show of compassion from Jesus to displace the confusion and despair in the hearts of His disciples.

As He comforts them, Jesus weaves together a beautiful portrayal of the Trinity. It is an eloquent account of the inseparable and divine relationship between Father, Son, and Holy Spirit. Jesus explains that He and the Father are one, that He is the Way, the Truth, the Life, and the only pathway that leads to His Father's house. Jesus assures them that He will return, and their unwavering faith in Him will be honored by the Father with a place in heaven prepared especially for them. And in His absence, the Holy Spirit will serve as their Counselor.

In the next several verses, we find a pathway connecting intentional desire to relationship with Jesus and the expectation to live as though we honor, respect, and love Him, the One who holds our eternal destiny. In other words, do what He says!

> I will not leave you as orphans; I will come to you. *19* Before long, the world will not see me anymore, but you will see me. Because I live, you also will live. *20* On that day you will realize that I am in my Father, and you are in me, and I am in you. *21* **Whoever has my commands and keeps them is the one who loves me.** The one who loves me will be loved by my Father, and I too will love them and show myself to them. (John 14:18-21)

I found that as I read and applied God's truth in my life, certain behaviors (sin, bad habits, and misconceptions) began to fall away one by one. I believe this to be true for most Christians. Every evil (sin) is sanctified at our salvation, but not every evil is immediately dismissed from our behavior (sin nature). That is part of spiritual warfare and our spiritual battle.

Some people have what is called a besetting sin. This can be described as a stubborn sin that is not easily dismissed even after much prayer and a heartfelt desire to free themselves from it (otherwise referred to as a stronghold). This may truly be a difficult struggle, or at times, it may be considered a compromise. ("I'm doing so well in other areas of my Christian walk, surely God won't be upset if I hold on to this one bad habit.") In either case, one of my mentors used to say, "If you are 99. 9% for God, you are 100% against Him." (Reference James 2:10-11)

Now, I am not advocating the necessity for a perfect life, for while we strive for perfection, we will never attain it while on this earth. However, pursuing spiritual maturity on a daily basis will dramatically change your world view and your life. As previously mentioned, Paul addresses this quest in his letter to the Philippians.

> I want to know Christ—yes, to know the power of his resurrection and participation in his sufferings, becoming like him in his death, and so, somehow, attaining to the resurrection from the dead. Not that I have already obtained all this, or have already arrived at my goal, but I press on to take hold of that for which Christ Jesus took hold of me.

> Brothers and sisters, I do not consider myself yet to have taken hold of it. But one thing I do: Forgetting what is behind and straining toward what is ahead, I press on toward the goal to win the prize for which God has called me heavenward in Christ Jesus. **All of us, then, who are mature should take such a view of things.** And if on some point you think differently that too God will make clear to you. Only let us live up to what we have already attained. (Philippians 3:10-16)

At this point, I trust we have concluded that spending time in God's Word is not only vital to establishing your personal relationship with Him (soul prosperity), but it is also the key to your spiritual maturity. If that is the case, how do you suppose Satan would go about trying to defeat that purpose? Might he try to distract you and steal that time away from you? Consider the literary work that follows.

The Devil's Convention (Author Unknown)

Satan called a worldwide convention. In his opening address to his evil angels, he said, "We can't keep the Christians from going to church. We cannot keep them from reading their Bibles and knowing the truth. We cannot even keep them from forming an intimate, abiding relationship experience in Christ. If they gain that connection with Jesus, our power over them is broken.

"So let them go to their churches; let them have their conservative lifestyles, **but steal their time, so they cannot gain that relationship with Jesus Christ.** This is what I want you to do angels .... Distract them from gaining hold of their Savior and maintaining that vital connection throughout their day!"

"How shall we do this?" shouted his angels.

"Keep them busy in the non-essentials of life and invent innumerable schemes to occupy their minds."

I won't post the entire letter, but it is interesting reading. Visit: http://ensignmessage.com/articles/devils-convention/. [4]

Satan's schemes are mentioned many times in the Bible and in this study. While there are certainly other efforts on his part to destroy your soul prosperity, rest assured, they all begin the same way—he attacks your thoughts.

In his book, *It's Not Working, Brother John,* John Avanzini outlines "25 things that close the windows of heaven." Reason number 16 is titled Improper Thinking. Early in the chapter, John says, "The relationship Christians have with God takes place primarily in the mind. (Of course, I speak of the Spirit-dominated mind.) Because of that, the devil puts forth an ongoing effort to influence what goes on in your thinking."[5]

In closing this introduction to our study, I would like to draw attention to The Lord's Prayer, and for you to consider the prayer in a new light. It has become the closing prayer in my daily devotions.

This, then, is how you should pray: "Our Father in heaven, hallowed be your name, your kingdom come, your will be done on earth as it is in heaven. Give us today our daily bread. And forgive us our debts, as we also have forgiven our debtors. And lead us not into temptation, but deliver us from the evil one." (Mathew 6:9-13)

Our Father in heaven, hallowed be your name.
God is our Father. Satan (the father of lies) is not.
God reigns in heaven. Satan temporarily reigns on the earth.
We are to revere and glorify God, not Satan.
In love, He predestined us for adoption to sonship, through Jesus Christ, in accordance with his pleasure and will. (Ephesians 1:5)

Your kingdom come, your will be done on earth.
God's will for your life should supersede and win out over any plans that Satan might attempt to incorporate in your life.
Beloved, I wish above all things that thou mayest prosper and be in health. (3 John 2)

Give us today our daily bread. - *Even as thy soul prospereth.* (3 John 2) Some commentaries suggest this is a reference to asking God to meet our standard daily needs for food, shelter, and clothing. Others offer this as petition for spiritual nourishment for the day. In Matthew 4:4, Jesus answers, "It is written: 'Man shall not live on bread alone, but on every word that comes from the mouth of God." Reference also John, Chapter 6:25-59.

And forgive us our debts, as we also have forgiven our debtors. - *Anyone you forgive, I also forgive. And what I have forgiven - if there was anything to forgive - I have forgiven in the sight of Christ for* *your sake, in order that Satan might not outwit us. For we are not unaware of his schemes.* (2 Corinthians 2:10-11)

And lead us not into temptation. - *Therefore, since we have these promises, dear friends, let us purify ourselves from everything that contaminates body and spirit, perfecting holiness out of reverence for God.* (2 Corinthians 7:1)

But deliver us from the evil one.
Other gospels record, 'deliver us from evil.'
John's gospel is definitive toward the source of all evil—Satan.
The thief comes only to steal and kill and destroy. (John 10:10)

NOTE: As recorded in John's Gospel, just before Jesus is arrested, he prays to his Heavenly Father, first for himself and then for his disciples. Notice the highlighted portion of that prayer below.

> *I will remain in the world no longer, but they are still in the world, and I am coming to you. Holy Father, protect them by the power of your name, the name you gave me, so that they may be one as we are one. While I was with them, I protected them and kept them safe by that name you gave me. None has been lost except the one doomed to destruction so that Scripture would be fulfilled. I am coming to you now, but I say these things while I am still in the world, so that they may have the full measure of my joy within them. I have given them your word and the world has hated them, for they are not of the world any more than I am of the world. **My prayer is not that you take them out of the world but that you protect them from the evil one.** They are not of the world, even as I am not of it. Sanctify them by the truth; your word is truth.* (John 17:11-16)

As we finish this chapter, take a moment to review our foundational verse.

For though we live in the world, we do not wage war as the world does. The weapons we fight with are not the weapons of the world. On the contrary, they have divine power to demolish strongholds. We demolish arguments and every pretension that sets itself up against the knowledge of God, **and we take captive every thought to make it obedient to Christ.** (2 Corinthians 10:3-5)

1. Francis P. Martin, *Hung by the Tongue* (Lafayette: F. P. M. Publications, 1979), 10-12
2. James Hastings, *The Great Texts of the Bible—Volume 11* (New York: Charles Scribner's Sons, T and T Clark, 1910–1915), 428
3. James Hastings, *The Great Texts of the Bible—Volume 11* (New York: Charles Scribner's Sons, T and T Clark, 1910–1915), 428
4. The Devil's Convention. (n. d.) Retrieved from http://ensignmessage.com/articles/devils-convention/
5. John Avanzini, *It's Not Working Brother John* (Tulsa: Harrison House, 1992), 141

Chapter 3: The Power of Association

As this chapter begins, I believe a brief reminder is in order. I have been deliberate in the frequent reference of Scripture to lay out a biblically accurate foundation for understanding God's intention for your life, as well as the battle plan of our enemy, Satan, to defeat you. Going forward, I will continue that practice so that God's Word will remain as our standard bearer. By following the simple diagram below, we were able to establish that our daily walk as Christians is primarily determined by our thoughts, and that our thoughts are influenced by three principal factors (our 5-senses, God, and Satan). We also clearly outlined God's agenda for us as believers, and how Satan's agenda is in direct opposition to the will of God for our lives. After reading the preceding chapter, I must ask, have you found yourself thinking about what you are thinking about?

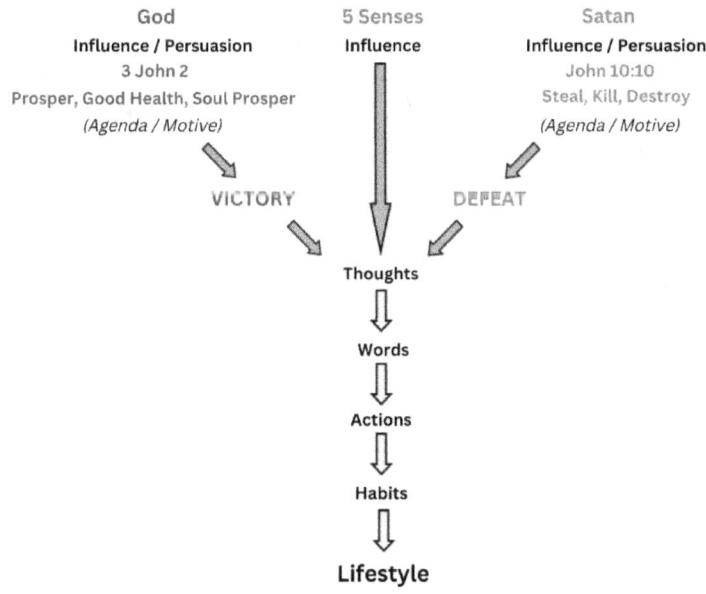

With great intention, the majority of this study has been, and will continue to be focused on the stark contrast between God's desire for our lives and Satan's attempt to prevent us from ever fulfilling any part of that plan. As we review our diagram, many Christians will be familiar with the concept of God's will for their lives as they remember and recite the Lord's prayer: "Our Father in heaven, hallowed be your name, your kingdom come, your will be done on earth as it is in heaven." This is how Jesus taught his disciples (and us) to pray.

Many years later, as the New Testament church began to prosper in Asia Minor, you find the Apostle Paul repeatedly drawing the attention of his readers to the personal implications of these contrasting agendas; God's will vs. Satan's will for our lives.

> *Do not conform to the pattern of this world but be transformed by the renewing of your mind. Then you will be able to test and approve what God's will is - **his good, pleasing, and perfect will**. (Romans 12:2)*

The above was written as an encouragement to honor God's supreme majesty and the gift of grace He had bestowed upon all those that had accepted Jesus Christ as their Savior. In a separate letter, as Paul is advising new believers in their conduct towards others, we see the opposite reference.

> *And the Lord's servant must not be quarrelsome but must be kind to everyone, able to teach, not resentful. Opponents must be gently instructed, in the hope that God will grant them repentance leading them to a knowledge of the truth, and that they will come to their senses and escape from the trap of the devil, **who has taken them captive to do his will**. (2 Timothy 2:24-26)*

There is an important transition point in these verses. Not only do they highlight Satan's ability to impose his will upon us, but they also draw our attention to his ability to influence others. As Paul is instructing Timothy in the appropriate way for a follower of Christ to address false doctrine and the potential argument that could ensue, take notice that he describes the false prophets as *opponents*. (The King James Version uses, "Those that oppose themselves," and The New American Standard Version uses "Those who are in opposition.")

No matter the translation, Paul leaves no room for doubt as to the source of false doctrine. So, while the first part of this study emphasized our personal struggle with spiritual warfare, it is now time to consider how Satan's schemes affect those around us as we focus on the power of association. As before, we will look closely at how God's Word instructs us in this vital area of our lives.

During our lifetime, we have probably all heard comments like this.
- If you lie down with dogs, you will wake up with fleas.
- If everyone else jumped off a bridge, I suppose you would do it too.
- You may not have been a direct participant, but you are assumed guilty by association.

Do any of these expressions sound familiar? At some point, you may have come to the realization that the people you choose to associate with have great potential to cast their influence upon you, be that positive or negative. In the framework of our study on spiritual warfare, this chapter will present a newfound significance to the concept of association. For I would suggest that other than the spiritual forces of evil in this dark world (as referenced in Ephesians 6:12), **the power of association has the most potential to negatively influence our lives.**

To do that, we are going to consider associations both within the church and with the outside world. If you are part of a vibrant church, it would be easy to assume that Christians are immune from any unhealthy associations within the warm fellowship of faithful believers. However, as we will see in 1 Corinthians, the church is not impervious to Satan's attacks.

In Paul's first letter to the church in Corinth, he addresses many of the ills and distractions that plague this body of new believers. His initial concern is division within the church, as the fellowship is beginning to fracture because of leadership preferences.

> *My brothers and sisters, some from Chloe's household have informed me that there are quarrels among you.* ¹² *What I mean is this: One of you says, "I follow Paul"; another, "I follow Apollos"; another, "I follow Cephas"; still another, "I follow Christ."* (1 Corinthians 1:11-12)

This is a common scheme from the 'father of lies' and highly effective at eroding church unity. Many of you have experienced church splits (for various reasons deemed important at the time), and this type of discord in the body tears at the fabric of Christianity. If left unattended, it can and will lead to the death of a church. It also does extensive damage to the gospel message. Knowing the potential outcome, Paul pleads with this congregation.

> *I appeal to you, brothers and sisters, in the name of our Lord Jesus Christ, that all of you agree with one another in what you say and that there be no divisions among you,* **but that you be perfectly united in mind and thought.** (1 Corinthians 1:10)

Following the premise of our study, you can't help but notice the reference to being united in mind and thought. As a side note, there is another verse in Romans that mirrors the one above. Of interest is that Paul's letter to the Romans was written in Corinth. Apparently, *those who cause divisions* (see below) were not exclusive to the church in Corinth. Imagine that!

*I urge you, brothers and sisters, to watch out for those who cause divisions and put obstacles in your way that are contrary to the teaching you have learned. Keep away from them. For such people are not serving our Lord Christ, but their own appetites. By smooth talk and flattery, they deceive **the minds** of naive people.* (Romans 16:17-18)

I want to take a minute to focus on Paul's words from this quote in Romans. "For such people are not serving our Lord Christ, but their own appetites." Remember our diagram. Serving our Lord Christ would mean that God (Jesus Christ in this instance) primarily influences our thought process, and that we are allowing His agenda to guide our lives, individually and collectively as the church.

I think it is obvious that when Paul refers to "those who cause divisions" serving "their own appetites," he is not referring to their physical hunger. One of the most common synonyms for appetite (when not referring to food) is desire. Paul is pointing directly to a spiritual problem—spiritual warfare. Their lives are under a different influence and following a different agenda. So, the question becomes this. If they are not serving Christ, who are they serving?

By allowing Satan's negative influence in their lives, they are serving Satan and promoting his agenda! Stop and think about that for a minute as it applies to our lives. Who do our words, actions, and habits glorify and what does that reflect to the world around us? And as Paul states in this verse, much like the father of lies, such people deceive the minds of naïve believers. Remember these verses from earlier in our study.

As for you, you were dead in your transgressions and sins, in which you used to live when you followed the ways *of this world and of the ruler of the kingdom of the air, the spirit who is now at work in those who are disobedient. All of us also lived among them at one time, **gratifying the cravings of our flesh** and **following its desires and thoughts**.* (Ephesians 2:1-3)

Now go back to Romans 16:17 and notice Paul's stark warning. "I urge you brothers and sisters – keep away from them." Paul already knows and has clearly outlined our struggle with spiritual warfare in Romans, Chapters 7 and 8. Because of this, he gives clear warning not to associate with those under Satan's influence.

*Those who live according to the flesh have **their minds** set on what the flesh desires (their own appetites); but those who live in accordance with the Spirit have **their minds** set on what the Spirit desires. ⁶**The mind** governed by the flesh is death, but **the mind** governed by the Spirit is life and peace. ⁷**The mind** governed by the flesh is hostile to God; it does not submit to God's law, nor can it do so. ⁸Those who are in the realm of the flesh cannot please God."* (Romans 8:5-8) (Bold added for emphasis.)

Please notice Verse 8: "Those who are in the realm of the flesh cannot please God." Why would you, as a Christian, called to glorify God, purposely and knowingly associate with those under Satan's influence if they are not willing to accept Christ in their lives, repent, and modify their behavior? When you look again at Paul's message, is it any wonder why he urges us to keep away from them? ("The mind governed by the flesh is **death.** The mind governed by the flesh is **hostile to God.**")

As we continue, you will notice that the power of association is a major emphasis in the New Testament. In Paul's letter to the Galatians, he was primarily chastising members of the church because they were abandoning the truth of the Gospel and returning to the Jewish law for sanctification. In Chapter 1, Verse 7, he states, "Evidently some people are throwing you into confusion and are trying to pervert the gospel of Christ." Later in Chapter 4, he says the following:

> Those people are zealous to win you over, but for no good. What they want is to alienate you from us, so that you may be zealous for them. (Galatians 4:17)

Reflecting on just the Scripture verses referenced so far, it becomes clear that Paul's concern over our associations is tied directly to our struggle with spiritual warfare. So much so that as he closes his letter to the church in Rome, he says this:

> I want you to be wise about what is good, and innocent about what is evil. The God of peace will soon crush Satan under your feet. (Romans 16:19^b-20)

The clear recognition of our battle with the evil one and the repeated warnings regarding the war for our souls are consistent themes in Paul's writing. Could it be that he is determined for his brothers and sisters in Christ to see the world through the same spiritual lenses that God had developed in him? To find out, let us go back to Paul's instructions to the Corinthians.

As his letter continues, Paul warns against other potential pitfalls and stumbling blocks. Among them are a lack of humility (arrogance), sexual immorality, infidelity, frivolous lawsuits, idolatry and more. Keep in mind that almost all the topics that Paul addresses in 1 Corinthians are sins within the church. But even among believers, Paul emphasizes the following.

> But now I am writing to you that **you must not associate** with anyone who claims to be a brother or sister but is sexually immoral or greedy, an idolater or slanderer, a drunkard or swindler. Do not even eat with such people. (1 Corinthians 5:11)

There are many similar warnings throughout this letter; however, for the purpose of our study, it can best be summed up by Paul's stern warning in Chapter 15.

> *Do not be misled: Bad company corrupts good character.* (1 Corinthians 15:33)

And that is the entire premise for this chapter. If each one of us is personally engaged in a spiritual battle, then it would be appropriate to suggest that those we choose to associate with are also prone to the same struggle, whether knowingly or unknowingly. **The truth is, for every person we have opportunity to interact with, there is a primary spiritual authority influencing that person's thought process, and as a result ruling that person's life.** (Read that again if you need to.)

In a broader context, this extends beyond personal interaction. Who was the primary spiritual influence behind the author of the book you are reading, the producer of the movies you watch, the creator of the internet sites you frequent, etc. ? Now, I am not suggesting that we ought to live in a bubble, but we are called to sharpen our awareness and our defenses. Note the warning in the Scripture reference below.

> *See to it that no one takes you captive through hollow and deceptive philosophy, which depends on human tradition and the elemental spiritual forces of this world rather than on Christ.* (Colossians 2:8)

Let me take a minute to unpack this verse.
The elemental spiritual forces of this world (Satan and his demons)

Human tradition (secular habits influenced and supported by Satan and his demons)

Deceptive philosophy (thinking or attitude built on lies—who is the father of lies?)

Takes you captive (enslaved by sin)

Paul warns these baby Christians that they are not to fall prey to those under the influence of Satan. Of course, this warning was not, and is not, limited to one body of believers nor limited to one point in time. It is as relevant in our lives today as it was to the Colossians. Once we understand this principle, it becomes our responsibility to discern the primary spiritual influence in everyone we encounter and then gauge our personal interaction with that individual or group based on that determination. Like Paul, we must begin to see the world through a new set of spiritual lenses.

> *We do, however, speak a message of wisdom among the mature, but not the wisdom of this age or of the rulers of this age, who are coming to nothing. No, we declare God's wisdom, a mystery that has been hidden and that God destined for our glory before time began.* (1 Corinthians 2:6-7)

> *What we have received is not the spirit of the world, but the Spirit who is from God, so that we may understand what God has freely given us.* (1 Corinthians 2:12)

> **But we have the mind of Christ.** (1 Corinthians 2:16[b])

Remember Mark 4:11 from the first part of our study? "The secret of the kingdom of God has been given to you." That same 'mystery' (God's wisdom) is referenced above. God has given us his Spirit, that we might have the mind of Christ! Can I get an amen? The gift of wisdom and discernment is available to us as believers, but we must pursue it. So, how do we do that?

If we go back to the Old Testament and the beginning of King Solomon's reign, we find an interesting and important interaction between God and the young king in 1 Kings 3:5-10.

> [5] At Gibeon the LORD appeared to Solomon during the night *in a dream*, and God said, "Ask for whatever you want me to give you." (Remember the previous reference to God's ability to influence our thoughts twenty-four hours a day.)
>
> [7] "Now, LORD my God, you have made your servant king in place of my father David. But I am only a little child and do not know how to carry out my duties. [8] Your servant is here among the people you have chosen, a great people, too numerous to count or number. [9] **So give your servant a discerning heart to govern your people and to distinguish between right and wrong**." (Other translations use 'good and evil' in place of 'right and wrong.')
>
> [10] The Lord was pleased that Solomon had asked for this.
>
> [12] I will do what you have asked. I will give you a wise and discerning heart.

As you read this, take special notice of Solomon's main concern. He asks for a discerning heart "to govern God's people,"' or in other words, manage or deal with a population "too numerous to count." Secondly, he is not asking for a general understanding between right and wrong. He is asking God to be able to distinguish the good or evil that is representative in the lives of God's people.

Now part of his anxiety is probably due to the fact that Solomon is only twelve years old when his father David appoints him as king. Perhaps another factor contributing to his anxiety is the chaos that surrounded the end of David's reign as king, not the least of which was David's own son Absalom, who plotted to kill David and take over the kingdom.

Solomon has witnessed the evil influence in those surrounding his father. It was as though he knows that he will face the same destructive force. And isn't it interesting that immediately following God's commitment and promises to Solomon in Verses 12—14, Solomon's wisdom is challenged by the story of two prostitutes claiming to be the mother of the same baby? Solomon must discern which mother is motivated by good (love) and which is motivated by evil. (1 Kings 3:16-28)

Just as Solomon asks God for a discerning heart (mind), we must also seek the wisdom and counsel of the Holy Spirit to guide us in all our interactions and transactions with other people. For just as our diagram outlined God's agenda verses Satan's agenda for us, **each person we meet or befriend has an agenda in mind for us as well.** And just as God works through people, Satan can and does use his influence to work through people.

> *Dear children, do not let anyone lead you astray. He who does what is sinful is of the devil, because the devil has been sinning from the beginning.* (1 John 3:7-8[a])

It is interesting to note that the letters in 1st, 2nd and 3rd John contain no hint of the identity of the Christian community to which they were addressed nor where these believers lived. However, based on the content of the letters, we can be confident in the following.

1. They are Christians.
2. They appear to have a mutual friendship and bond with the writer.

3. They are facing a threat from false teaching, a threat which was both serious and which appears to have arisen from within their Christian community. (1 John 2:18-19)

As you read them, all three of John's letters draw a stark contrast between good and evil. Good is represented by God (Father, Son, and Holy Spirit) and the gift of new life available through Jesus Christ. The many promises outlined by John because of that new life are a reminder of God's agenda for this faith community.

But pay attention! When he writes, "Do not let anyone lead you astray. He who does what is sinful is of the devil," it is a clear warning that those who cling to this false teaching have a completely different agenda for the faithful in Christ. Satan is the primary ruling authority in the lives of these false teachers, and as such, they must be avoided. If you have any doubts about the serious nature of this warning, notice the last half of Verse 8.

The reason the Son of God appeared was to destroy the devil's work. (1 John 3:8[b])

Again, I am not suggesting that we completely isolate ourselves or disengage from those who need salvation or a closer walk with their Savior. However, we are to sharpen our spiritual discernment and walk in wisdom, clarity, and a keen sense of awareness. Allow me to illustrate in a story.

Some of you may remember an old TV series from the early 1970s called *Kung Fu*. In the series, Kwai Chang Caine (David Carradine) is the orphaned son of an American man and a Chinese woman. After his maternal grandfather's death he is accepted for training at a Shaolin Monastery in China, where he grows up to become a Shaolin priest and martial arts expert.

In the pilot episode, Caine's beloved mentor, Master Po, is murdered by the emperor's nephew. Outraged, Caine retaliates by killing the nephew. With a price on his head, Caine flees China to the western United States, where he seeks to find his family roots and, ultimately, his half-brother. Flashbacks are often used to recall specific lessons from Caine's childhood training in the monastery. In these flashbacks, Master Po calls his young student "Grasshopper." However, another Shaolin Monk, Master Kan, refers to him by his Chinese name, Kwai Chang.

This was one of my favorite shows growing up, and even though I cannot remember any other episodes, there is one lesson that stuck with me all these years. I think it might be a good illustration of how we are to develop a discerning spirit. Of course, it has been a long time since I watched this show, but I was able to find the following transcript online from Episode #5, titled "The Tide."

In this episode, Master Kan sends Grasshopper (Kwai Chang) and another young priest, Ho Fong, on a short journey to the market. On the road to the market, they meet a kind old beggar who suggests they take an alternate path as he warns of bandits on the main road.

The young priests head down the alternate path into an ambush, and they are beat up and robbed by five bullies near the marketplace. Kwai Chang and Ho Fong return to the monastery to tell Master Kan that they had been lied to by the beggar and ambushed by a group of strangers.

Kwai Chang reports: "They took our money, our cart, our clothes, everything we had of value."
Master Kan: "Except that which is irreplaceable—your lives. How did you come to leave the main road?"
Ho Fong: "Because we were fooled, we trusted a stranger."
Kwai Chang: "He was an old man, with a kind face and a gentle manner.
Master Kan: "Ho Fong, what lesson have you learned from this?"
Ho Fong: "Never trust a stranger."

Master Kan: "Kwai Chang, what lesson have you learned from this?"

Kwai Chang: **"To expect the unexpected."**

Master Kan: "Ho Fong, in the morning when you are well and rested, you will leave the temple."

Ho Fong: "When shall I return Master Kan?"

Master Kan: "To us, never."

Master Kan: (to Kwai Chang); "You are troubled about your friend, Ho Fong?"

Kwai Chang: "I do not understand why he was asked to leave and not I, when I was equally responsible for trusting the old man."

Master Kan: "We do not punish for trust. If while building a house, a carpenter strikes a nail, it proves faulty by bending, does the carpenter lose faith in all nails and stop building his house?"

Kwai Chang: "Then we are required to trust, even if we are often reminded of the existence of evil."

Master Kan: "Deal with evil through strength. But affirm the good in man through trust. In this way, we are prepared for evil, but we encourage good."

Kwai Chang: "And is good our great reward for trusting?"

Master Kan: "In striving for an ideal, we do not seek rewards. Yet trust does sometimes bring with it a great reward. Even greater than good."

Kwai Chang: "What is greater than good?"

Master Kan: "Love."

Transcript copied from: https://kungfu1953. wordpress.com/television-episodes-main/season-1-1972-73/5-the-tide/ [1]

"To expect the unexpected." That was the lesson! If we return to 1st John, you will see nearly the same thought process outlined in Chapter 4. (See also 1 Thessalonians 5:19-22)

> *Dear friends, do not believe every spirit, **but test the spirits to see whether they are from God**, because many false prophets have gone out into the world. [2]This is how*

you can recognize the Spirit of God: Every spirit that acknowledges that Jesus Christ has come in the flesh is from God, ³but every spirit that does not acknowledge Jesus is not from God. This is the spirit of the antichrist, which you have heard is coming and even now is already in the world. (1 John 4:1-3)

Scripture encourages us to expect the unexpected, even among those who claim to be Christians (identified by Paul in these verses as false prophets). However, Paul also tells us in no uncertain terms how to identify the influence of Satan in these individuals. Just as Solomon did, we must ask God for wisdom and discernment to clearly distinguish between good and evil in those we encounter.

To this point in the chapter, we have focused primarily on the warning against false teachers and those within the church who have not fully matured in Christ. However, we are also called to exercise the same level of discernment when engaged with non-believers outside the body of Christ.

Do not be yoked together with unbelievers. For what do righteousness and wickedness have in common? Or what fellowship can light have with darkness? (2 Corinthians 6:14)

First, let me repeat that I am not suggesting that we ignore our calling to the Great Commission and completely avoid all non-believers. We were all lost at one point, and thank God, a faithful follower of Christ shared the good news with us. However, the Scripture above instructs us not to be "yoked" (or bound together) with unbelievers. For even as Jesus was preparing the disciples to share in his ministry, he warned, "If anyone will not welcome you or listen to your words, leave that home or town and shake the dust off your feet." (Matthew 10:14)

Remember my point that each person we encounter has an agenda in mind for us. I want us to think about that for a minute because it is an important part of the discernment process. As we come into contact with each individual or group, we should seek to approach that interaction with guidance from the Holy Spirit.

The main priority is to discern if their primary influence is that of righteousness or wickedness. Of course, the caution above is to avoid wickedness. Sometimes the clues are obvious. Other times they are more subtle. I have found that listening to what people say (the words that come out of their mouths) is usually the best indicator of where their heart is.

> *Does not the ear test words as the tongue tastes food?* (Job 12:11)

> *With the tongue we praise our Lord and Father, and with it we curse human beings, who have been made in God's likeness.* ¹⁰ *Out of the same mouth come praise and cursing. My brothers and sisters, this should not be.* (James 3:9-10)

Next, if the evidence of wickedness is apparent, and darkness is the ruling authority in their lives, proceed with caution. They might not be aware of it, but Satan could be working through them to cause you harm. If you sense that there may be a hidden agenda behind their actions, then immediately step away. James 4:7 teaches, "Submit yourselves, then, to God. Resist the devil, and he will flee from you."

I would caution that not every agenda of a non-believer is worrisome or treacherous. Sometimes the agenda can be benign, such as a genuine longing for friendship that looks past any differences. I still have friends like that. They know where I stand in my faith, and I know they are comfortable in their current lifestyles. We don't try to influence each other. We just enjoy each other's company. I still pray for them, and expect at some point an event in their life may cause them to inquire about the peace I have in Christ.

But because Satan can and still does work through people, it is best to be continually on guard. Have you ever been in a social gathering or one-on-one with someone and heard the following?

"Oh, come on, one little drink is not going to hurt you."

"Just try it this one time, nobody is ever going to find out."

"It is just a dinner meeting, why do you need to tell your spouse?"

"You are such a goody two shoes. It's okay to let your hair down on occasion."

That type of temptation comes in many forms, and it takes only one instance to start a downward spiral. **Every bad habit, every destructive behavior, every stronghold, begins with a single thought or a single surrender to temptation.** Follow the temptation and you provide an opportunity for Satan to guide you one step closer to defeat.

Perhaps one of the best examples of this can be found when we return to 1 Kings and the story of Solomon's fall from grace. God promises King David that his offspring will be the one to build God's temple. Solomon is that offspring, and God establishes the throne of Solomon's kingdom (2 Samuel 7:12-13). Then, as we read earlier, God honors Solomon's wish and he is blessed with wisdom and discernment. "So that there will never have been anyone like you, nor will there ever be." This is emphasized twice in the following passages.

> [29] God gave Solomon wisdom and very great insight, and a breadth of understanding as measureless as the sand on the seashore. [30] Solomon's wisdom was greater than the wisdom of all the people of the East, and greater than all the wisdom of Egypt. [34] From all nations people came to listen to Solomon's wisdom, sent by all the kings of the world, who had heard of his wisdom. (1 Kings 4:29-34)

> King Solomon was greater in riches and wisdom than all the other kings of the earth. The whole world sought audience

with Solomon to hear the wisdom God had put in his heart. (1 Kings 10:23-24)

Before we continue, the opportunity exists here to make an especially important point. There is a dangerous attitude that can beset anyone who is not careful. It is the perception, whether out of arrogance or ignorance, that we are somehow immune to Satan's temptation (direct or indirect), or that a certain portion of God's law does not apply to us (which of course is also a lie from the father of lies). We find a striking example of this stumbling block in a most unusual place in Scripture. Take careful notice of the verses below.

1 Kings 11:

¹King Solomon, however, loved many foreign women besides Pharaoh's daughter.

² They were from nations about which the LORD had told the Israelites, "You must not intermarry with them, because they will surely turn your hearts after their gods." Nevertheless, Solomon held fast to them in love.

³ He had seven hundred wives of royal birth and three hundred concubines, and his wives led him astray.

⁴ As Solomon grew old, his wives turned his heart after other gods, and his heart was not fully devoted to the LORD his God, as the heart of David his father had been.

⁶ So Solomon did evil in the eyes of the LORD; he did not follow the LORD completely, as David his father had done.

⁹ The LORD became angry with Solomon because his heart had turned away from the LORD, the God of Israel, who had appeared to him twice.

¹⁰ Although he had forbidden Solomon to follow other gods, Solomon did not keep the LORD's command.

*[11] So the L**ORD** said to Solomon, "Since this is your attitude and you have not kept my covenant and my decrees, which I commanded you, I will most certainly tear the kingdom away from you and give it to one of your subordinates."*

My friends, if the wisest man that ever was, or ever will be, can fall short of God's plan due to temptation and the power of association, we ought not think too highly of ourselves.

As we get ready to close, I would like to share a personal story that I believe illustrates the power of association and the need for discernment in our relationships. My specific struggle is not as important as the pattern of temptation and eventual fall into sin.

When I was a child, our home was in the center of a large neighborhood with hundreds of houses within a two-mile radius. I was two years old when we moved there and made many friends through elementary and middle school. The elementary school closest to our home had a large sports field, and we never had a problem assembling enough neighborhood kids for an impromptu game of football, baseball, basketball, or dodge ball. (We called it murder-ball back then—it was so much fun!) In fact, we would challenge other neighborhoods to sporting contests and rarely lost.

As you can imagine, I developed a core group of friends, and we did everything together. In fact, the only time we were at home was when it was time to eat. And even then, I usually had three or four buddies outside my kitchen window, waiting for me to join them in whatever the activity was for the day. These were deep-rooted friendships. We loved each other, we trusted each other, and we had each other's backs. We even accepted each other's shortcomings. We were a team!

As we entered high school, we retained the bond that had developed over all those years. It was 1972, and as freshmen in a much larger school, we were exposed to a much larger sphere of influence. Like many in their mid-teens, drinking beer and wine (when we could get our hands on it) became fashionable. At the same time, the drug culture was growing in popularity and frequently advertised as a new form of counter cultural freedom from society. It was cool, it was fun, and marijuana was the drug of choice.

As a close-knit group of friends, now spread throughout different classes and beginning to establish new acquaintances, we were each exposed to the temptation to join in and be part of the 'in' crowd. Outside of school, I can remember banding together with a common commitment and saying, "We'll never do that." As naïve as we were, drugs still had an extremely negative connotation and quite frankly, scared the heck out of us. They were illegal, they were dangerous, they could get you suspended if not kicked out of school, or they could kill you!

Over time, some of our core group surrendered to temptation, and I can still remember what a shock it was to learn that they had given in to this perilous persuasion. At first, it was just one of our friends, and we all tried to convince him to stop. Then two, then three, and soon many of my closest friends were smoking pot on a regular basis. As the habit embedded itself, they were getting high at what used to be our normal outings. And now we had a subset of 'cool users' within our band of brothers.

Well, eventually it came down to one other friend and me as the only hold outs. We made a promise to each other that we would not, under any circumstance, participate in this drug culture. We would do things together while the rest of our friends enjoyed their new lifestyle. Then one day, the two of us went to a party with our original group of friends, and as they were passing a joint around, he took a hit and offered it to me. I was shocked. He had fallen to the temptation too. Now all my friends had given into the same temptation. I was the lone holdout and the voices I mentioned earlier began:

"Oh, come on, one little toke is not going to hurt you."
"Just try it this one time, nobody is ever going to find out."
"Oh, you are such a goody two shoes. Everybody else is doing it."

I was seventeen years old. These were all my closest friends, some of whom I had known and trusted since kindergarten. Now a senior, I had not participated in sports or any social activities during high school. I had not felt the need to. I had a group of friends, and we all entered the same high school at the same time. Not having the personality at the time to seek out new relationships, I continued to hang out with the same friends. I would attend the parties and still play pick-up games at the schoolyard, but things were different than they had been before. I felt like an outsider with people I had known most of my life.

I stood my ground for a while, trying to enjoy the past camaraderie, but continuing to decline the invitation to get high. But over time, my determination began to wane. One by one, most of the fears I had about drugs were fading away, like bricks being removed from a wall. I did not realize it then, but Satan was whispering in my ear.

"Are your friends really that different from before? Surely you can see that smoking pot is not dangerous. Why should this be illegal? It is no different from drinking alcohol. Nothing bad is happening to your friends. Why don't you join in the fun? It is just marijuana. It is not going to kill you. You can control it." (One of Satan's biggest lies!)

Eventually, I gave into the temptation. I allowed the slow drip of Satan's temptation to influence my life in the wrong direction. I did not realize it at the time, but he had already succeeded in the lives of my friends and was now working through them to accomplish the same agenda in my life. What was once inconceivable became common place and then acceptable through the power of association. When sin becomes normalized in your sphere of influence, it is a clear indication that you are in trouble and need to step away before the enemy ensnares you for his objective.

That one decision led to years of substance abuse, experimenting with other drugs, and many close calls with the law. As I look back at it now, I believe it was only God's grace and the fervent prayers of my parents that kept me alive and out of jail. Praise the Lord!

I share this story to make the following points.

1. As stated previously, the specific struggle is not as important as the pattern of temptation and eventual fall into sin. As Paul warned in 1 Corinthians, Chapters 5 and 6, the pattern can be applied to drug or alcohol abuse, sexual immorality, infidelity, lawlessness, physical or verbal abusiveness, foul language, idolatry, gambling, etc.
2. Satan can and will tempt you directly, but he will also use the power of association to his advantage.
3. Satan is cunning, subtle, and patient. He will whisper in your thoughts for as long as you allow him to. (But as we continue our study, you will not be unaware of his schemes.)
4. At the first surrender to temptation and during the downward spiral, **YOU** are allowing Satan to open wide the path to destruction. And the eventual outcome will not be pretty. "For the wages of sin is death." (Romans 6:23)
5. We may not realize it, but we all have the potential to influence other people. Whose side are you on? "But the gift of God is eternal life in Christ Jesus our Lord." (Romans 6:23)

I have referenced Solomon quite a bit in this section of our study; however, his father David is aware of the power of association. Just look at his words as he cries out to the Lord in prayer.

> *Test me, O LORD, and try me, examine my heart and my mind; for your love is ever before me, and I walk continually in your truth. I do not sit with the deceitful, nor do I associate with hypocrites. I abhor the assembly of evildoers and refuse to sit with the wicked.* (Psalm 26:2-5)

You know, sometimes a simple proclamation is the best. With that said, we will close this chapter with words of wisdom from The Book of Proverbs.

> **A righteous man is cautious in friendship, but the way of the wicked leads them astray.** (Proverbs 12:26)

As I have done at the close of prior chapters, I will ask you to reflect on the foundational verse of this study.

> *For though we live in the world, we do not wage war as the world does. The weapons we fight with are not the weapons of the world. On the contrary, they have divine power to demolish strongholds. We demolish arguments and every pretension that sets itself up against the knowledge of God,* **and we take captive every thought to make it obedient to Christ.** (2 Corinthians 10:3-5)

1. Kung Fu - The Tide. (1972) Retrieved from https://kungfu1953.wordpress.com/television-episodes-main/season-1-1972-73/5-the-tide/

Chapter 4: The Danger of Sin and Hypocrisy!

In the previous chapter, we focused on the potential danger of association, both with non-believers as well as those within the body of Christ that are not fully aware of evil's influence, still maturing in their faith, or deliberately acting as false prophets. The emphasis was identifying, through discernment from the Holy Spirit, the primary spiritual influence in those we encounter and then forming an appropriate course of action based on that determination.

In this chapter, we are going to focus exclusively on those who have placed their faith in Jesus Christ and are attempting to live out the Christian lifestyle. When we claim to be Christians, we must understand that there is an entire world looking through that glass house just waiting to judge us. And much of that world seems to think that just because we accept Christ as our Savior, we automatically become pure, and holy, and sinless. What we know to be true is that God does not expect us to be sinless, for we will never attain perfection in this life. We are however, as we mature in our Christian faith, compelled by love and gratitude for the gift we have been given (salvation) to sin less.

As part of the salvation that has been granted unto us, we are called to actively engage in the Great Commission. We are called to set ourselves apart from the world and set an example that would not only draw nonbelievers to know the truth of the gospel, but also glorify God. Whether casual or deliberate, this commitment to live a Christian lifestyle is reason enough for Satan to draw a big target on your back. God's purpose for us is clear, but you can rest assured that Satan will attempt to defeat that agenda with one of his own. Let's take a minute to review our diagram again.

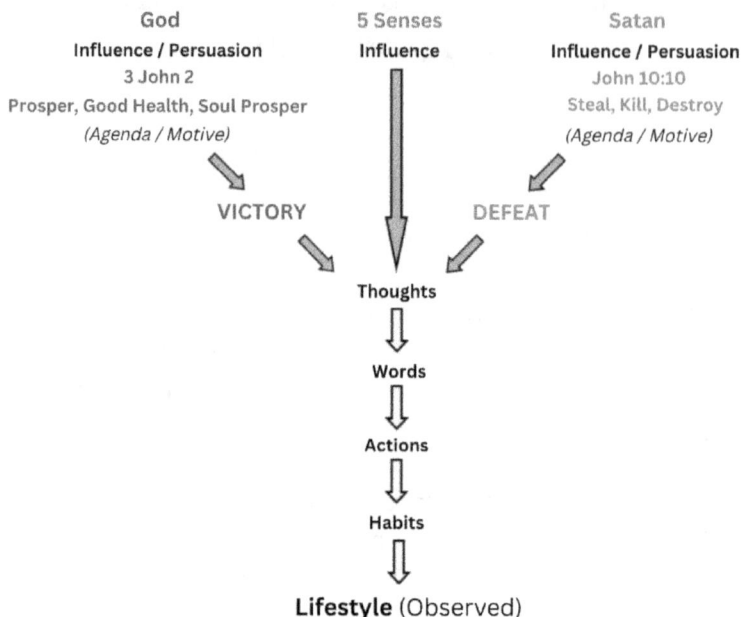

Notice that I have added the word *observed* to the diagram. In your struggle with spiritual warfare and the battle for our thoughts and minds, Satan has more than one agenda for you. Yes, it is always a personal attack, and we discussed that part of his agenda at length in the previous chapters, but it goes beyond your personal struggle. For if we are called to set an example, and Satan causes us to fall to temptation, then the promise of the gospel becomes a fallacy to those observing us. The devil's goal is for unbelievers to view us as hypocrites, thus denying the gospel message and tarnishing God's image.

Falling prey to sin and this part of the devil's scheme is the primary danger of hypocrisy. To better understand this danger, it will be helpful to examine a definition of hypocrisy. I borrowed the explanation below from *Layman's Bible Commentary Set*.

Hypocrisy can take many forms:

1. *Hypocrisy can be a conformity to the values and expectations of someone else, bowing to the idol of other people's values, which are not really our own. Hypocrites adjust and accommodate their appearance to what other people think or feel.*
2. *Hypocrisy can be an inconsistency. It is the discrepancy between what appears and what is, between the way things seem and the way they are.*
3. *Hypocrisy can be a deception by our actions or our words, acting in such a way that people will come to the wrong conclusion.*

One of the temptations we face as Christians is to focus on outward acts or appearances rather than on <u>inward motivation</u>. We are often guilty of taking new Christians aside and trying to rid them of their evil behaviors, as though cleaning up the outside purifies the inside. Jesus teaches us that when we clean up the inside, <u>when our attitudes and motives are pure</u>, our outward lives will clean up. Often, cleaning up only the outside tends to corrupt the inside more. Now, having cleaned up the outside, we find pride and self-righteousness to be added to our list of inner evils. Let us learn from our Lord that holiness begins inside and works outward, and not the reverse. [1]

There are several points worth noting in this commentary.

1. Notice the reference to inward motivation. This is directly in line with the premise of this study and who is influencing your thoughts.
2. Jesus teaches us that when we clean up the inside, <u>when our attitudes and motives are pure</u>, our outward lives will clean up. This is a mind influenced by God!

3. Often, cleaning up only the outside tends to corrupt the inside more. Have you ever noticed that one lie leads to another? In an attempt to cover our sin, the level of deception grows. This is a mind influenced by Satan, the father of lies.
4. We find pride and self-righteousness to be added to our list of inner evils. These are two of Satan's most powerful tools!
5. Holiness begins inside and works out, and not the reverse.

Let me provide a practical example of this point by reflecting on my past. Drinking beer was almost a cultural necessity in Milwaukee and practically a daily activity for me, starting in my late teens, and then following me as I moved to Atlanta at the age of twenty-three. My parents would visit me at least twice a year, and because beer was more expensive in Atlanta, my dad would always bring two cases which quickly found their way to the refrigerator in my garage. This went on for years, and each delivery was well received and put to good use.

After my profession of faith in Jesus Christ, my consumption of alcohol began to decrease significantly. I can honestly say that this was not a well thought out or intentional decision. I hadn't prayed about it, nor did I feel like it affected my daily walk with the Lord. It just became less important to me as I matured in my faith and my circle of influence began to change (the power of association).

During one visit, as we unloaded two cases of beer from my dad's car and carried them to the garage, the two cases that he delivered six months earlier were still in the refrigerator. I can still remember the puzzled look on my dad's face as he asked me, "Son, have you stopped drinking?"

I really hadn't thought about it until he asked me that question. But sure enough, as my walk with the Lord became more consistent and grew stronger, the Holy Spirit was transforming me from the inside out. My life was becoming a reflection of my faith. Many of you have probably experienced the same thing. It may have been foul language, drug abuse, or any one of a number of bad behaviors. As your faith matured, the Holy Spirit began to convict you, and either suddenly or over time, your behavior changed.

It may come as no surprise that the Bible commentary above was written in regard to Jesus' interaction with the Pharisees and Sadducees as recorded in Luke, Chapters 11 and 12. In Luke's gospel account, Jesus has been invited to dinner by one of the Pharisees. While at dinner, Jesus sharply criticizes the Pharisees for their hypocritical behavior (the six woes). After the dinner, and while a crowd of many thousands had gathered around Jesus, he gave this warning, specifically to his disciples.

> *Jesus began to speak first to his disciples, saying; "**Be on your guard against the yeast of the Pharisees, which is hypocrisy.**" (Luke 12:1*^{b}*)

I borrow again from the *Layman's Bible Commentary Set*.

> *Jesus states clearly that the 'yeast' of the Pharisees is hypocrisy. They tend to know little about true religion and act as if they do. On the outside they look fine. They have long, pious-sounding prayers, and they have all the trappings of men of dignity and holiness. But inside, Jesus says, they are full of greed and wickedness. (Referring to Luke 11:39)*

> *Hypocrisy is a problem no matter what the motivation. Whether we are hypocritical to achieve men's praise or to avoid their persecution, Jesus calls us to something different.* [2]

Returning to Scripture, in addition to the above warning in Verse 1, Jesus said this to his disciples.

There is nothing concealed that will not be disclosed, or hidden that will not be made known. What you have said in the dark will be heard in the daylight, and what you have whispered in the ear in the inner rooms will be proclaimed from the roofs. (Luke 12:2-3)

We will come back to this verse later, but for now, look closely at what Jesus is telling his disciples (and us). No matter how clever you think you are at hiding your sin, when you succumb to Satan's temptation, the eventual outcome is that **you will be exposed**. Your sin, whether developed over days, months, or years, will be 'heard in the daylight' and 'proclaimed from the rooftops.' Jesus was clear in His warning; you can be confident that Satan's agenda will achieve its original intent!

Now, as some of you may know, this same warning from Jesus is referenced a little differently in the gospel of Mark and the gospel of Matthew.

"Be careful," Jesus warned them. "Watch out for the yeast of the Pharisees and that of Herod." (Mark 8:15)

Jesus said to them. "Be on your guard against the yeast of the Pharisees and Sadducees." (Matthew 16:6)

In both gospels above, the religious elite, having already witnessed many of the miracles performed by Jesus, ask him for another sign from heaven to prove that he is the Messiah. Of course, Jesus chastises the Pharisees and Sadducees directly, but later, when he shares his warning with the disciples, they mistakenly think Jesus is chastising them because they did not bring enough bread to eat on their journey. (Remember, in both gospels, this exchange is shortly after Jesus feeds the five thousand and then feeds the four thousand.)

In both accounts, Jesus reminds the disciples of these two miracles. And in both accounts, Jesus asks, "Do you still not understand?" However, only in Matthew do you see the following exchange.

> "How is it you don't understand that I was not talking to you about bread?" Then they understood that he was not telling them to guard against the yeast used in bread, <u>but against the teaching of the Pharisees and Sadducees</u>. (Matthew 16:11-12)

The obvious question here is what is the teaching of the Pharisees and Sadducees, and why is it so dangerous? The answer is twofold as the religious elite are hampered by their pride and their religion.

1. Up to this point, even after all the miracles they had witnessed, <u>they refuse to place their faith in Jesus</u>. NOTE: This is also true of Herod Antipas as referenced in Mark, Chapter 6. When Herod hears about Jesus, he thinks that Jesus is John the Baptist "come back from the dead" (<u>Mark 6:16</u>). Herod is obviously impressed by Jesus, yet he does not believe in him or his message of the kingdom of God.

2. <u>The Pharisees still hold onto a 'righteousness by keeping the law' mentality.</u> In other words, a salvation by works attitude. Paul later writes about this in Romans 9:30-32 and confirms Jesus as the abolishment of the law in Chapter 10, Verse 4.

   a. *What then shall we say? That the Gentiles, who did not pursue righteousness, have obtained it, a righteousness that is by faith; but the people of Israel, who pursued the law as the way of righteousness, have not attained their goal. Why not? <u>Because they pursued it not by faith but as if it were by works</u>. They stumbled over the stumbling stone.* (Romans 9:30-32)

b. *Christ is the end of the law so that there may be righteousness for everyone who believes.* (Romans 10:4)

Here is the danger. The disciples are being groomed to be saved by grace, a salvation secured by faith in Jesus Christ, who by His death, burial, and resurrection, later grants His righteousness to them before the Father. Eventually, this leads to Jesus' command to go and make disciples of all nations (The Great Commission (Matthew 28:18-20), and the indwelling of the Holy Spirit at the day of Pentecost (Acts 2:1-4). For the disciples to preach the gospel of Jesus Christ and still hold to any part of the Pharisees' teaching in regard to 'pursuing the law as the way of righteousness' will be the height of hypocrisy.

As we continue in the New Testament, Paul addresses this same topic in 1 Corinthians, Chapter 10. In the text titled "Warnings from Israel's History," Paul warns the new church not to repeat the disobedience and hypocrisy of the exiled Jewish nation.

*For I do not want you to be ignorant of the fact, brothers and sisters, that our ancestors were all under the cloud and that they all passed through the sea. ² They were all baptized into Moses in the cloud and in the sea. ³ They all ate the same spiritual food ⁴ and drank the same spiritual drink; for they drank from the spiritual rock that accompanied them, and that rock was Christ. ⁵ Nevertheless, God was not pleased with most of them; their bodies were scattered in the wilderness. ⁶ **Now these things occurred as examples to keep us from setting our hearts on evil things as they did**. ⁷ Do not be idolaters, as some of them were, as it is written: "The people sat down to eat and drink and got up to indulge in revelry. ¹² So, if you think you are standing firm, be careful that you don't fall!* (1 Corinthians 10:1-7, 12)

The Israelites benefit from God's grace as they are set free from Egypt. They witness God's miracles and are happy to partake of his blessings of food and water while in the desert. However, their hearts are set on evil as they later complain, practice immoral behavior and idolatry, and long to return to Egypt and do not place their faith in the Lord God Almighty. As a result, "God was not pleased with most of them."

God is not pleased with their hypocritical behavior and lack of faith. Paul is warning that "these things" are examples to be avoided, and to beware of the temptation that is sure to come from Satan and his demons. Paul closes with perhaps his strongest statement against hypocrisy.

> *You cannot drink the cup of the Lord and the cup of demons too; you cannot have a part in both the Lord's Table and the table of demons.* (1 Corinthians 10:21)

When studying ancient Scripture, it almost seems natural that we separate ourselves from the practical application to everyday life in the 21st century. After all, Jesus, in the text, speaks to his disciples not us. Paul speaks to the new church in Corinth not us. This misguided attitude often results in the familiar assertion that we've come a long way since then and times have changed. Well, it may be true that our culture is different today, but the devil's schemes remain the same, and one of his primary goals (to shame all Christians) also remains the same. Ironically, the remedy for this misguided thought process is a deeper understanding of Scripture.

> *As iron sharpens iron, so one person sharpens another.* (Proverbs 27:17)

As we sharpen our understanding of Scripture, we will begin with an overview from the book of Acts. This is the story of the birth and infancy of the new church of Jesus Christ. Jesus commissioned His disciples, the Father anointed them with the Holy Spirit, they begin to preach boldly, and the new church was born. Upon Saul's conversion in Chapter 9, his story begins to dominate the rest of the book. Mostly, it is the story of a church planter, now called Paul, who travels from town to town spreading the gospel and starting churches in Antioch, Philippi, Thessalonica, Corinth, Ephesus, and elsewhere. At every part of his journey, he chronicles how he is opposed by the enemy and those under Satan's control.

I think it is important to our study, and to a general understanding of Paul's letters to the various churches, that we look a little closer at the beginning of Paul's walk with Jesus Christ. While Saul's conversion is detailed by Luke in Acts, Chapter 9, it is referenced twice more in the same book. Reviewing all three references collectively brings clarity to Christ's intent for calling on this man who considered himself the worst of sinners. "Here is a trustworthy saying that deserves full acceptance: Christ Jesus came into the world to save sinners—of whom I am the worst." (1 Timothy 1:15) The story begins in Acts 9:3-6.

> As he neared Damascus on his journey, suddenly a light from heaven flashed around him. He fell to the ground and heard a voice say to him, "Saul, Saul, why do you persecute me?" "Who are you, Lord?" Saul asked. "I am Jesus, whom you are persecuting," he replied. "Now get up and go into the city, and you will be told what you must do."

Blinded by his encounter with Jesus, Saul is led into Damascus by his companions. Without sight for three days, the Lord sends a disciple named Ananias to restore Saul's vision. He is immediately baptized and receives the indwelling of the Holy Spirit. After spending several days with the disciples, Saul begins to preach in the synagogues that Jesus is the Son of God. All who hear him are astonished and his testimony that Jesus is the Christ grows more and more powerful. But Scripture then records the following.

After many days had gone by, there was a conspiracy among the Jews to kill him, but Saul learned of their plan. Day and night, they kept close watch on the city gates in order to kill him. But his followers took him by night and lowered him in a basket through an opening in the wall. (Acts 9:23-25)

Saul returns to Jerusalem and joins the disciples where he continues to boldly proclaim Jesus as the Messiah. But once again his message is ill received.

He talked and debated with the Grecian Jews, but they tried to kill him. When the believers learned of this, they took him down to Caesarea and sent him off to Tarsus. (Acts 9:29-30)

Sometime later, Barnabas travels to Tarsus looking for Saul, and together they travel to Antioch to teach and support the growing church there. After traveling through much of the region to preach the gospel, Paul, prompted by the Holy Spirit, returns to Jerusalem and an uproar quickly develops among the devout Jews. Ridiculed, beaten, and in chains, he finds himself before the angry crowd and describing his original encounter with the Lord and defending his call to preach the gospel. This is referenced in Acts 22:6-11.

About noon as I came near Damascus, suddenly a bright light from heaven flashed around me. I fell to the ground and heard a voice say to me, "Saul! Saul! Why do you persecute me?" "Who are you, Lord?" I asked. "I am Jesus of Nazareth, whom you are persecuting," he replied. My companions saw the light, but they did not understand the voice of him who was speaking to me. "What shall I do, Lord?" I asked. "Get up," the Lord said, "and go into Damascus. There you will be told all that you have been assigned to do."

After describing the incident to the crowd, Paul is taken to the guard's barracks for his safety and once again, a plot develops among the Jews to kill him. As Chapter 23 begins, we see Paul called before the Sanhedrin (a counsel of the religious elite) challenging their understanding of the Jewish law. Upon stating his belief in the resurrection of the dead, the debate among the Pharisees and Sadducees becomes so heated that the guards, now fearing for Paul's life, again escort him into the barracks until he can be transferred to Caesarea the next evening. In Verse 11, you find this encouragement and direction from the Lord. *The following night the Lord stood near Paul and said, "Take courage! As you have testified about me in Jerusalem, so you must also testify in Rome."*

While in Caesarea, Paul defends himself in the court of Governor Felix but remains under guard in Herod's palace for two years. Paul is then called before the new Governor, Porcius Festus, and eventually granted an appearance before King Agrippa. Before the king, it is Paul's final reference of his encounter that has the most relevance to our study.

> *On one of these journeys I was going to Damascus with the authority and commission of the chief priests. About noon, as I was on the road, I saw a light from heaven, brighter than the sun, blazing around me and my companions. We all fell to the ground, and I heard a voice saying to me in Aramaic, "Saul, Saul, why do you persecute me? It is hard for you to kick against the goads."*

> *Then I asked, "Who are you, Lord?"*

> *"I am Jesus, whom you are persecuting," the Lord replied. "Now get up and stand on your feet. I have appeared to you to appoint you as a servant and as a witness of what you have seen and will see of me. I will rescue you from your own people and from the Gentiles. **I am sending you to them to open their eyes and turn them from darkness***

*to light, **and from the power of Satan to God**, so that they may receive forgiveness of sins and a place among those who are sanctified by faith in me."*(Acts 26:12-18)

The significance and application of these verses is central to understanding Paul's passion and commitment to proclaiming the gospel. In our prior discussion regarding 'The Power of Association' I wrote the following. The clear recognition of our battle with Satan and the war for our souls are consistent themes in Paul's letters. Could it be that he is determined for his brothers and sisters in Christ to see the world through the same spiritual lenses that God had developed in him?

It is in this third reference by Paul that we are given insight into his spiritual discernment. It is Jesus who details the specific purpose for Paul's ministry and Jesus who clearly identifies Satan as the enemy. But it is more than that. The highlighted verse above is exactly what Jesus does in Paul's life. Jesus opens his eyes from darkness to light (giving him new spiritual lenses), allowing Paul to clearly recognize the enemy's schemes and turn from the power of Satan to the power of God.

As the father of lies, Satan's *power* is the ability to influence, persuade, deceive, and hold captive the thoughts of man, which inevitably leads to acts of unrighteousness. With that one statement, Jesus pierces Paul's heart with the truth that his previous hatred of those professing Christ as Savior was influenced by the power of Satan's deception. Prior to his conversion, Paul perceived the gospel as blasphemous and thought he served God by persecuting the followers of Jesus. In truth, he was advancing Satan's agenda by torturing and oppressing new Christians. As retched as that felt, the greater realization is that God had completely forgiven him of his sins, sanctified him by his new faith in Jesus Christ, and commissioned him to share that good news with others.

When you see Saul's conversion from that perspective, you begin to understand his passion and boldness in proclaiming the gospel. After all, the gospel message is Saul's personal and powerful testimony. But more importantly, it is Paul's unique insight into spiritual warfare (made visible by Jesus in their first and subsequent encounters) that is fervently preached in each of his letters to the new believers as he attempts to open their eyes from darkness to light, while exposing Satan as the church's primary adversary. (I'll share more on Paul's *subsequent encounters* with Jesus later in the study.

The Book of Romans starts this series of letters from Paul to the churches he planted in these various cities. It is the first such letter in the New Testament and as such, holds a unique level of importance. The intensity with which Paul identifies Satan and his schemes seems to grow with each letter. But as you will see, the references, while subtle, begin in the early part of this first letter.

Remember, these letters were meant to be read aloud to the church body and then passed along from town to town. And now they have been passed down to you. What you find recorded in your Bible is Paul's letter to **YOU!** The beginning of this letter is significant because it holds direct application to our lives as well as a clear direction for our lives. Paul begins with our calling as born-again Christians.

> *Paul, a servant of Christ Jesus, called to be an apostle and set apart for the gospel of God - the gospel he promised beforehand through his prophets in the Holy Scriptures regarding his Son, who as to his earthly life was a descendant of David, and who through the Spirit of holiness was appointed the Son of God in power by his resurrection from the dead: Jesus Christ our Lord. Through him we received grace and apostleship to call all the Gentiles to the obedience that comes from faith for his*

*name's sake. And **you** also are among those Gentiles who are called to belong to Jesus Christ.* (Romans 1:1-6)

There is that word again—**you!** You (we) are among *those Gentiles* who are called to belong to Jesus Christ. We are all called to be apostles (by his grace and according to our spiritual gifts) and set apart to advance the salvation gospel. But there is more—look closely. When we accept the gift of salvation and claim the title *Christian*, we are called "to the obedience that comes from faith in Jesus Christ."

Therein lies our greatest challenge. The foundation of our calling, to apostleship and to advancing the Gospel, rests in our ability to be obedient to the faith we claim in Jesus Christ. The problem is, apart from the power of God and the indwelling of the Holy Spirit, we do not have the ability to remain obedient. And even with God's help, we are not immune to Satan's temptations.

This crossroad serves as the perfect breeding ground for hypocrisy. For if our claim does not match up with our behavior, what type of example are we setting? No one knew this better than Paul as he wrote about struggling with sin.

> *So, I find this law at work: Although I want to do good, evil is right there with me. For in my inner being I delight in God's law; but I see another law at work in me, **waging war against the law of my mind** and making me a prisoner of the law of sin at work within me. What a wretched man I am! Who will rescue me from this body that is subject to death? Thanks be to God, who delivers me through Jesus Christ our Lord! So then, I myself **in my mind** am a slave to God's law, but in my sinful nature a slave to the law of sin.* (Romans 7:21-25)

Perhaps more than any other reference in the Bible, the Scripture above illustrates our perpetual struggle with spiritual warfare and the battle for our thoughts and minds. Even as we refer to our diagram, Paul perfectly describes the conflict of influence in our lives, God's agenda vs. Satan's agenda. **"Although I want to do good, evil is right there with me."** And notice Paul's powerful language: *waging war, making me a prisoner, wretched man, slave,* and *subject to death.* This battle is not to be taken lightly.

But there is more in these verses that demands our attention. As prominent as the contrast between good and evil, there is another startling claim in Paul's language. Please notice how he starts this passage. "So, I find this <u>law</u> at work." **Paul is not proposing a theory. He's stating a fact!** As he does through the first ten chapters of Romans, Paul repeatedly points to the disparity between God's law and the law of sin. As adults, we know a law is absolute until it is revoked. And a law can be revoked only by a higher authority. As mature Christians, we lay claim to the highest authority, as does Paul. "Thanks be to God, who delivers me through Jesus Christ our Lord!"

In this passionate letter to the church in Rome, Paul dedicates Chapters 5-8 to an imperative theological truth. We are caught in a battle between good and evil, and we become slaves to that which we choose to follow or obey. I've included a brief summary in the verses below; however, a determined self-study of these chapters will help clarify this disparity.

> *16 Don't you know that when you offer yourselves to someone as obedient slaves, you are slaves of the one you obey - whether you are slaves to sin, which leads to death, or to obedience, which leads to righteousness? 22 But now that you have been set free from sin and have become slaves of God, the benefit you reap leads to holiness, and the result is eternal life.* (Romans 6:16, 22)

For we know that our old self was crucified with Him so that the body of sin might be done away with, that we should no longer be slaves to sin. (Romans 6:6)

*Therefore, there is now no condemnation for those who are in Christ Jesus, ² because through Christ Jesus the **law** of the Spirit who gives life has set you free from the **law** of sin and death.* (Romans 8:1-2)

Paul offers us great hope in these promises, yet the question remains; where does this absolute law originate? Return with me to Genesis.

> The Lord God took the man and put him in the Garden of Eden to work it and take care of it. And the Lord God commanded the man, "You are free to eat from any tree in the garden; but you must not eat from the tree of the knowledge of good and evil, for when you eat from it you will certainly die. " (Genesis 2:15-17)

We are not given the exact arrival time of evil in the creation account. Many theologians believe Satan's fall from grace and expulsion from heaven happened between Genesis 1:1 and Genesis 1:2. We are not here to debate that issue. What we can conclude from Genesis 2:17, is that the **law** of good and evil existed when God placed man in the Garden of Eden. Evil (Satan) was already there, and although Adam and Eve wanted to do good, evil was right there with them.

The presence of evil is also referenced in Genesis 4:6-7 in the story of Cain and Abel. Again, although Cain wanted to do good, evil was right there with him.

*Then the L*ORD *said to Cain, "Why are you angry? Why is your face downcast? If you do what is right, will you not be accepted? But if you do not do what is right,* **sin is crouching at your door; it desires to have you, but you must rule over it."** (Genesis 4:6-7)

Imagine if you would that God is having this conversation with you. He is not discussing a theory with you. He is trying to explain this universal law. Sin is crouching at your door, and it desires to have you. **YOU** must rule over it! And just in case we haven't quite cemented this truth in our conscience, we discover the potential consequence of our disobedience to God's command to rule over sin in Genesis 6:5.

*The L*ORD *saw how great the wickedness of the human race had become on the earth, and that* **every inclination of the <u>thoughts</u> of the human heart was only evil all the time**. (Genesis 6:5)

Now, we know that God has always been, and will always be, in control of his creation. However, in each of these examples, the law of sin prevailed. Satan's agenda succeeded. We are born with the Adamic nature as a consequence of Adam and Eve's disobedience. Cain was cursed as a result of his failure to rule over sin. And in probably one of the saddest commentaries in the Bible (Genesis 6:6), the great flood occurred because all of mankind (except for Noah and his family) was seduced by the law of sin.

*The L*ORD *regretted that he had made human beings on the earth, and his heart was deeply troubled.* (Genesis 6:6)

There is a purpose for venturing down this rabbit hole. Remember our calling according to Paul? We are called to belong to Jesus Christ, to join as apostles in advancing the gospel, and to the obedience that comes from faith in His name. As we attempt to carry out this calling *(Although I want to do good...)*, **we must**

acknowledge that the law of sin is real *(...evil is right there with me)*. And as God commanded Cain; **we must rule over it.** It cannot be ignored, and it cannot be minimized.

You may not believe in or be able to physically take hold of the law of gravity, but I do not recommend walking off a ten-story building to test its validity. Likewise, you may not be aware of or believe in the law of sin, but I don't recommend that you attempt to live out the Christian lifestyle without attesting to its validity. To do so will only expose you to an increased danger of hypocrisy.

Now that we have a clear-cut definition of hypocrisy, as well as vigorous warnings from our Heavenly Father, our Savior Jesus Christ, and the apostle Paul to guard against it, we are going to take a closer look at three specific dangers of sin and hypocrisy.

1. Being "Punk'd" (2 Corinthians 11:13-15)
2. Ruining God's Reputation (Romans 2:17-24)
3. The Point of No Return (Romans 1:18-32 and 2:5-8)

On the issue of being *Punk'd*, I would like to use a contemporary analogy to illustrate this specific danger of hypocrisy. You may be familiar with this short-lived reality show on MTV. Punk'd was an American, hidden camera-practical joke reality television series that first aired on MTV in 2003. It was created by Ashton Kutcher and Jason Goldberg, with Kutcher serving as producer and host. It bears a resemblance to the classic hidden camera shows, *Candid Camera* and *TV's Bloopers & Practical Jokes*, which also featured pranks on celebrities. Being "punk'd" referred to being the victim of such a prank. (Borrowed from Wikipedia.com.)

You may think this is an odd analogy for spiritual warfare, but I trust you will find the similarities as we explore a little further. There are many examples to choose from when it comes to the subject of hypocrisy among Christians.

For the purpose of this study, I chose to focus first on perhaps the most damaging to both the individual and to the church at large; the fall of someone in a leadership position.

While we are all at risk for temptation, I believe Satan purposely targets those with which he can cause the greatest amount of damage. For this reason, pastors, deacons, missionaries, and church staff are prime targets. And if we include televangelists, there are probably a few names that come to mind quite readily.

The tactics are not new, and as we have already discussed, the father of lies is cunning, devious, and patient. The temptation may seem innocent and insignificant at first, an initial thought introduced by Satan or through someone already under his influence (the power of association). If there is a level of pride involved, it will only make matters worse. As is referenced so many times in the Bible, sexual sin seems to be a favorite weapon of the enemy. As the sin evolves, pride usually steps in, and one of Satan's biggest lies begins to take hold within the individual. "I can control this."

What was once inconceivable can quickly develop into a tangled mess. One lie leads to another, and the level of deception grows as the vicious cycle of maintaining both identities becomes an unbearable necessity. Some feel trapped and ashamed, not sure how to break free. Others, through a false sense of pride, feel they can maintain the charade and continue in their capacity to serve God. In either case, Paul has a dire warning for these hypocrites.

> *For such people are false apostles, deceitful workers, masquerading as apostles of Christ. And no wonder, for Satan himself masquerades as an angel of light. It is not surprising, then, if his servants also masquerade as servants of righteousness. Their end will be what their actions deserve.* (2 Corinthians 11:13-15)

Did you notice the reference Paul uses here? While *'such people'* may still believe they are carrying out the Lord's work, Paul calls them Satan's servants! How much more deceived can you get? Then, the final warning is frightening! **"Their end will be what their actions deserve."** What most do not realize is that *'their end'* is what Satan had in mind at the beginning of his deception (the first thought).

Whether this process has taken weeks, months, or years, the enemy has been licking his chops and patiently waiting to arrange the carnage. ("Be alert and of sober mind. Your enemy the devil prowls around like a roaring lion looking for someone to devour.") (1 Peter 5:8) And when the lies are exposed, and the cameras come out, Satan steps out of the shadows with a sinister yet prideful proclamation.

"YOU'VE BEEN PUNK'D! I set up this whole charade from the beginning. I wrote the script, selected the actors, arranged all the props, and invited you to play the lead role. I want to thank you for participating. You took the bait and played the part magnificently. And now I have destroyed your ministry, your reputation, your family, your self-esteem, and most likely your chance of ever serving in a similar capacity, not to mention placing another stain on God's reputation. Remember that verse in 2 Corinthians 10:5 ... something about capturing every thought and making it obedient to Christ? Oh wait, I guess you missed that one. Well too bad, have a nice life. I have another appointment waiting for me."

Of course, the premise of the TV show is that being Punk'd is a laughing matter—it is all good fun. However, in the realm of spiritual warfare, the only one laughing is Satan. And while the victim is left stunned and ruined, Satan is off to target his next victim. For the most part, these are well-intentioned people. They just did not fully comprehend the law of sin, nor did they take God's advice and learn to rule over that sin.

While I focused first on positions of leadership, there are of course, many other examples.

- The spouse who entertains and then commits adultery
- Sexual promiscuity outside of marriage and any of its non-intended consequences
- The slippery slope that leads to alcoholism or drug addiction
- Financial improprieties (gambling, embezzlement, theft, etc.)
- Spreading lies (gossip, innuendos, rumors, slander)
- Idolatry in its many forms

The obvious point here is that we all have the potential to be 'Punk'd.' And whether we are boldly proclaiming our faith, or just quietly doing our best to live out a Christian lifestyle, Satan will use any ploy to discredit you to a world that is watching. (Remember the Wikipedia definition, in which being 'punk'd' refers to being the victim of such a prank.) Don't allow yourself to be fooled. Don't allow yourself to fall victim to the enemy. I mentioned earlier that I would come back to the verses below. Perhaps they have more relevance after reflecting on Satan's pattern of deceit and intentional destruction.

> *There is nothing concealed that will not be disclosed, or hidden that will not be made known. What you have said in the dark will be heard in the daylight, and what you have whispered in the ear in the inner rooms will be proclaimed from the roofs.* (Luke 12:2-3)

- - -- - - - - - - - - - - Ruining God's Reputation - - - - - - - - - - - - - -- - - -

There is of course an aspect to hypocrisy that extends beyond the personal damage it causes. Every personal indiscretion has the potential to harm the reputation of God and His church. As Paul continues in Chapter 2 of his letter to the church in Rome, he speaks directly to this specific danger of hypocrisy. (Please notice the revisions as a contemporary commentary of Paul's message.)

> *Now you, if you call yourself a ~~Jew~~ (Christian); if you rely on the ~~law~~ (Holy Spirit) and boast in God; if you know his will and approve of what is superior because you are instructed by the ~~law~~ (Holy Spirit); if you are convinced that you are a guide for the blind, a light for those who are in the dark, an instructor of the foolish, a teacher of little children, because you have in the ~~law~~ (Spirit) the embodiment of knowledge and truth - you, then, who teach others, do you not teach yourself? You who preach against stealing, do you steal? You who say that people should not commit adultery, do you commit adultery? You who abhor idols, do you rob temples? You who boast in the ~~law~~ (salvation through Jesus Christ), do you dishonor God by ~~breaking the law~~ (your hypocrisy)? As it is written: "God's name is blasphemed among ~~the Gentiles~~ (all non-believers) because of you."* (Romans 2:17-24, strikethroughs are mine for emphasis)

To place these verses in context, you may remember that after the Day of Pentecost, the gospel is preached first to the Jews. After Peter's vision in Acts, Chapter 10, the disciples begin to share the gospel with the Gentiles as well. This continues throughout Paul's travels, and when he first arrives in Rome, he gathers the Jewish leadership to share the good news of Jesus Christ. A handful believe, but most of the Jews turn their backs to Paul's teaching. Even so, Paul stays in Rome for two years, preaching to all who come to see him (Acts 28:17-31). Later, as he writes these verses from Corinth, Paul is addressing the hypocritical behavior of the Jews in Rome.

It's important to note that at this point in history, the majority of Jews considered the Gentiles as dogs. The Jews held a racial animosity toward the Gentiles based on the Jews' self-appointed air of spiritual superiority. What Paul is referencing above is that the Jews had been called by God to be a light to the Gentiles, but rather than witnesses of God's love, all the Gentiles saw was spiritual snobbery, prejudice, and pride. (Adapted from the *Layman's Bible Commentary Set*) [3]

Regardless of who this letter is addressing, the result of the hypocrisy is clear. God's name and his church are being dishonored. Before we move on, there is one more passage in Ephesians that is worth noting. In Chapters 4 and 5 of this letter, Paul instructs church members on how they ought to live their lives as believers in Jesus Christ. He warns them "to put off your old self" and then lists former behaviors they should avoid. In Chapter 4, Verse 30, Paul says this; "And do not grieve the Holy Spirit of God, with whom you were sealed for the day of redemption." Our actions can not only cause harm to God's reputation, but they can also break His heart.

I can remember when I was a little boy, and continuing through my teenage years, a phrase that my parents would repeat every time I left the house. "Remember whose son you are!" That was their way of saying, "Don't do anything stupid or illegal that would tarnish our family name." Of course, I did, and of course, it broke their hearts. Culturally, it seems like carrying on the family name was a much bigger deal back then than it is now. But trust me; it is still a big deal to God!

- - - - - - - - - - - - - - - - - The Point of No Return - - - - - - - -- - - - - - - - -

I call the third danger of hypocrisy The Point of No Return. Again, this comes early in Paul's letter to the Roman church, and we will focus on Romans 1:18-32 and 2:5-8. Paul begins his letter with a warm and gracious greeting to the church and even praises them as 'their faith is being reported all over the world.' As he wraps up this short, five-paragraph introduction, he states the following.

> For I am not ashamed of the gospel, because it is the power of God that brings salvation to everyone who believes: first to the Jew, then to the Gentile. For in the gospel the righteousness of God is revealed—a righteousness that is by faith from first to last, just as it is written: "The righteous will live by faith. (Romans 1:16-17)

By the sixth paragraph, Paul's tone changes dramatically as he outlines 'God's Wrath Against Mankind.' Since this study is premised on thoughts being the first step to determining our lifestyle, it is interesting to note all the references below to thoughts, mind, heart, and understanding.

> [18] The wrath of God is being revealed from heaven against all the godlessness and wickedness of people, who suppress the truth by their wickedness, [19] since what may be known about God is plain to them, because God has made it plain to them. [20] For since the creation of the world God's invisible qualities—his eternal power and divine nature—have been clearly seen, being **understood** from what has been made, so that people are without excuse.

> [21] For although they knew God, they neither glorified him as God nor gave thanks to him, but their **thinking** became futile and their foolish **hearts** were darkened. [22] Although they claimed to be wise, they became fools [23] and exchanged the glory of the immortal God for images made to look like a mortal human being and birds and animals and reptiles.

> [24] Therefore God gave them over in the sinful desires of their **hearts** to sexual impurity for the degrading of their bodies with one another. [25] They exchanged the truth

about God for a lie and worshiped and served created things rather than the Creator—who is forever praised. Amen.

*²⁶ Because of this, God gave them over to shameful lusts. Even their women exchanged natural sexual relations for unnatural ones. ²⁷ In the same way the men also abandoned natural relations with women and were **inflamed** with lust for one another. Men committed shameful acts with other men and received in themselves the due penalty for their error.*

*²⁸ Furthermore, just as they did not **think** it worthwhile to retain the knowledge of God, so God gave them over to a depraved **mind**, so that they do what ought not to be done. ²⁹ They have become filled with every kind of wickedness, evil, greed and depravity. They are full of envy, murder, strife, deceit and malice. They are gossips, ³⁰ slanderers, God-haters, insolent, arrogant and boastful; they invent ways of doing evil; they disobey their parents; ³¹ they have no **understanding**, no fidelity, no love, no mercy. ³² Although they know God's righteous decree that those who do such things deserve death, they not only continue to do these things but also approve of those who practice them."*

As a believer in Jesus Christ, this is a difficult passage to read. It is hard to comprehend how some people can know God and His truth, and yet turn their backs on Him and purposely follow Satan's lies. However, we dare not judge, for prior to God's saving grace, many of us (me included) acted in similar fashion. Notice in this passage of Paul's letter, we once again see his express and powerful acknowledgement of spiritual warfare in Verse 21.

*For although they knew God, they neither glorified him as God nor gave thanks to him, but their **thinking** became futile and their foolish **hearts** were darkened.*

This is a direct manifestation of the diagram we have been studying. Not only do they lose the battle for their thoughts, but also, they are so determined that they lose the war. *Although they claimed to be wise, they became fools.* Please do not overlook the dire consequences of their sin.

- *They exchanged the **truth** about God for a **lie.***
- *Therefore, God gave them over in the **sinful desires** of their **hearts.***
- *Because of this, God gave them over to shameful **lusts.***
- *God gave them over to a depraved **mind.***
- *They have become filled with every kind of wickedness, evil, greed and depravity.*
- *They not only continue to do these things but also approve of those who practice them.*

Do you see the dangerous progression of listening to the wrong influence and allowing Satan to set the agenda for your life? But there is a greater danger still. It is an eternal separation from God announced on the Day of Judgment if there is no repentance.

But because of your stubbornness and your unrepentant heart, you are storing up wrath against yourself for the day of God's wrath, when his righteous judgment will be revealed. God will repay each person according to what they have done. To those who by persistence in doing good seek glory, honor, and immortality, he will give eternal life. But for those who are self-seeking and who reject the truth and follow evil, there will be wrath and anger. (Romans 2:5-8)

You may think it harsh that we referenced this danger of hypocrisy as The Point of No Return, but look closely at the contrast in these verses and rest assured, apart from salvation through faith in Jesus Christ. God will repay people, individually, according to what they have done.

1. *To those who by persistence in doing good seek glory, honor and immortality, he will give eternal life.*
2. *But for those who are self-seeking and who **reject the truth and follow evil**, there will be wrath and anger.*

We know that all truth is revealed to us through the Holy Spirit. It is the Holy Spirit that convicts us of our sin and leads us to accept Jesus Christ as our Savior. It is the Holy Spirit that makes God's Word come alive and penetrate our hearts. Lastly, it is the Holy Spirit that allows us to mature in our faith and then directs us in how we should serve in God's community according to our spiritual gifts.

God speaks into our thoughts through the Holy Spirit. **Think about that for just a minute.** God is sharing his love, his truth, and his agenda for your life through the Holy Spirit. There is no greater hypocrisy than to know (have a full understanding of) God's truth yet choose to follow the sinful desires placed in your heart by the enemy. Jesus describes this purposeful, intentional, and continual denial of the Holy Spirit as the unforgivable sin.

And so I tell you, every kind of sin and slander can be forgiven, but blasphemy against the Spirit will not be forgiven. [32] Anyone who speaks a word against the Son of Man will be forgiven, but anyone who speaks against the Holy Spirit will not be forgiven, either in this age or in the age to come. (Matthew 12:31-32)

Brothers and sisters, I have devoted several chapters now to the study of spiritual warfare, outlining Satan's schemes, and identifying his opposing agenda to God's will for your life. However, before I close this chapter, there is one more parable that Jesus shares with his disciples that should remove any doubt that *our struggle is not against flesh and blood, but against the rulers, against the authorities, against the powers of this dark world and against the spiritual forces of evil in the heavenly realms.* (Ephesians 6:12)

Mentioned previously in Chapter 1, take another look at "The Parable of the Weeds" in a different context.

*Jesus told them another parable: "The kingdom of heaven is like a man who sowed good seed in his field. But while everyone was sleeping, **his enemy** came and sowed weeds among the wheat, and went away. When the wheat sprouted and formed heads, then the weeds also appeared. The owner's servants came to him and said, 'Sir, didn't you sow good seed in your field? Where then did the weeds come from?' 'An enemy did this,' he replied."* (Matthew 13:24-28)

*His disciples came to him and said, "Explain to us the parable of the weeds in the field." He answered, "The one who sowed the good seed is the Son of Man. The field is the world, and the good seed stands for the people of the kingdom. **The weeds are the people of the evil one, and the enemy who sows them is the devil.** The harvest is the end of the age, and the harvesters are angels. "As the weeds are pulled up and burned in the fire, so it will be at the end of the age. The Son of Man will send out his angels, and they will weed out of his kingdom everything that causes sin and all who do evil. They will throw them* *into the blazing furnace, where there will be weeping and gnashing of teeth."* (Matthew 13:36-42)

This parable clearly defines the direct opposition we face from Satan as we attempt to live out a Christian lifestyle. My hope is that this study, at least to this point, has opened your eyes to where the opposition comes from and the exact intent of the devil's schemes. For some of you, it may be the first serious discussion of the spiritual realm. In either case, as human beings, we are caught up in both dominions, and it is imperative that we acknowledge that fact and learn how to navigate through both.

There is another book I would recommend that illustrates this point in a unique style. The following is from *The Rules of Engagement* by Charles Kraft and David DeBord and is subtitled *Understanding the Principles That Govern the Spiritual Battles in Our Lives*. The authors discuss various topics regarding spiritual warfare and present their conclusions by way of 'Principles' and 'Observations.'

> Observation #2.1 is titled, "Any analysis of a given event in the human sphere needs to take into account both human and spiritual dimensions."
>
> It is typical of Westerners, including westernized Christians, to evaluate the significant events of their lives totally at the human level, as if no supernatural activity were involved. Whether it is war, arguments in families, accidents, or natural disasters, analyzing events only on the human level is to miss the equally important supernatural dimension.
>
> The author of a *Time* magazine cover story (May 16, 1994), that dealt with the 1994 Rwandan massacres inadvertently revealed the fact that there was a spiritual dimension to the massacres, though we doubt that the writer realized the significance of [the] observations. [1] She quoted Daniel Bellamy of the United

Nations High Commission for Refugees concerning the young men of the Hutu death squads: "If you look in their eyes, there is something there that is not in the eyes of normal people." Concerning the same event, a missionary observed, "There are no devils left in hell. They are all in Rwanda."

Each of these remarks takes note of the fact that there is a spiritual dimension as well as a human dimension to such atrocities. This is more than a case of man's inhumanity to man. **It involved the cooperation of human beings with the satanic kingdom.** To try to understand what happened in Rwanda without understanding the spiritual dimension of this event leads to misanalysis. Both human and spiritual dimensions need to be recognized for full understanding.

Though an understanding of human motivations, decisions and actions is crucial to analyzing an event, so is an understanding of the activities of spirit beings that relate to it. An analysis is incomplete if it does not deal with both factors. ([1]Nancy Gibbs, "Why? The Killing Fields of Rwanda." – Time, May 16, 1994, Vol. 143, No. 20)[4]

Earlier, I described this concept as developing a new set of spiritual lenses by which to view the world. Full acknowledgment of this reality coupled with an increased level of discernment will empower you to live the Christian lifestyle victoriously. However, there is still work to do, and that is where we will start in our next chapter.

We have spent a good deal of time studying danger and defeat. The remainder of this study will focus on the safety and victory available to us through Jesus Christ.

I look forward to sharing that good news with you. Before we close, another quick review of our foundational verse is in order.

For though we live in the world, we do not wage war as the world does. The weapons we fight with are not the weapons of the world. On the contrary, they have divine power to demolish strongholds. We demolish arguments and every pretension that sets itself up against the knowledge of God, **_and we take captive every thought to make it obedient to Christ_**. (2 Corinthians 10:3-5)

1. *Layman's Bible Commentary Set, Vol. 9—Luke and John* (Uhrichsville: Barbour Publishing, 2008) 62-63 *
2. *Layman's Bible Commentary Set, Vol. 9—Luke and John* (Uhrichsville: Barbour Publishing, 2008) 62-63 *
3. *Layman's Bible Commentary Set, Vol. 10—Acts thru 2 Corinthians* (Uhrichsville: Barbour Publishing, 2008) 120
4. Charles Kraft and David DeBord, *The Rules of Engagement* (Eugene: Wipf and Stock, 2000) 41-43

Chapter 5: Press on Toward the Goal

The introductory chapters of this book focus on the potential for danger and defeat directed at all Christians if we allow Satan's influence to monopolize our thoughts. The remainder of this study will focus on the safety, power, and victory available to us through Jesus Christ. Earlier, we described it as developing a new set of spiritual lenses by which to view the world. My hope is that as we make this transition, it will empower you to live a victorious Christian lifestyle.

By nature, we are all creatures of habit. Since habits are familiar and comfortable, making any transition, especially a lifestyle change, is never easy. What complicates the process for many of us is that when we finally decide to modify our behavior, we focus our energy by first trying to change our habits (see below). As we have learned in our study, the appropriate starting point is in our minds by allowing the proper spiritual influence to direct our thoughts.

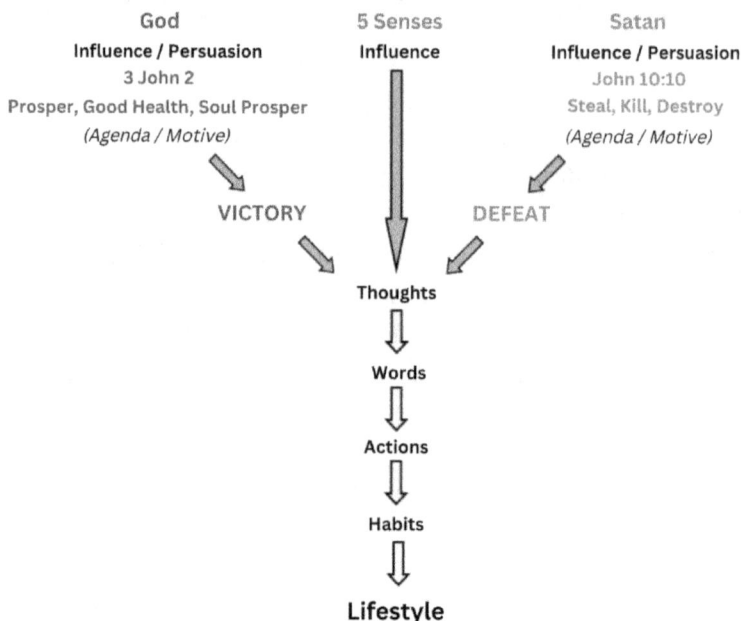

If you are struggling in any part of your Christian walk and want to make the transition to living victoriously in Christ Jesus, Scripture is precise and deliberate in telling us where to begin. We have already studied dozens of verses that clearly define the battle for our minds. As we begin this chapter, I would recommend that we first focus on Paul's recommendation in the book of Romans.

> *Do not conform any longer to the pattern of this world,* ***but be transformed by the renewing of your mind****. Then you will be able to test and approve what God's will is— His good, pleasing, and perfect will.* (Romans 12:2)

This single verse offers such a strong confirmation of everything we have been studying in the previous chapters. The *'pattern of this world'* is created by the ruler of this world. Satan and his demons are constantly trying to influence your thought process and lead you into sin, doubt, and distress. **Your key to being transformed is**

in the renewing of your mind. As you begin to identify Satan's schemes and tactics, you will be able to test those lies against God's perfect will for your life. Remember the quote from 3 John 2. "Above all things I wish that you prosper and be in good health, even as your soul prospers."

So, while this portion of the study will focus on *what* we need to do next, I would like to offer some additional motivation as to *why* we might want to fortify our faith and strengthen our spiritual resolve. As a general observation, there are many things in life that we start and don't finish. For most of us, the diminishing determination to reach our goal or ambition is the absence of a strong reason why we need to achieve that specific target. Making the determination to mature in our understanding of Scripture and its application to our lives is no different.

For myself, I found some of the most valuable motivation in Peter's letters to what is believed to be the persecuted church in Rome. Many consider Peter as the leader among Christ's apostles. The gospel writers emphasize this in Scripture by placing his name at the head of each list of apostles and including more information about him in the four gospels than any other person other than Christ.

As examples, in Matthew 16:18, Jesus makes this statement about Simon Peter. "And I tell you that you are Peter, and on this rock I will build my church, and the gates of Hades will not overcome it." After the resurrection and ascension, Peter initiates the plan to replace Judas. Upon the indwelling of the Holy Spirit at Pentecost, Peter is empowered to become the leading gospel preacher among the disciples and leads 3,000 people to accept Christ with his first sermon. He also performs many miracles in the early days of the church and is the first to preach the gospel to the Gentiles. The following commentary from *The MacArthur Bible Handbook* sheds light on Peter's role in the early church.

*Since the believers addressed in 1 Peter were suffering increasing persecution, **the purpose of this letter was to teach them how to live victoriously** in the midst of that hostility: (1) without losing hope; (2) without becoming bitter; (3) while trusting in their Lord; (4) while looking for His second coming. Peter wished to impress on his readers that by living an obedient, victorious life under duress, a Christian can actually evangelize his hostile world.*

Believers are constantly exposed to a world system energized by Satan and his demons. Their effort is to discredit the church and to destroy its credibility and integrity. One way these spirits work is by finding Christians whose lives are not consistent with the Word of God, and then parading them before the unbelievers to show what a sham the church is. Christians, however, must stand against the enemy and silence the critics by the power of holy lives. Their citizenship is in heaven, and they are strangers in a hostile, Satan energized world. [1]

The purpose for Peter's letters and the purpose for the remainder of this study are one in the same, but it still requires a dogged determination on our part to succeed in that which Christ intends for our lives. The motivation for that determination is suggested throughout Peter's writing. He starts his first letter to the church with this greeting:

To God's elect..., [2] *who have been chosen according to the foreknowledge of God the Father, through the sanctifying work of the Spirit, to be obedient to Jesus Christ and sprinkled with his blood: Grace and peace be yours in abundance.* (1 Peter 1:1-2)

Does it help you to know that you've been chosen (personally selected) by the Creator of the universe and empowered by the

Holy Spirit to reflect Jesus Christ and the truth of the gospel to a lost and dying world? Does it also help to know that your sins have been forgiven—paid for in full by the blood Jesus shed on the cross? Has it ever struck you in these verses that you have been invited and fully accepted (by claiming Jesus Christ as your Savior) to partake in the Holy Trinity of God? Now that's motivation!

Because of these truths (and despite our trials), Peter can offer this most wonderful greeting. "Grace and peace be yours in abundance." I also found it interesting how closely this greeting mirrors the emotion and intention of John's greeting which I have referenced repeatedly. "Above all things I wish that you prosper and be in good health, even as your soul prospers." Both are based on the marvelous truth below as Peter continues in his letter.

> Praise be to the God and Father of our Lord Jesus Christ!
> In his great mercy he has given us new birth into a living
> hope through the resurrection of Jesus Christ from the
> dead,[4] and into an inheritance that can never perish, spoil,
> or fade. This inheritance is kept in heaven for you, [5] who
> through faith are shielded by God's power until the
> coming of the salvation that is ready to be revealed in the
> last time. (1 Peter 1:3-5)

As noted in the quote from *The MacArthur Bible Handbook*, our permanent citizenship is in heaven, and even though we walk as strangers in this hostile world, we can live victoriously in the midst of that hostility. But even with that motivation and the power of the Trinity standing beside us, Peter understands the depth of the struggle and strongly urges us to continue in our fight against evil.

> But you are a chosen people, a royal priesthood, a holy
> nation, God's special possession, that you may declare the
> praises of him who called you out of darkness into his
> wonderful light. [10] Once you were not a people, but now
> you are the people of God; once you had not received

*mercy, but now you have received mercy. **¹¹ Dear friends, I urge you, as foreigners and exiles, to abstain from sinful desires, which wage war against your soul.** ¹² Live such good lives among the pagans that, though they accuse you of doing wrong, they may see your good deeds and glorify God on the day he visits us.* (1 Peter 2:9-11)

There are both victory and worldly struggle in these verses. As born-again Christians, we have attained the ultimate victory over sin and death, and our inheritance to the kingdom of heaven is assured. However, we struggle to reflect the light of Christ to a broken world that consistently falls prey to Satan's deception. For us to prosper in this calling from God, it is imperative that we remember the prerequisite for victorious service, which is our soul prosperity.

Before we can attain victory in our own personal walks with Christ, and in reaching the lost, we must learn to defend against the constant onslaught from Satan to distract and discredit us. It is these "sinful desires"—the negative influence of the enemy, conceived first in our minds, that "wage war against our souls." So, how do we learn to fight effectively and advance the cause of Christ? We do what any army does, we practice. As Peter continues, please note his first call to action.

__Therefore, prepare your minds for action__; be self-controlled, set your hope on the grace to be given you when Jesus Christ is revealed. ¹⁴ As obedient children, do not conform to the evil desires you had when you lived in ignorance. ¹⁵ But just as he who called you is holy, so be holy in all you do; ¹⁶ for it is written: "Be holy, because I am holy." (1 Peter 1:13-16)

Arguably, Paul and Peter are the two most prominent apostles as recorded in the New Testament. I trust you will find it as noteworthy as I did, that as both addressed the new believers in Rome, the first encouragement to their readers was to win the battle over their thought life.

- **Paul**: "**Be transformed by the renewing of your mind.**"
- **Peter**: "**Therefore, prepare your minds for action...**"

Their message remains the same in our spiritual battles today. Having said that, many believers may still feel the need to ask, "How do we go about the process of renewing our minds?" For the answer to that question, we are once again directed to the foundational verse of this study.

*We demolish arguments and every pretension that sets itself up against the knowledge of God, and **we take captive every thought to make it obedient to Christ**.* (2 Corinthians 10:5)

Let me take just a minute to emphasize several important points here.

1.) These two verses completely capture *what* we need to do (Romans 12:2) and *how* we need to do it (2 Corinthians 10:5). Is there more to learn? Absolutely, but this is the firm foundation upon which that knowledge rests.
2.) Make no mistake, we are in a war for our souls. This is spiritual warfare, and don't think for a minute that just because you decide to engage in the fight, Satan is going to fold his hands and move on. Be prepared for an extended battle to gain your freedom.
3.) Be encouraged! The weapons we fight with are God's weapons, and they have divine power to demolish Satan's strongholds and his arguments against God's truth.
4.) The renewing of your mind and the ability to test and approve God's will for your life are not part of a casual

quest! Before you can identify Satan's lies, you must know God's truth. Winning this war will take a determined and consistent effort to study God's Word until it becomes the rock you stand on and your principal point of reference (a new set of spiritual lenses by which to view the world).

So, we still have some work ahead of us. If you have truly made the decision to live a victorious Christian lifestyle, let me be the first to congratulate you. However, no single decision stands in isolation. It usually requires a series of additional decisions to either support or refute the original premise. The verse, 2 Corinthians 10:5, doesn't say that we should capture a single thought. It says that we should capture EVERY thought and make it obedient to Christ. And while the premise may sound simple, it is not easy. That is why Paul encourages us to **press on toward the goal**.

Whether your quest for victory through Jesus Christ is a new goal or a renewed commitment to a previous vow, the reality of what that entails will be different for everyone reading this book. We all have our own struggles and our own shortcomings. And if you are like me, there will be a case or two of poor judgment as you venture down life's trail. However, whatever temptation or condemnation Satan throws your way, you have learned that the battle begins in your mind. As mentioned previously, no one illustrates this struggle better than Paul.

> Those who live according to the flesh have **their minds** set on what the flesh desires; but those who live in accordance with the Spirit have **their minds** set on what the Spirit desires. **The mind** governed by the flesh is death, but **the mind** governed by the Spirit is life and peace. **The mind** governed by the flesh is hostile to God; it does not submit to God's law, nor can it do so. Those who are in the realm of the flesh cannot please God. (Romans 8:5-8)

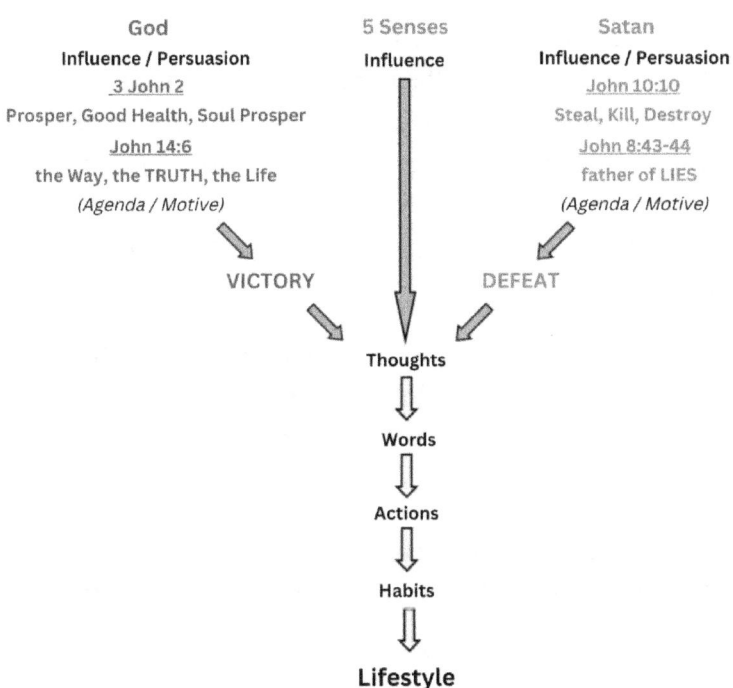

	God	5 Senses	Satan

Using our diagram as a reference point, I want us to focus on these two statements from the verses above.

1.) *The mind <u>governed by the flesh</u> is death*
2.) *The mind <u>governed by the Spirit</u> is life and peace*

I have added additional Scripture references to the diagram to illustrate Paul's statement in these verses. Upon further review, please notice that "those who live according to the flesh" are also referred to as "those who are in the realm of the flesh." In that realm, their desires (thoughts) are a direct result of Satan's influence and therefore "the mind governed by the flesh is hostile to God." Why would a mind governed by the flesh result in death (separation from God)? The answer can be found in the gospel of John.

Why is my language not clear to you? Because you are unable to hear what I say. **44** *You belong to your father, the devil, and you want to carry out your father's desires. He was a murderer from the beginning, not holding to the truth, for there is no truth in him. When he lies, he speaks his native language, for he is a liar and **the father of lies**.* (John 8:43-44)

In contrast, "those who live in accordance with the Spirit have their minds set on what the Spirit desires." We all live in the same earthly realm, but those whose minds are governed (influenced) by God's Spirit live in His peace.

*Jesus answered, "I am the way and **the truth** and the life. No one comes to the Father except through me."* (John 14:6)

Throughout this study, we have highlighted the diametrically opposed agendas for our lives that originate in the heavenly realms. These passages from John's gospel once again expose that opposition as reality. Note the contrasts. Our heavenly Father (through Jesus Christ) offers us all that is true, holy, and proper. Jesus does not just offer the truth; He is the truth! Satan has no truth in him. He is lies. In fact, he is referred to as the father of lies.

I am not trying to over-simplify this, but your Christian walk will be completely determined by what, or who, you allow to influence your thoughts and control your mind. Suppose I were to introduce you to a pastor, a salesperson, a financial planner, a teacher, a doctor, or anyone for that matter, by saying, "I want you to know that this person is a genuine, professional liar. Anything that comes out of his mouth is a lie. In fact, lying is his native language. I've known him for a long time, and I can guarantee that there's not an ounce of truth in him."

I doubt any of us would be anxious to take advice from that person. Sadly, many Christians seek the devil's counsel on a daily basis by the television shows they watch, by the books they read, by the movies they attend, by the internet sites they visit, by the friends they keep, etc. They seek out Satan's influence (his lies) by pursuing what the culture of the day displays as normal and/or natural. Make no mistake, for some this pursuit is intentional. (Remember one of Satan's greatest lies—"I can control this.") For others, they simply do not identify (think about) the subtle message of disobedience that is injected into these media or by those with whom they associate.

You see, most of us do not think of spiritual warfare in those terms because that is too abstract. Yes, we have heard the references to Satan in the Bible, but many think he is just a character utilized to make important points or a scapegoat upon whom to lay blame for our shortcomings. But this struggle for our freedom is real. Note the quote from Jesus in the verses below.

> To the Jews who had believed him, Jesus said, "If you hold to my teaching, you are really my disciples. **Then you will know the truth, and the truth will set you free."** They answered him, "We are Abraham's descendants and have never been slaves of anyone. How can you say that we shall be set free?" Jesus replied, "Very truly I tell you, everyone who sins is a slave to sin." (John 8:31-34)

Have you ever taken the time to really understand what Jesus is telling us in these verses? "If you hold to my teaching" (if you allow me to influence your thoughts and apply my instruction to your life). "Then you will know the truth, and the *truth will set you free.*" Have you ever asked yourself, "Free from what?"

If not, now is the appropriate time to begin our conversation about victory, for here is the freedom that Jesus offers.

- Freedom from Satan's lies
- Freedom from Satan's influence
- Freedom from Satan's persuasion
- Freedom from Satan's condemnation
- Freedom from the guilt and penalty for sin
- Freedom from Satan's ability to steal, kill, and destroy
- Freedom from the fear of illness and the finality of death

For clarification, please note that I did not include freedom from Satan's temptation or accusation. For that is the devil's nature, and his desire to lure you into sin or accuse you of past transgressions will not cease this side of heaven. Many of us, in our ignorance, me included, answer as the Jews in this passage. We think to ourselves, I *live in a free country. I have never been a slave to anyone. I am free to make my own decisions and determine my own path in life.* That may appear accurate in the temporal world; however, there is a definitive spiritual component to our lives, and that spiritual influence is more powerful than any of us can imagine.

The purpose of this study is to heighten our awareness of the spiritual realm, identify the potential for truth to overcome evil, and to sharpen our ability to walk victoriously in Christ Jesus. As we continue, we are going to focus on three key components of our victory walk.

1.) Developing our spiritual awareness (wisdom and discernment)
2.) Developing disciplined thinking skills (conscious vs. subconscious)
3.) Learning how to fully appropriate our identity in Christ

Wisdom and discernment are acquired skills in any profession. Learning how to develop those skills in the spiritual realm is no different. For this first section, Romans 12:2 will serve as the foundational verse: "Be transformed by the renewing of your mind." Romans 12:2 clearly instructs us on **what** we are to do. Earlier, I said that the renewing of your mind and the ability to test and approve God's will for your life is not a casual quest. Before you can identify Satan's lies, you must know God's truth. Winning this war will take a determined and consistent effort to study God's Word until it becomes the rock you stand on and your principal point of reference. **The pursuit of Godly wisdom is the task.**

> For the LORD gives wisdom; from his mouth come knowledge and understanding. He holds success in store for the upright; he is a shield to those whose walk is blameless, for he guards the course of the just and protects the way of his faithful ones. Then you will understand what is right and just and fair - every good path. For wisdom will enter your heart, and knowledge will be pleasant to your soul. Discretion will protect you, and understanding will guard you. (Proverbs 2:6-11)

We begin our pursuit by exploring both the offer and the promise found in these verses. First, notice that God *gives* wisdom. Just like the offer of salvation, He offers the gift of wisdom free of charge. "From his mouth come knowledge and understanding." When you read the Bible, do you think of it that way? Do you recognize that God has given instruction for every aspect of your life in His word? To a Christian hungry for truth, the Bible is a priceless resource. If you have yet to discover that truth, please do not let the value of God's precious gift be determined by the purchase price of a Bible.

"For wisdom will enter your heart." This is a promise that if you pursue wisdom, God will allow it to penetrate and permeate your thoughts, your mind, your heart, your life, and your soul. When I first began my walk with the Lord, I not only had trouble reading the Bible, but also understanding it. If that has been the case for you, may I share the suggestion I received from my mentor? God provided a personal tutor to help us understand His word. Before you begin to read, ask the Holy Spirit to reveal God's truth to you. For the Holy Spirit is the Counselor Jesus promised to his disciples (and to us).

> But the Advocate, the Holy Spirit, whom the Father will send in my name, will teach you all things and will remind you of everything I have said to you. (John 14:26)

"Discretion (discernment) will protect you, and understanding (wisdom) will guard you." This final verse is simply a summary of the promises found in the preceding verses.

- He offers _success_ for the upright (victory over Satan's agenda for your life).
- He is a _shield_ to those whose walk is blameless (against Satan's fiery arrows).
- He _guards_ the course of the just (against Satan's schemes).
- He _protects_ the way of his faithful ones (providing a hedge of protection against Satan's attacks).
- He _provides_ understanding of what is right and just and fair (against Satan's lies).
- He will _guide_ you down every good path (avoiding Satan's pitfalls and strongholds).

The book of Proverbs was written by Solomon, King David's son. God answered Solomon's prayer and blessed him with wisdom and discernment ("...so that there will never have been anyone like you, nor will there ever be." 1 Kings 3:12). While the entire book of Proverbs is a confirmation of that which the Lord provided to Solomon, the first four chapters are a powerful statement and constant reminder of that which we should also seek. Reading all four chapters would be an excellent idea in your private time, but for now, I will highlight a few verses that are relevant to our current theme.

Please pay special attention as Solomon describes several key benefits of attaining Godly wisdom and how these benefits perfectly align with God's agenda for our lives as summarized in John's third letter and as outlined in our study diagram (prosperity, good health, even as your soul prospers). I found this quite fascinating!

> My son, do not forget my teaching, but keep my commands in your heart, for they will prolong your life many years and bring you peace and **prosperity**. (Proverbs 3:1-2)
>
> Do not be wise in your own eyes; fear the LORD and shun evil. This will bring **health** to your body and nourishment to your bones. (Proverbs 3:7-8)
>
> [1]My son, if you accept my words and store up my commands within you, [2] turning your ear to wisdom and applying your heart to understanding - [5] then you will understand the fear of the LORD and find the knowledge of God. [10] For wisdom will enter your heart, and knowledge will be pleasant to your **soul**. (Proverbs 2:1-2, 5, 10)

Have you ever connected these verses from Proverbs with God's agenda for your life as stated in 3 John 2, Deuteronomy, and elsewhere in Bible? Take special notice of Verse 5: "Then you will understand the fear of the LORD and find the knowledge of God." **What a promise!** Proverbs 1:7 states, "The fear of the Lord is the beginning of wisdom." My friend, would you make this your quest?

If you are struggling with spiritual warfare, would you commit to studying God's Word until the "knowledge of God' becomes the rock you stand on and the principal point of reference in renewing your mind? Please understand that your heavenly Father is patiently waiting for you to ask for His help. Note the words of Jesus as he taught his disciples to pray.

> *So I say to you: Ask and it will be given to you; seek and you will find; knock and the door will be opened to you. For everyone who asks receives; the one who seeks finds; and to the one who knocks, the door will be opened. Which of you fathers, if your son asks for a fish, will give him a snake instead? Or if he asks for an egg, will give him a scorpion? If you then, though you are evil, know how to give good gifts to your children, **how much more will your Father in heaven give the Holy Spirit to those who ask him!** (Luke 11:9-13)*

There is victory available, and waiting for us to ask for it. Of course, in western culture, we are shy about asking for gifts. I would offer that most of us have probably been taught that asking for a gift is ill-mannered. But have you noticed yet that God's kingdom operates differently?

- *For God so loved the world that he **gave** his only Son... (John 3:16)*
- *For the LORD **gives** wisdom... (Proverbs 2:6-11)*
- *How much more will your Father in heaven **give** the Holy Spirit to those who ask him. (Luke 11:9-13)*

Somehow when God said, "Ask for whatever you want me to give you," Solomon, at age twelve, already knew that he would need God's wisdom to rule as king. Years later, he documents this in the book of Proverbs, reflecting the blessings received from the diligent pursuit and application of that which he sought. Solomon titles Chapter 4 "Wisdom Is Supreme." Take careful notice of his encouragement for us to follow his example.

*Get wisdom, get understanding; do not forget my words or turn away from them. Do not forsake wisdom, and she will protect you; love her, and she will watch over you. **Wisdom is supreme; therefore, get wisdom. Though it cost all you have, get understanding.*** (Proverbs 4:5-7)

*My son, pay attention to what I say; turn your ear to my words. Do not let them out of your sight; keep them within your heart; for they are life to those who find them and health to one's whole body. **Above all else, guard your heart** (your mind)**, for it is the wellspring of life.*** (Proverbs 4:20-23) (Bold added for emphasis.)

Before we go further, there is an essential construct built into all these verses. I have defined this construct as the "Prerequisite Principle." It is the same principle that was introduced early in this study, has held true in all that we have discussed so far, and is prominent in Solomon's writing as well. If you have not picked up on it yet, all these promises (yes, God's promises) are contingent upon first seeking and attaining God's wisdom.

- *Beloved, I wish above all things that thou mayest prosper and be in health, even **as thy soul prospereth**.* (KJV)
- *...but be transformed by the renewing of your mind. **Then** you will be able to test and approve what God's will is.*
- *If you hold to my teaching, **then** you will know the truth, and the truth will set you free.*
- *For the LORD gives wisdom; **then** you will understand what is right and just and fair - every good path.*
- *My son, if you accept my words and store up my commands within you, **then** you will understand the fear of the LORD and find the knowledge of God.*

Remember the main premise of this study. **God wants you to be victorious in your Christian walk!** He has an agenda for your life and earnestly wants you to succeed. That "success" is different for each one of us and most likely requires a series of small successes along the way, but one thing is certain. God cannot steer a parked car! It is inherent upon you to develop a habit of seeking God's wisdom before he can complete His plan in you.

Many consider the Sermon on the Mount, as recorded in Matthew's gospel, to be some of Jesus' most prominent teaching. The select words of Jesus below, first in the Beatitudes and continuing in Chapters 6 and 7, reinforce both the encouragement to seek wisdom and the promise to those who develop this discipline.

> *Blessed are those who hunger and thirst for righteousness, for they **will be** filled.* (Matthew 5:6)

> *25 Therefore I tell you, do not worry about your life, what you will eat or drink; or about your body, what you will wear. 32 For your heavenly Father knows that you need them. 33 But seek first his kingdom and his righteousness, and (then) **all these things will be given to you as well**.* (Matthew 6:25, 32ᵇ, 33) (Bold added for emphasis.)

The *Layman's Bible Commentary Set* includes an interesting quote regarding Matthew 6:33.

> This is the climatic teaching of the whole section, and perhaps of the entire Sermon on the Mount—seek first His kingdom, and everything else will follow. Perhaps these words are some of the best known of all Jesus' teachings. But what do they mean? **The first priority of the disciple is to seek the reign of God in one's own life.** This whole section is an encouragement to refocus one's life and seek a right relationship with God. *2*

As Jesus completes the Sermon on the Mount, he offers one last encouragement to seek wisdom, one last emphasis on application, and one last promise to build a solid foundation against evil.

Therefore, everyone who hears these words of mine and puts them into practice is like a wise man who built his house on the rock. (Matthew 7:24)

I believe the words of Jesus are clear—we are called to pursue and practice our faith. In other words, press on toward the goal. As we started this session, I stated, "If you have truly made the decision to live a victorious Christian lifestyle, let me be the first to congratulate you. However, no one decision stands by itself. It usually requires a series of additional decisions to either support or refute the original premise." The original premise is to study God's Word (get wisdom). The corresponding and necessary decision is to repeatedly act upon what you have learned and how the Holy Spirit is leading you.

Do not merely listen to the word, and so deceive yourselves. Do what it says. (James 1:22)

If you have not already established the habit of setting aside time each day to study God's Word, will you make the repeated decisions necessary to build that consistency? Are the gifts and promises we have just studied enough motivation for you to build that habit starting today? It is generally accepted that anything you do consistently for twenty-one days will develop into a habit. There are thirty-one chapters packed full of wisdom in the book of Proverbs. Might I suggest that you start immediately and set aside the same time every day to read one chapter until you create the habit that leads to victorious Christian living?

If you find yourself struggling to make that commitment, may I ask you another question? Where do you suppose the thoughts come from that are preventing you from maintaining that commitment?

Do you suppose that Satan would be opposed to you studying your Bible every day and might offer up every kind of excuse to sidetrack you? Unfortunately, many Christians treat this pursuit of knowledge as a casual quest.

The reasons may vary, but the search for God's truth is just not a priority for them. However, there is alarming spiritual consequence for remaining ignorant of this spiritual battle. Returning to the first chapter of Proverbs, Solomon offers a "Warning Against Rejecting Wisdom." Notice how Solomon's words align with John's gospel (10:10) and focus on Satan's agenda for your life (**steal, kill, destroy**) as illustrated in our diagram.

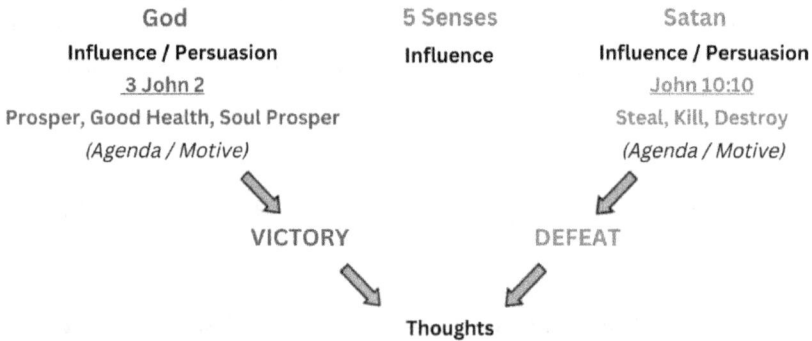

God	5 Senses	Satan
Influence / Persuasion	**Influence**	**Influence / Persuasion**
3 John 2		John 10:10
Prosper, Good Health, Soul Prosper		Steal, Kill, Destroy
(Agenda / Motive)		*(Agenda / Motive)*

VICTORY   DEFEAT

Thoughts

²⁹ *Since they hated knowledge and <u>did not choose</u> to fear the LORD. ³⁰ Since they would not accept my advice and spurned my rebuke, ³² the waywardness of the simple will* **kill** *them, and the complacency of fools will* **destroy** *them.* (Proverbs 1:29, 30, 32)

As we all know, the choice is up to us. We can choose victory, or we can choose defeat. Since we are now focused on the victory available to us through Jesus Christ our Savior, let me share another quote inspired by the Holy Spirit. (I find this to be of interest; note how the prerequisite principle is reinforced in these verses.)

> [20] *Wisdom calls aloud in the street, she raises her voice in the public square;* [22] *How long will you who are simple love your simple ways? How long will mockers delight in mockery and fools hate knowledge?* [23] *Repent at my rebuke!* **Then** ***I will pour out my thoughts to you****, I will make known to you my teachings.* (Proverbs 1:20, 22, 23)

I trust that this brief focus on a specific segment of God's Word has provided an adequate case for seeking wisdom and discernment. Before we move on, I will offer one last bit of encouragement from God as he spoke to the Israelites in Deuteronomy.

> [11] *Now what I am commanding you today is not too difficult for you or beyond your reach.* [19] *This day I call the heavens and the earth as witnesses against you that I have set before you life and death, blessings and curses.* ***Now choose life****, so that you and your children may live* [20] *and that you may love the LORD your God, listen to his voice, and hold fast to him.* (Deuteronomy 30:11, 19, 20)

The second component of our victory walk is developing disciplined thinking skills (our conscious vs. our subconscious mind). For this section, 2 Corinthians 10:5 will serve as the foundational verse as it clearly instructs us on **how** we are to accomplish our transformation and "take captive every thought to make it obedient to Christ."

In the last segment, I quoted from the *Layman's Bible Commentary Set* regarding Matthew 6:33. A portion of that quote read as follows; "This whole section is an encouragement to refocus one's life and seek a right relationship with God." This segment revolves around that premise, however, since our lifestyle is determined by our thoughts, this will be an encouragement to first refocus your thoughts to seek, acquire, and then maintain a victorious Christian lifestyle.

In the fifth chapter of Deuteronomy, as God is preparing the Israelites to take possession of the promised land, Moses begins with a review of the Ten Commandments. Because the application of God's Word transcends the boundaries of time, it is important to remind ourselves of the following.

> *The LORD our God made a covenant with us at Horeb. It was not with our ancestors that the LORD made this covenant, but with us, with all of us who are alive here today.* (Deuteronomy 5:2-3)

The covenant at Horeb is God's promise to the Israelites to take possession of a land flowing with milk and honey. As we have just discussed, God's covenant with us ("all of us who are alive here today") is that if we refocus our thoughts, seek His wisdom, and develop a right relationship with God, we have the ability to live victoriously through His new covenant, Jesus Christ.

As if the Israelites needed it, after all they had witnessed, Moses reminds them of who their God really is and His compassion for them as His chosen people (Deuteronomy 4:32-40). Included in this passage is another important reminder of the prerequisite principle.

> *Acknowledge and take to heart this day that the LORD is God in heaven above and on the earth below. There is no other. Keep his decrees and commands, which I am giving you today, <u>so that it may go well with you and your children after you</u> and that you may live long in the land the LORD your God gives you for all time.* (Deuteronomy 4:39-40)

As a reminder, I encourage you to read all of Chapters 5 and 6 in Deuteronomy, for this same promise is repeated seven more times; "So that it may go well with you." What is the prerequisite you may ask? It is a call to refocus our thoughts on Almighty God!

> *Hear, O Israel: The LORD our God, the LORD is one. Love the LORD your God with all your heart and with all your soul and with all your strength. These commandments that I give you today are to be on your hearts. Impress them on your children. Talk about them when you sit at home and when you walk along the road, when you lie down and when you get up. Tie them as symbols on your hands and bind them on your foreheads. Write them on the doorframes of your houses and on your gates.* (Deuteronomy 6:4-9)

Repetition is often used in Scripture to emphasize a point. Clearly, God intends for us to internalize these declarations, as we see them repeated a few chapters later in Deuteronomy.

> *Fix these words of mine in your hearts and minds; tie them as symbols on your hands and bind them on your foreheads. Teach them to your children, talking about them when you sit at home and when you walk along the road, when you lie down and when you get up. Write them on the doorframes of your houses and on your gates.* (Deuteronomy 11:18-20)

At this point, you may be asking, "How does all this tie in with developing our attentive skills and the conscious mind vs. the subconscious mind?" To answer that question, let me illustrate these principles through a common life event that most of us have experienced.

At the age of fifteen or sixteen, most of us were excited about getting a driver's license. It is probably the one thing we wanted most at that age (and the one thing our parents feared most). If only we had studied algebra as diligently as we studied the guide for the written test. With passing grades on the written test, we were all destined for the dreaded road test. Can you clear your mind for just a minute and think back to that stressful day?

Where I grew up, state law required a skilled Department of Motor Vehicle (DMV) instructor to accompany me on the road test. (Keep in mind, this included the assessment of my parallel parking skills— UGH!) Let me paint the picture for you. There I sat, nervous as an alley cat, next to my dad as all the rules of the road kept running through my mind. To this point, Mom or Dad had always been in the car with me as I practiced my driving skills. Now, out came some stranger in a pressed white shirt, dark slacks, and a pencil thin black necktie. (Think *The Matrix*.) Standing outside his small office, clipboard in hand and scanning the room of anxious teenagers, he called my name.

"JEFF ROWE? "

I raised my hand (gulp) and said, "Over here. That's me."

He sized me up as he walked over and introduced himself. "Well young man, are you ready to take your road test? "

"Yes," I said rather sheepishly.

"Okay then," he said, "Dad, we'll be back in about fifteen minutes."

I am sure there was the normal small talk as I followed him out to the car, but I honestly don't remember. My mind was racing a mile a minute trying to avoid the mistakes I hadn't even made yet. He gave me the go ahead to start the car and, thank God, I remembered to buckle my seat belt. I think that was the first check mark he made on his clipboard just to intimidate me.

"Okay young man, let's pull out of the parking lot and turn right."

Palms sweaty, I put the car in drive and inched forward. Hands at ten and two, I successfully navigated out of the DMV lot and into traffic. Whew!

We hadn't gone far when he said, "About three blocks ahead, I want you to make a left-hand turn at that four-way stop intersection." And then it happened. My mind began to run through the checklist.

- ✓ "Watch your speed."
- ✓ "Heck, what is the speed limit here?"
- ✓ "Am I going to fast?"
- ✓ "Look at the speedometer."
- ✓ "No, no—don't take your eyes off the road!"
- ✓ "Slow down to prepare for the turn."
- ✓ "No, not yet, it's too early."
- ✓ "When do I turn on the blinker?" *(That's a turn signal for everybody who is not from Milwaukee.)*
- ✓ "Am I supposed to stick my arm out the window too?"
- ✓ "Arm straight or bent for a left-hand turn?"
- ✓ "We're getting close—start applying the brakes."
- ✓ "Nice and slow now, you don't want him to go flying through the windshield."
- ✓ "I WISH HE'D PUT THAT DARN CLIPBOARD AWAY!"
- ✓ "Okay, we're stopped at the intersection."
- ✓ "Oh no, there's a car to my right."
- ✓ "Who got here first?"
- ✓ "Who's got the right of way? Does it matter that I'm turning left?"
- ✓ "Here I go. No, wait! Look left and right one more time."
- ✓ "Okay, it's my turn, accelerate nice and slow."
- ✓ "Keep two hands on the steering wheel—hand over hand."

✓ "Is it over yet?"
✓ "It feels like we've been in the car for an hour."
✓ **"I WISH HE'D PUT THAT DARN CLIPBOARD AWAY!"**

Can any of you relate? Well, I did pass the road test that day and walked out of the DMV with my driver's license. But that's not the point of this story. You see, on that day, and for that moment in time, the only thing I could think about was the task at hand, which was making a left-hand turn. **It took 100% of my conscious effort to focus my mind on successfully completing that one task.** There was no way I could have thought about or done anything else while engaged in that test.

If you can relate to that story, may I ask you an important question? How do you drive now? If you are like me, I think it is probably safe to say that multitasking while driving is an understatement. You have got one hand on the wheel while the other is playing with the radio or the navigation system. "Oh wait, the phone is ringing. Let's see who that is." "I'm running late—out of my way while I exceed the speed limit, weave through traffic, and eat my lunch." Sound familiar?

Would it be safe to say that ninety percent of your driving skills are now done at the subconscious level? Why is that? It is the principle of repetition. You have done it so many times before that it becomes engrained in your subconscious, and the effort now takes little conscious thought. In fact, I would be willing to bet that if you drive the same route to work or school each day, you automatically know when to switch lanes to avoid that annoying pothole. Am I right?

Well guess what? It is the same reason God instructed the Israelites in Deuteronomy 6:4-9, "Fix these words of mine in your hearts and minds." God wants us to consciously focus on His instructions until His law is fixed in our subconscious minds. ("Write them, tie them, bind them, talk about them, impress them.")

Now apply that same principle of sharpening your disciplined thinking skills to the realm of spiritual warfare. What if you make a conscious effort to "take captive every thought to make it obedient to Christ?" Wait, am I asking you to make an all-out conscious effort to think about every thought that comes into your mind? Yes, if that is what it takes. At the least, I'm suggesting that it will, at first, require a conscious effort to focus on any negative thought that contradicts the will of God in your life.

> Brothers and sisters, stop **thinking** like children. In regard to evil be infants, but in your **thinking** be adults. (1 Corinthians 14:20)

I have no way of knowing where you are in developing your Christian walk, nor do I know what kind of spiritual attack you may be experiencing. Some may have walked in darkness so long that their subconscious default is evil. Others may be experiencing a specific attack by the enemy based on a recent failure in life. That was my situation when the Lord began to reveal this truth to me.

> So I tell you this, and insist on it in the Lord, that you must no longer live as the Gentiles do, **in the futility of their thinking**. You were taught, with regard to your former way of life, to put off your old self, which is being corrupted by its deceitful desires; to be made new in the attitude of your minds and to put on the new self, created to be like God in true righteousness and holiness. (Ephesians 4:17 and 22-24)

What is Paul referring to when he says, "You must no longer live as the Gentiles do, in the futility of their thinking?" The answer can be found as you read Verse 18, which was not included above.

They are darkened in their understanding and separated from the life of God because of the ignorance that is in them due to the hardening of their hearts. (Ephesians 4:18)

Please note that Paul is not calling the Gentiles stupid. However, by hardening their hearts (minds) to the light of the gospel (God's wisdom), they are ignorant of the truth and have lost out on the 'knowledge of God' that we spoke of earlier. Without that knowledge, they are relegated to darkness and separated from the influence of God and God's agenda for their lives.

Paul is practically pleading with his brothers and sisters in Christ (you and me) to "put off your old self" which has been corrupted by futile thinking and deceitful desires (Satan's lies). Then he reminds them, "You were taught," just as you are being taught in this study, "to be made new in the attitude of your minds." This is Paul's directive to consciously focus on capturing and changing each thought that contradicts the will of God in their (our) lives, and to then "put on the new self, created to be like God in true righteousness and holiness."

That last statement is a statement of victory! Your conscious effort to identify, capture, and refute the lies of the enemy, if sustained, will lead to a new self. Just like in the driving test story, what once seemed deliberate, calculated, and burdensome becomes a matter of habit by way of repetition. Your battle against Satan's lies is now fought and overcome at a subconscious level. The devil's fiery arrows now bounce off the shield that is your newfound identity and confidence in Christ.

Thus far, we have assembled a solid biblical argument for disciplining our thoughts. Additionally, there is an abundance of scientific research and literature to support this premise. Now, I'm not a scientist, nor am I an expert on how the brain works, but a basic understanding of the interaction between our conscious and our subconscious mind will prove extremely helpful as we explore Paul's directive to "take captive every thought to make it obedient to Christ" and then apply this directive to our lives.

I was fortunate to find a simple and easy to understand analogy online that also held some unique commentary applicable to our study. The following was condensed from, "A Walk Through the Human Mind," as found on The Mind Unleashed. Use this link to find more information: (https://themindunleashed.com/) [3]

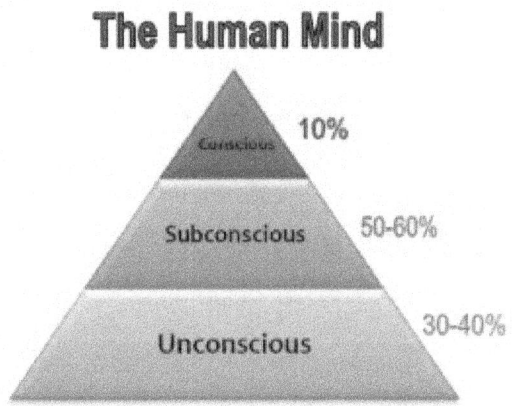

*The tip of the triangle is your **conscious mind**. The middle is your **subconscious**. The bottom is the **unconscious mind**.*

Your conscious mind is where people live daily. It communicates to the outside world and the inner self through speech, pictures, writing, physical movement, and thought.

The subconscious mind is the storehouse of all memories and past experiences and forms our beliefs, habits, and behaviors.

Your conscious mind is like a computer keyboard and monitor. Data (internal or external stimulus) is inputted on the keyboard and shown on the monitor.

Your subconscious is like the RAM in your computer - data currently in use that can quickly be accessed by the computer processor. It also holds recurring thoughts, behavior patterns, habits, and feelings.

Your unconscious is like the hard disk drive in your computer. It is the long-term storage place for all your memories and programs that have been installed since birth.

The ability of your conscious mind to direct your attention and awareness is one of the most important powers you have. To *create change in your life you must learn to <u>control what you consciously focus on</u>. Deciding how you will think and what thoughts you will* allow *into your mind will determine your destiny. It can literally be used for good or evil, for constructive or destructive means.*

Our mental thoughts are probably the one true freedom we have in this world that we can actually control. By continuously being in charge of your own thoughts through directing your focus, you can influence what programs the subconscious mind constantly runs. Do this often enough (and with enough emotional energy) and it will start to reprogram your unconscious internal representation and belief system. And when that happens, you will experience change on a very deep level!

My friend, please do not easily dismiss what we have just discovered. In fact, take some time later if needed to review both the scriptural and scientific validations that reinforce the foundation of this entire study which is to *'take captive every thought to make it obedient to Christ.'* Remember, God wants you to win but the decision is yours. Seek wisdom, refocus your thought life, and ask the Holy Spirit to reveal God's truth to you. Then enjoy the fruits of living victoriously in Christ Jesus.

> *Then he turned to his disciples and said privately, "Blessed are the eyes that see what you see. For I tell you that many prophets and kings wanted to see what you see but did not see it, and to hear what you hear but did not hear it."*
> (Luke 10:23-24)

Before we move on to the conclusion of this chapter, might I suggest a quick review? We have discussed **what** we are to do; "Be transformed by the renewing of your mind." We have discussed **how** we are to do it; "Take captive every thought to make it obedient to Christ." Now we need to discover **who** we really are and **why** all this matters.

> [9] *God is faithful, who has called you into fellowship with his Son, Jesus Christ our Lord.* [30] *It is because of him that **you are in Christ Jesus**, who has become for us wisdom from God - that is, our righteousness, holiness, and redemption.* (1 Corinthians 1:9, 30)

As we continue, we will explore how to fully appropriate our identity in Christ. For me, this was a topic I had not given much thought to as a new Christian, and even years into exploring God's truth, I wasn't able to fully comprehend the depth of His love and compassion for me. However, as I continued to mature in my understanding of God's Word, I began to fully appropriate all that He had done for me.

So, what does it mean to "fully appropriate my identity in Christ?" As a verb, the Merriam-Webster dictionary defines *appropriate* as "to set apart for or assign to a particular recipient, purpose, or use." When applying that definition for the purpose of our study, it is God's Word that has been set apart for each one of us, **we are the recipients**. The Bible is God's love letter to us and His instruction manual on how to manage every part of our lives, including our battle with Satan. (You know—when all else fails, read the directions.)

> *Search me, O God, and know my heart; test me and know my anxious thoughts. See if there is any offensive way in me and lead me* (influence me) *in the way everlasting.* (Psalm 139:23-24) (Emphasis added.)

The Bible's purpose is to allow us to mature in our faith and continually deepen our fellowship with God, while at the same time guiding our relationships with our fellow human beings.

> *"Teacher, which is the greatest commandment in the Law?" Jesus replied: "'Love the Lord your God with all your heart and with all your soul and with all your mind.' This is the first and greatest commandment. And the second is like it: 'Love your neighbor as yourself.'"* (Matthew 22:36-39)

The Bible is to be used to advance the gospel in our own hearts, to share the good news with others, and to refute the lies of the enemy.

> *All Scripture is God-breathed and is useful for teaching, rebuking, correcting, and training in righteousness, so that the servant of God may be thoroughly equipped for every good work.* (2 Timothy 3:16-17)

I would like to dwell here for just a minute to take a quick inventory of what our Heavenly Father has "set apart and assigned" to each one of us, in addition to His word.

- He granted His grace and mercy while we were still sinners, and His grace is extended to us daily as believers.
  > *In him we have redemption through his blood, the forgiveness of sins, in accordance with the riches of God's grace.* (Ephesians 1:7)

- He gave us His Son.
  > *For God so loved the world that he gave his one and only Son, that whoever believes in him shall not perish but have eternal life.* (John 3:16)

- He gave us His Holy Spirit.
  > *But the Advocate, the Holy Spirit, whom the Father will send in my name, will teach you all things and will remind you of everything I have said to you.* (John 14:26)

- He gave us Eternal Life.
  > *For my Father's will is that everyone who looks to the Son and believes in him shall have eternal life, and I will raise them up at the last day.* (John 6:40)

- He promised us an inheritance to the Kingdom of Heaven.
  > *The Spirit himself testifies with our spirit that we are God's children. Now if we are children, then we are heirs - heirs of God and co-heirs with Christ, if indeed we share in his sufferings in order that we may also share in his glory.* (Romans 8:16-17)

  > *Do not let your hearts be troubled. You believe in God; believe also in me. My Father's house has many rooms; if that were not so, would I have told you that I am going there to prepare a place for you? And if I go and prepare a place for you, I will come back and take you to*

be with me that you also may be where I am. (John 14:1-3)

And you also were included in Christ when you heard the message of truth, the gospel of your salvation. When you believed, you were marked in him with a seal, the promised Holy Spirit, who is a deposit guaranteeing our inheritance until the redemption of those who are God's possession—to the praise of his glory. (Ephesians 1:13-14)

- He provides for us and protects us while we are in this earthly tent.

  Our Father in heaven, hallowed be your name, your kingdom come, your will be done, on earth as it is in heaven. Give us today our daily bread. And forgive us our debts, as we also have forgiven our debtors. And lead us not into temptation, but deliver us from the evil one. (Matthew 6:9-13)

May I ask at this point, what has God held back from you? If you have never taken this inventory before, I encourage you to dwell on this truth in your quiet time and let the depth of God's love flood into your heart. As we continue in this section of our study, please remind yourself as often as necessary that this same God is your advocate and stands continually by your side in this battle we call spiritual warfare.

> *You have searched me, LORD, and you know me. You know when I sit and when I rise; you perceive my thoughts from afar.* (Psalm 139:1-2)

One of the best books I've read on who we are in Christ and how to take inventory of that fact is *Lifetime Guarantee*, written by Dr. Bill Gillham. The subtitle is *Making Your Christian Life Work and What to Do When It Doesn't*. Dr. Gillham is a former professor of psychology at Southeastern Oklahoma State University. He and his wife Anabel have spoken worldwide through Gillham Ministries out of Fort Worth, Texas.

In the first sentence of his book, Dr. Gillham states; "This book is written to the Christian who is struggling in his/her attempt to live the life of victory in Jesus." A few paragraphs later, while still in the introduction, he adds, "Your problem is twofold:"

> *Number 1, you are trying to live the Christian life instead of understanding how to collaborate with Christ to live the Christian life for you and through you.*
>
> *Number 2, you are not comprehending <u>how to appropriate</u> your true identity as the new creation you already are in Christ. You are still attempting to face each day using your old ID pass. The key to experiencing victory in Christ lies in learning how to literally 'walk in the newness of life' as described in the Word." [4]*
>
> *As with every spiritual principle, this victory will not be so much a matter of fighting against the power of the Evil One, but rather a matter of starting up a new method of walking, moment by moment, experiencing Christ as your very life while simultaneously you "act dead" <u>to those thoughts</u> that will be served up to your mind through the flesh in the brain. Let's look at just a few of the many astounding and glorious things God has to say about our true identity, the new people we are in Christ.*
>
> - *I am holy. (We're not discussing performance; we're discussing identity.)*
> - *I am accepted. (Hebrews 13:5)*
> - *I am totally forgiven. (Colossians 2:13)*
> - *I am not condemned. (Romans 8:1)*
> - *I am a conqueror over evil. (Romans 8:37)*

*In essence, God says in Colossians 3:1-4, "Now then, Son, I want you to understand what your true identity is **and the method I have designed to enable you to live it out**. If you have been raised up with Christ, <u>set your mind on the things above, not on the things that are on the earth</u>." ⁵*

NOTE: The bolded statement in the above paragraph (*and the method I have designed to enable you to live it out*) is referring to 2 Corinthians 10:3-5 ('...take captive every thought to make it obedient to Christ.'), which is written in the book just above this paragraph. There is a similar reference in Romans 13:14. "Rather, clothe yourselves with the Lord Jesus Christ, and do not think about how to gratify the desires of the flesh."

In this third component of our preparation for victory, we set out to discover **who** we are **in** Christ. I hope that this relatively small representation of God's abundant grace has helped you to fully appropriate your new identity in Christ. Yet, the question remains, **why** does all this matter? I'm quite sure that the answer(s) to that question could be discussed for hours. However, in the context of this study, I will refer to Peter's second letter to "God's elect." Please take your time and let this incredible summary penetrate your heart and mind.

His divine power has given us everything we need for a godly life through our knowledge of him who called us by his own glory and goodness. Through these he has given us his very great and precious promises, so that through them you may participate in the divine nature, having escaped the corruption in the world caused by evil desires.
(2 Peter 1:3-4)

These powerful verses hold an even greater impact when we take the time to examine each individual component in the early part of

Peter's second inspired letter warning against false teachers in the early church.

- ❖ *His divine power*—The same power that raised Jesus from the dead.
- ❖ *Has given us everything we need for a godly life*— "But seek first his kingdom and his righteousness, and all these things will be given to you as well." (Matthew 6:33). We only need to look to God to walk victoriously as Christians.
- ❖ *Through our knowledge of him*—The fear of the LORD is the beginning of knowledge. (Proverbs 1:7)
- ❖ *Who called us by his own glory and goodness*—The God of all creation pursues you with loving intent.
- ❖ *He has given us his very great and precious promises*— Salvation, redemption, and an eternal inheritance.
- ❖ *So that you may participate in the divine nature*— "The knowledge of the secrets of the kingdom of God has been given to you." (Luke 8:10)
- ❖ *Having escaped the corruption in the world caused by evil desires*— "You shall know the truth and the truth shall set you free." (John 8:32)

As you continue to read this same letter, Peter begins Chapter 3 by writing the following.

> Dear friends, this is now my second letter to you. I have written both of them as reminders **to stimulate you to wholesome thinking.** (2 Peter 3:1)

As we close out this section, I would like to share one more incredible passage of Scripture with you. This is one of those passages that I read many times without fully grasping its meaning or importance. Then one day, as He tends to do, the Holy Spirit opened my eyes to the truth that was represented in this part of

Paul's letter to the Ephesians. It is another powerful statement of *why* we should pursue wisdom and discernment, discipline our thought process, and appropriate our identity in Christ.

> *I became a servant of this gospel by the gift of God's grace given me through the working of his power. Although I am less than the least of all the Lord's people, this grace was given me: to preach to the Gentiles the boundless riches of Christ, and to make plain to everyone the administration of this mystery, which for ages past was kept hidden in God, who created all things. His intent was that now, <u>through the church</u>, the manifold wisdom of God should be made known to the rulers and authorities in the heavenly realms, according to his eternal purpose that he accomplished in Christ Jesus our Lord.* (Ephesians 3:7-11)

Did that just hit you like it hit me? God's intent is that now, through us (the church), the previous mystery that was and is a combination of forgiveness, redemption, and salvation through Jesus Christ, should be made known to the rulers and authorities in the heavenly realms. My dear friends, when you walk victoriously in and through Jesus Christ, your life is a beacon of truth and a definitive statement of God's eternal rule and authority to the enemy who is trying to steal, kill, and destroy you! You are not only an example to unbelievers, but also, as a mature and confident follower of Jesus Christ, part of your responsibility is to make apparent the 'manifold wisdom of God' to all those in the heavenly realms (angels and demons). See 1 Peter 1:12. **Your life counts—and God wants you victorious!**

As I mentioned at the beginning of this chapter, we have begun our march toward a victorious Christian lifestyle. "Press on toward the goal" was the preparation for battle. In the next several chapters, I will uncover God's essential weapons to engage and ultimately defeat the enemy. I look forward to sharing that good news with you. As this chapter ends, allow our foundational verse to focus your mind once again on God's truth.

> *For though we live in the world, we do not wage war as the world does. The weapons we fight with are not the weapons of the world. On the contrary, they have divine power to demolish strongholds. We demolish arguments and every pretension that sets itself up against the knowledge of God, **and we take captive every thought to make it obedient to Christ**. (2 Corinthians 10:3-5)*

1. John MacArthur, *The MacArthur Bible Handbook—The New Testament* (Nashville: Thomas Nelson, 2003), 201-202
2. *Layman's Bible Commentary Set, Vol. 8—Matthew and Mark* (Uhrichsville: Barbour Publishing, 2008) 43-44
3. The Mind Unleashed - A Walk Through the Human Mind. (n. d.) Retrieved from http://themindunleashed.com/2014/03/conscious-subconscious-unconscious-mind-work.html
4. Bill Gillham, *Lifetime Guarantee* (Eugene: Harvest House Publishers, 1993), 9-12
5. Bill Gillham, *Lifetime Guarantee* (Eugene: Harvest House Publishers, 1993), 125-128

Chapter 6: Your Authority to Win Through Jesus Christ

In the previous chapter, we began our march toward a victorious Christian lifestyle by focusing on a deliberate, dedicated, and determined effort to study the Bible as the best preparation to equip you for this spiritual battle. In fact, the examination of Scripture is a necessary and lifelong quest for knowledge and understanding until it becomes the rock you stand on and the principal point of reference in defeating the enemy and ultimately glorifying your Heavenly Father.

So, while the last chapter was offered as a spiritual boot camp, the next several chapters are intended as a continuance of your combat training relevant to spiritual warfare. As stated above, I believe the effort to equip and protect yourself will require a lifelong commitment. To some that might sound burdensome, but trust me, the deeper you delve into God's Word, the more exciting it becomes, as His truth penetrates your heart and new levels of understanding are revealed to you. Contrary to what many would expect from such an effort, which is an increase in head knowledge, what you will find is a personal relationship with Father, Son, and Holy Spirit that grows in intimacy and establishes a clear sense of what God desires for you in your life. **Remember, God wants you to be victorious!**

> *For everything that was written in the past was written to teach us, so that through the endurance taught in the Scriptures and the encouragement they provide we might have hope.* (Romans 15:4)

As we move forward, we will gather all that we have learned so far regarding our battle with Satan and combine it with a plan to engage and defeat the enemy. The continued study of God's Word

176

will help us to further understand His provision for our defensive posture as well as our ability to employ and maintain a spiritual offensive.

But before we continue, allow me to share with you how God has blessed the process of writing this study and confirmed my part in sharing His truth with you. I am sure there are many reading this study who have experienced the sometimes mysterious and yet definitive way that God chooses to give direction in our lives. For those that have not, I can only encourage you to stay consistent in seeking wisdom daily in His Word and communicating with Him continually in prayer. For when you sincerely seek Him, God will reveal Himself to you, for He longs to be your Counselor.

Your statutes are my delight; they are my counselors. (Psalm 119:24)

For to us a child is born, to us a son is given, and the government will be on his shoulders. And he will be called Wonderful Counselor, Mighty God, Everlasting Father, Prince of Peace. (Isaiah 9:6)

There have been many times in my life that I wanted God to just sit across the table from me and say, "Jeff, this is what I want you to do." While He could certainly do that, I have found that most of His direction, at least in my life, has come more in the form of subtle hints. The secret to discerning their meaning, like any other relationship, is in communication. The more you communicate with someone (sincerely listening and sharing your thoughts) the easier it is to pick up on subtle hints sent your way. (If you've been married for any length of time, I'm sure you can relate.)

As I mentioned in the introduction to this study, I am not formally trained in theology. My relationship with the Lord has been built by focusing on the basics—daily reading of God's Word and seeking

His counsel through prayer. Through that consistent communication, God began to heighten my awareness of spiritual warfare and the personal battle the enemy had been waging against me. In my defense, I began to catalog Scripture verses that had anything to do with the topic, eventually compiling eight pages of Old and New Testament Scripture as a reference guide. With that material and a basic outline of the spiritual influence in our lives, God prompted me to write about the subject.

Like Moses, I resisted at first and offered numerous excuses as to why I was not equipped to write a book. Over time, I would occasionally grant casual consideration to the idea, but I continued to bargain with God. I thought, *Perhaps I could solicit the help of my former pastor and mentor to assist me. Surely the content of the study would be more respected with a Ph. D. in theology and forty years in ministry attached as a co-author.* But as had happened many times before, I set the idea aside.

Then one day, a casual business acquaintance invited me to lunch. During our conversation, he disclosed the purpose for our meeting. He was writing a book about a heartbreaking experience in his life and wanted to run a few ideas past me. You see, I was an executive recruiter, and he had been laid off after serving with one company for twenty years. While unemployed and searching for answers, he realized that no one had ever written a book about the emotional trauma surrounding job loss. He was a technical person and had never done anything like this before. The manuscript was 90% done, and as he was searching for a title, he asked if I would read the entire draft and offer an opinion. The book was self-published several months later.

Now, I'm not sure how you would interpret that, but after years of sidestepping God's leading, I was not about to ignore this rather obvious hint. To me, it was a clear directive. **God was not interested in my ability or my spiritual intellect. He was interested in my availability.** I would not be writing this material, He would. I just needed to say yes, sit down at my computer, and start the process. God would do the rest! Remember this verse?

But the Advocate, the Holy Spirit, whom the Father will send in my name, will teach you all things and will remind you of everything I have said to you. (John 14:26)

As I was writing this chapter, the project was about sixty percent complete and I must tell you, it had been an amazing journey to experience God working through me up to that point. I hope that the information I have shared so far has been helpful, but trust me, the process of weaving eight pages of individual Scripture verses into a coherent and valid thesis is something only God could have accomplished. There are so many ways that the Holy Spirit has guided me through this process, but I would like to mention one that has special relevance to this chapter on authority.

As I have noted throughout this study, my research has included many different resources in addition to the Bible itself. These include books that I read and highlighted years ago, Bible commentaries, and of course the Internet. What has been truly remarkable is how God has led me to the exact resource I needed, when I needed it, and how that piece of the puzzle seemed to fit perfectly into the content I was working on at the time. I pray that His guidance has been evident as I have tried to follow His lead.

In my preparation for writing this entire section on how to fight and win, God intervened again. You see, I had what I considered to be the major emphasis outlined in my head for years, which was the power of the spoken word. What I did not realize was there was an extremely important building block that I had inadvertently neglected. If fact, it was more than that. It was, and is, the cornerstone of this chapter and several to follow. Let me share with you how God made sure that I did not miss what He had intended as the foundation of our victory through Jesus Christ.

I have read and collected dozens of books from secular and Christian authors. Over the years, I would share certain books with our daughters to encourage them or to provide additional guidance through life's trials. When our youngest daughter moved to Knoxville, Tennessee, I began to share one or two books a month with her and she developed an excellent reading habit. Two years later, when she moved into an apartment of her own, I suggested to my wife that we give her a box of books that had been sitting on our garage shelf, **unopened, for the past six years**.

I was somewhat confident that the box contained mostly motivational and self-help books, but my wife suggested we open it to make sure. To my surprise, buried in the middle of the box was a book on spiritual warfare that I had completely forgotten about. As I pulled it out, I remembered how the title not only captured my attention and caused me to buy the book, but also aggravated me a bit. You see, during all my wrestling with God, I had envisioned a title for "my" book (should I ever write it). And there, right in front of me, was a book on spiritual warfare with "my" title—*Rules of Engagement*.

After discovering the book again, I left it idle on my desk for a few days, but when I finally began to browse through the chapters and focus on the areas of text that I had highlighted years earlier, it became evident to me that this was not a coincidence. There on page 149, was a vital lesson on understanding authority as it applies to our daily walk as Christians and our battle with Satan and his demons.

As only He could do, God had orchestrated the exact timing of all these events. I believe now that without this cornerstone, the power available to us through the spoken Word of God (the primary topic of this section) would not achieve the intended results. So, let us begin with that cornerstone as together we learn **how to fight and how to win!**

The excerpt below comes from *Rules of Engagement* by Derek Prince. The first paragraph was referenced at the beginning of this study. In Chapter 18, "Principles of Spiritual Protection," he writes the following.

When we are born again as Christians into the Kingdom of God, we discover that we are caught up in a war with an opposing spiritual kingdom – the kingdom of Satan. We discover, too, that we have various kinds of enemies, but the most powerful and the most formidable is a kingdom of rebellious angels in the heavenly places, under the rule of God's archenemy, Satan.

Because we have such powerful enemies, we all need to avail ourselves of the protection that God has provided. Every Christian needs the protection of being under appropriate scriptural authority. Luke 7:1-10 records how a Roman centurion sent some Jewish elders to Jesus to ask for the healing of his servant, who was at death's door. Jesus offered to go and pray for the healing of the servant, but the centurion responded:

> *"Lord, do not trouble Yourself, for I am not worthy that You should enter under my roof. I therefore, I did not even think myself worthy to come to You. But say the word, and my servant will be healed. For I also am a man placed under authority, having soldiers under me. And I say to one, 'Go,' and he goes; and to another, 'Come,' and he comes; and to my servant, 'Do this,' and he does it."* Luke 7:6-8 (NKJV)

By saying, "I *also* am a man placed under authority," the centurion recognized that the authority of Jesus in the spiritual realm was analogous to the authority that he had in the military realm as a centurion in the Roman army. In each case, their authority was derived from submission to a higher source. For the centurion, the source was the Roman Emperor. For Jesus, the source was God the Father.

Note, too, that the centurion did not say – as many have done – "I *have* authority," but "I am *under* authority." He affirmed a basic principle of Scripture: to *have* authority one must be *under* authority. Authority always flows *downward*. There are chains of authority that descend from God the Father through Jesus the Son into every situation in the universe. Every Christian needs the protection of being under the appropriate authority. A Christian not under authority is an unprotected Christian.[1]

Let that last sentence sink in for just a minute. "A Christian not under authority is an unprotected Christian." I don't care what kind of fight you are about to engage in, not one of us would want to enter a battle unprotected, especially not this conflict. We have invested valuable time identifying our spiritual battle and discussing the consequences of allowing Satan's agenda to influence our lives. We cannot, and must not, expect to win this battle on our own, unprotected, and without the authority of a spiritual advocate on our side.

Well, I have good news. That was not, and is not, God's plan for us. Earlier, I referenced John 14:26, in which Jesus promises an advocate (the Holy Spirit) to assist the disciples in their mission of spreading the Gospel. In 1 John, there is the promise of another advocate.

*My dear children, I write this to you so that you will not sin. But if anybody does sin, we have an **advocate** with the Father—**Jesus Christ**, the Righteous One.* (1 John 2:1)

In the context of John's letter, Jesus is represented as a mediator, appointed by God the Father, and with the Father's authority, to come alongside those that fall into sin. Jesus serves as the atoning sacrifice that turns away God's divine wrath by offering his own punishment as payment for our sins.

> *Which is easier: to say to this paralyzed man, 'Your sins are forgiven,' or to say, 'Get up, take your mat and walk'? But I want you to know that the Son of Man **has authority** on earth to forgive sins." So, he said to the man, "I tell you, get up, take your mat and go home."* (Mark 2:9-11)

However, as we will see in the Scripture verses referenced below, Jesus is not just given authority for the singular purpose of forgiving our sins. He is granted authority over all things by God the Father.

> *Then the eleven disciples went to Galilee, to the mountain where Jesus had told them to go. When they saw him, they worshiped him; but some doubted. Then Jesus came to them and said, **"All authority in heaven and on earth has been given to me.** Therefore, go and make disciples of all nations, baptizing them in the name of the Father and of the Son and of the Holy Spirit, and teaching them to obey everything I have commanded you. And surely, I am with you always, to the very end of the age."* (Matthew 28:16-20)

> *The reason my Father loves me is that I lay down my life— only to take it up again. No one takes it from me, but I lay it down of my own accord. **I have authority to lay it down and authority to take it up again.** This command I received from my Father.* (John 10:17-18)

*Don't you believe that I am in the Father, and that the Father is in me? The words I say to you **I do not speak on my own authority**. Rather, it is the Father, living in me, who is doing his work.* (John 14:10)

*After Jesus said this, he looked toward heaven and prayed: "Father, the hour has come. Glorify your Son, that your Son may glorify you. **For you granted him authority** over all people that he might give eternal life to all those you have given him."* (John 17:1-2)

As an aside to this study, I encourage you to read John's gospel with a fresh purpose in mind. In John's account, Jesus is quoted time and time again regarding the four-fold relationship between God the Father, Jesus his Son, the Holy Spirit, and those born again ("all those you have given him"). Throughout this gospel, Jesus praises his Father, thanks his Father, glorifies his Father, and then on our behalf, pleads with his Father that we may fully accept Jesus Christ as the Son of God and as the promised Messiah and Savior. And while most of His conversation and intercessory prayer is directed toward the disciples, **Jesus also prays for us** just before being arrested.

*My prayer is not for them alone. **I pray also for those who will believe in me through their message**, that <u>all</u> of them may be one, Father, just as you are in me and I am in you. May they also be in us so that the world may believe that you have sent me. I have given them the glory that you gave me, that they may be one as we are one - I in them and you in me - so that they may be brought to complete unity. Then the world will know that you sent me and have loved them even as you have loved me. Father, I want those you have given me to be with me where I am, and* *to see my glory, the glory you have given me because you loved me before the creation of the world.* (John 17:20-24)

When we accept Jesus as our personal Lord and Savior, we are united as one with the Trinity, and Jesus not only serves fully as our advocate, but also passes the authority given to Him by his Father, to those who remain in Him.

> *Jesus called his twelve disciples to him **and gave them authority** to drive out impure spirits and to heal every disease and sickness.* (Matthew 10:1)

> *Calling the Twelve to him, he began to send them out two by two **and gave them authority** over impure spirits.* (Mark 6:7)

> *When Jesus had called the Twelve together, **he gave them power and authority** to drive out all demons and to cure diseases, and he sent them out to proclaim the kingdom of God and to heal the sick.* (Luke 9:1-2)

> ***I have given you authority** to trample on snakes and scorpions and to overcome all the power of the enemy; nothing will harm you.* (Luke 10:19) (Jesus sends out the Seventy-Two.)

In the context of our study, it is interesting to note the primary reasons we are granted this authority.

- *To drive out impure spirits*
- *To drive out all demons*
- *To overcome <u>all</u> the power of the enemy*

If we return to 1 John, we have an even more definitive declaration of Jesus' purpose in God's plan for eternity.

*The one who does what is sinful is of the devil, because the devil has been sinning from the beginning. **The reason the Son of God appeared was to destroy the devil's work.*** (1 John 3:8)

We have now established the vertical authority structure as outlined in Scripture and how it is passed downward from God the Father to His Son, Jesus Christ, and then to those who claim Jesus as Lord and Savior. However, there is a vital acknowledgement and prerequisite that cannot be overemphasized.

Most Christians acknowledge and accept the path to salvation as outlined in Paul's letter to the Romans, commonly referred to as "The Roman Road to Salvation."

- *As it is written: "There is no one righteous, not even one."* (Romans 3:10)
- *For all have sinned and fall short of the glory of God.* (Romans 3:23)
- *But God demonstrates his own love for us in this: While we were still sinners, Christ died for us.* (Romans 5:8)
- *If you confess with your mouth, "Jesus is Lord" and believe in your heart that God raised him from the dead, you will be saved. [10] For it is with your heart that you believe and are justified, and it is with your mouth that you profess your faith and are saved.* (Romans 10:9-10)
- *Everyone who calls on the name of the Lord will be saved.* (Romans 10:13)

The most important proclamation in that journey is your personal profession of faith in Jesus Christ. You cannot just confess your belief in Jesus and who he is *(even the demons know and confess that He is the Son of God—James 2:19/Matthew 8:28-29)*. You must accept Him in your heart as your personal Lord and Savior and submit to His authority in your life. Remember the quote from

Derek Prince, "He (*the centurion*) affirmed a basic principle of Scripture: to **have** authority one must be **under** authority. Authority always flows downward." Is Jesus your Lord? Have you given Him authority in your life?

> *Submit yourselves, then, to God. Resist the devil, and he will flee from you.* (James 4:7)

This is the same prerequisite principle mentioned in the last chapter. Perhaps this verse should read, "Submit yourselves to God, <u>then</u> resist the devil, and he will flee from you." The act of submission is to allow Jesus to have complete authority and control in your life. For some, that action may seem overly restrictive and counterintuitive to their sense of personal freedom, but a *continued attitude* of spiritual submission will allow you to exercise your God given authority over any demonic attack.

SIDE NOTE: I know there will be some who take issue with the idea of submission. The dictionary defines this term as "an act or instance of yielding control to a more powerful or authoritative entity." Henceforth, the challenge. As human beings, we like to be in control of our lives, or at least we like to *think* we are in control. If that describes you, there is a bit of wise counsel (shared with me years ago) that may lower any apprehensions.

If you divide the word into two parts, you find that "sub" is the act of "yielding control." "Mission" is defined as "an important goal or purpose that is accompanied by strong conviction; the business with which such a group is charged." Most often, our challenge with submitting is that we do not have a clear understanding of the mission's purpose (how it will benefit us or others) or cannot correctly identify the authoritative entity behind the directive, or both. In being asked to submit to God's authority through Jesus Christ, the answers are clearly identified. God is the ultimate authority. His charge is to seek holiness and righteousness to gain your personal salvation, to share the gospel message with others, and to garner His power to defeat Satan's agenda for your life.

Notice the reference above to a 'continued attitude' of spiritual submission. Your personal profession of faith and acceptance of Jesus as Lord is the beginning of knowledge and strength in this battle against evil. Will we falter at times and attempt to win this war using our limited abilities and inadequate knowledge of the spiritual realm? Yes! However, Jesus encourages us to remain in Him.

> *[1] I am the true vine, and my Father is the gardener. [4] Remain in me, as I also remain in you. No branch can bear fruit by itself; it must remain in the vine. Neither can you bear fruit unless you remain in me. [5] I am the vine; you are the branches. If you remain in me and I in you, you will bear much fruit;* **apart from me you can do nothing.** *[7] If you remain in me and my words remain in you, ask whatever you wish, and it will be done for you. [8] This is to my Father's glory, that you bear much fruit, showing yourselves to be my disciples.* (John 15:1, 4, 5, 7, 8)

In these verses, Jesus once again establishes the correct vertical alignment. He is the vine, but his Father is the gardener. If we remain grafted into the vine, then the power and authority passed down from Father to Son remains available to us. In regard to spiritual warfare, we see an example of this in Luke's Gospel.

> *[1] After this the Lord appointed seventy-two others and* **sent them** *two by two ahead of him to every town and place where he was about to go. [17] The seventy-two returned with joy and said, "Lord, even the demons submit to us in your name."* (Luke 10:1, 17)

The key words in Verse 1 are *sent them*. Jesus sent them with His authority. In Verse 17 we see that the demons submitted to them because they professed the name of Jesus as their authority. As previously referenced, Jesus explains their experience in Verse 19, teaching, "I have given you authority to trample on snakes and scorpions and to overcome all the power of the enemy."

There is another key element relevant to this discussion. While the knowledge of Jesus' authority and our submission to His authority are important in this battle, so is **our faith** in His authority. Accordingly, the belief in our authority through Christ must also be firmly established. Remember, the seventy-two had been following Jesus long enough to establish their faith in Him as the Messiah. (Had that not been the case, I don't believe Jesus would have sent them out.)

We find a reference to the faith factor as it relates to this subject in Matthew's gospel. It is interesting to note that in Matthew's gospel, the following happens after the disciples have witnessed many miracles including the feeding of the five thousand, Jesus walking on water, and the transfiguration. This is also after Peter's confession of Christ as recorded in Matthew 16:15-16, "You are the Christ, the Son of the living God."

When they came to the crowd, a man approached Jesus and knelt before him. "Lord, have mercy on my son," he said. "He has seizures and is suffering greatly. He often falls into the fire or into the water. I brought him to your disciples, but they could not heal him." "You unbelieving and perverse generation," Jesus replied, "how long shall I stay with you? How long shall I put up with you? Bring the boy here to me." Jesus rebuked the demon, and it came out of the boy, and he was healed at that moment. Then the disciples came to Jesus in private and asked, "Why couldn't we drive it out?" **He replied, "Because you have**

189

so little faith. *Truly I tell you, if you have faith as small as a mustard seed, you can say to this mountain, 'Move from here to there,' and it will move. Nothing will be impossible for you. But this kind does not go out except by prayer and fasting."* (Matthew 17:14-21)

So why does it seem that some demons would obey the disciples while others would not? Because the authority necessary to defeat any and all spiritual battles is accessed through faith. Jesus gave His disciples authority over all powers of the enemy, but when they reached a demon they could not cast out, He told them it was because of an insufficiency in their faith. He went on to say that some demons are so strong and stubborn that prayer and fasting is required to drive them out.

Well, that invokes this question. What is the significance of prayer and fasting? The answer is, "Remain in me!" Jesus promises, "I am the vine; you are the branches. If you remain in me and my words remain in you, ask whatever you wish, and it will be done for you." A time of prayer and fasting is a focused effort to be nearer to God, a time to be regrafted into the vine, a time to not only study God's Word but also allow Him to speak to you through His word.

A dedicated time of prayer and fasting will always bring you closer to God and strengthen your faith. As Jesus professed to His disciples, a confident and assured faith is necessary to drive out the stronger demons (lies, temptations, accusations, condemnations) that plague us. As your faith increases, so will your ability to exercise your authority against demonic spirits. During his ministry, Jesus repeatedly stepped away from his disciples and the crowds to fast and pray (to *remain* in God the Father).

How do we build our faith and remain in Him? Go back to the simple truths outlined in "Press on Toward the Goal." By reading the Bible, we know the disciples to be eyewitnesses. They lived with Jesus, talked with him, witnessed his miracles, and saw him raised from the dead. So, you may ask, how could we possibly have the same faith?

Consequently, faith comes from hearing the message,
and the message is heard through the word about Christ.
(Romans 10:17)

We too can live with Jesus, talk with him, witness his miracles, and believe in him resurrected. That can be, and hopefully will be, part of your daily routine going forward. The simple commitment to spend time in God's Word each day and to continually ask for Godly wisdom and discernment will allow you to remain in Him. And as we have just discussed, it is of primary importance in defeating the enemy and establishing a victorious Christian lifestyle.

As we come to a close on the topic of authority, Scripture does warn of the danger of acting upon your own authority. The text below comes from the apostle Paul in the Book of Acts.

Some Jews who went around driving out evil spirits tried
to invoke the name of the Lord Jesus over those who were
demon-possessed. They would say, "In the name of the
Jesus whom Paul preaches, I command you to come out."
Seven sons of Sceva, a Jewish chief priest, were doing this.
One day the evil spirit answered them, "Jesus I know, and
Paul I know about, but who are you?" Then the man who
had the evil spirit jumped on them and overpowered them
all. He gave them such a beating that they ran out of the
house naked and bleeding. (Acts 19:13-16)

In the same passage where Jesus encourages us to remain in Him *(the vine)*, he also shares this warning.

If you do not remain in me, you are like a branch that is
thrown away and withers; such branches are picked up,
thrown into the fire and burned. (John 15:6)

Before we move on, may I offer a brief summary of the protection and authority granted us in Jesus Christ?

1.) Recognize that we are caught up in a spiritual battle. In this we have no option.
2.) Recognize that Jesus offers the only option to overcome; *all the power of the enemy* (Luke 10:19).
3.) Confess with your mouth and believe in your heart that Jesus is your personal Lord and Savior.
4.) Upon that confession, repent of your sins and submit yourself to God and His authority through Jesus Christ.
5.) With the proper vertical alignment in place, remain in Him (study God's Word).
6.) In faith, exercise your God given authority to; *drive out all demons and to cure diseases* (Luke 9:1-2).

There is one more important point to remember. **In this ongoing battle, we are not fighting _for_ victory—we are fighting from a position of victory!**

For God hath not given me the spirit of fear; but of power, and of love, and of a _sound mind_." (2 Timothy 1:7) (KJV)

For visual continuity, I have expanded our diagram and introduced the opposing agendas of God's authority and Satan's attempt to defeat us.

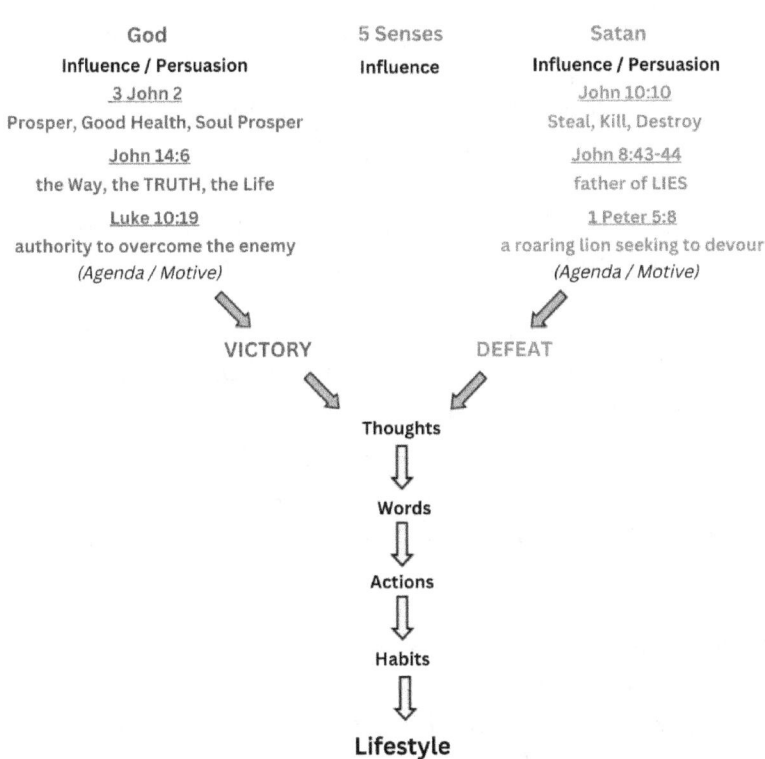

Remember, we are in a battle that not only includes our attempt to live the Christian lifestyle but can also determine the eternal destiny of those that do not know Jesus Christ as their Savior. In the first two chapters of Job, we see this exchange repeated twice.

One day the angels came to present themselves before the LORD, and Satan also came with them. The LORD said to Satan, "Where have you come from?" Satan answered the LORD, "From roaming throughout the earth, going back and forth on it." (Job 1:6-7, 2:1-2)

As the story of Job clearly details, Satan is not roaming the earth looking for a good picnic spot. He is looking for spiritual beings, trapped in a corrupted earth suit, that he can deceive and keep separated from their heavenly Father. We now know his primary weapon is the invasion of our thought life.

If you still have any doubts as to where our spiritual battle is won or lost, I invite you to contrast the Scripture verses below.

*Jesus went on: "What comes out of a person is what defiles them. For it is from within, out of a person's heart, **that evil thoughts come**—sexual immorality, theft, murder, adultery, greed, malice, deceit, lewdness, envy, slander, arrogance, and folly. All these evils come from inside and defile a person." (Mark 7:20-23) (See also Matthew 15:17-19.)*

*[8] Finally, brothers and sisters, whatever is true, whatever is noble, whatever is right, whatever is pure, whatever is lovely, whatever is admirable - if anything is excellent or praiseworthy - **think about such things**. [7] And the peace of God, which transcends all understanding, will guard your hearts and your minds in Christ Jesus. (Philippians 4:7-8 in reverse order)*

In his letter to the Galatians, Paul references this same contrast as he leads up to an often-quoted Scripture verse regarding the fruit of the Spirit.

For the flesh desires what is contrary to the Spirit, and the Spirit what is contrary to the flesh. They are in conflict with each other. (Galatians 5:17)

Just as our diagram illustrates, there are conflicting agendas for your life being encouraged in the spiritual realm. The good news is that God has given you free will to decide which agenda you will follow. The bad news is that God has given you free will to decide which agenda you will follow.

Now what I am commanding you today is not too difficult for you or beyond your reach. It is not up in heaven, so that you have to ask, "Who will ascend into heaven to get it and proclaim it to us so we may obey it?" Nor is it beyond the sea, so that you have to ask, "Who will cross the sea to get it and proclaim it to us so we may obey it?" No, the word is near you; it is in your mouth and in your heart so you may obey it. See, I set before you today life and prosperity, death and destruction. For I command you today to love the LORD your God, to walk in obedience to him, and to keep his commands, decrees, and laws; then you will live and increase, and the LORD your God will bless you in the land you are entering to possess.

But if your heart turns away and you are not obedient, and if you are drawn away to bow down to other gods and worship them, I declare to you this day that you will certainly be destroyed. You will not live long in the land you are crossing the Jordan to enter and possess.

This day I call the heavens and the earth as witnesses against you that I have set before you life and death, blessings, and curses. **Now choose life**, *so that you and your children may live and that you may love the LORD your God, listen to his voice, and hold fast to him.* (Deuteronomy 30:11-20)

Remember, we are now focused on marching toward a victorious Christian lifestyle and how we attain that victory. As our journey continues, we will explore each of the topics below.

1.) The Hope We Have in Christ Jesus
2.) The Power and Privilege of Prayer
3.) Spiritual Weapons to Defend Against the Enemy
4.) Offensive Weapons (The Power of the Spoken Word by Example)
5.) Offensive Weapons (The Power of the Spoken Word by Practical Application)
6.) The Power of the Spoken Word (Faith Supported by Science)

1. Derek Prince, *Rules of Engagement* (Grand Rapids: Chosen Books, 2016), 148-150

Chapter 7: The Hope We Have in Jesus Christ

Now that we have established our authority structure as outlined in Scripture and reviewed not only the choices available to us, but also the potential consequences of those choices, it is worthwhile to reaffirm the hope, trust, and faith that are offered to us in and through Jesus Christ our Savior. To help in our understanding of that truth, there is no better place to start than the beginning of John's gospel.

> *In the beginning was the Word, and the Word was with God, and the Word was God. He was with God in the beginning. Through him all things were made; without him nothing was made that has been made.* (John 1:1-3)

This is a familiar verse to many Christians and points back to one of the crucial doctrines of the Christian faith as outlined in the beginning of this study by R. Albert Mohler, specifically the full deity and full humanity of Jesus Christ. In Verses 1—3, John clearly establishes the Deity of Jesus and His role in creation. Later in the same gospel, Verse 14 testifies to the humanity of Jesus.

> *The Word became flesh and made his dwelling among us. We have seen his glory, the glory of the one and only Son, who came from the Father, full of grace and truth.* (John 1:14)

In-between the above quotes from John's gospel, there are several verses relevant to this portion of our study that deserve our attention as well.

> *⁴ In him was life, and that life was the light of all mankind. ⁵ The light shines in the darkness, and the darkness has not overcome it. ¹¹ He came to that which was his own, but his*

own did not receive him. [12] Yet to all who did receive him, to those who believed in his name, he gave the right to become children of God. (John 1:4, 5, 11, 12)

There are three main points I would like to emphasize as we strengthen our hope and faith in Jesus.

1. *In him was life, and that life was the light of all mankind.* **His light is our hope!** Jesus is the only truth that leads to repentance and salvation for all of mankind.
2. *The light shines in the darkness, and the darkness has not overcome it.* **His light is our victory!** To all who receive him, Jesus is the only truth that leads to victory.
3. *To those who believed in his name, he gave the right to become children of God.* **His light is our inheritance!** To those who have accepted Jesus Christ as their Savior, their place in the family of God is assured for all eternity.

These few verses only scratch the surface of the relationship between the hope and faith available to us through Jesus Christ, but just this brief look at the first chapter of John ought to provide a new confidence in your soul. I purposely used the word *confidence* here to make a point. If you are not familiar with it, there is a specific relationship in Scripture that weaves together the ideas of hope, faith, and confidence.

*Now **faith** is **confidence** in what we **hope** for and **assurance** about what we do not see.* (Hebrews 11:1)

As many of you know, Hebrews 11 is commonly referred to as The Faith Chapter. The NIV Bible titles the chapter; "By Faith" and begins with the definition of faith already outlined in Verse 1. As stated earlier, our ability and authority to overcome our spiritual enemies is rooted in our faith and submission to Jesus Christ as our Lord and Savior. But as evidenced above, our faith is developed by a confidence in what we hope for and an assurance in what we do not see. That confidence and assurance are attained by the study of God's Word, both individually and corporately.

> *Consequently, faith comes from hearing the   message, and the message is heard through the word about Christ.* (Romans 10:17)

As is common in any other endeavor in life, there is a maturing process that accompanies our growth as Christians. Our entrance into the family of God typically begins with a lot of questions. As we pursue the truth of the gospel, the Holy Spirit begins to reveal the meaning of Scripture to us little by little. For me, some of the answers to my questions were made clear early in my walk, but there were other more complicated revelations and promises that I could only hope were true.

The significance of that hope is that it kept me engaged. I wanted to know more, learn more, and understand more. I kept coming back to the Scriptures for confirmation of that which I hoped for. If you think about it, most of our endeavors in life are no different. In your relationships, your career, your athletic or recreational activities, there is frequently an ambition to improve, to get to the next level. Without the potential to achieve, there is no hope.

> *Know also that wisdom is like honey for you: If you find it, there is a future **hope** for you, and your **hope** will not be cut off.* (Proverbs 24:14)

God had given me an ambition to know more about Him. And as God had promised, the more I sought Him, the more He trusted me and the more He revealed his truth to me through his Holy Spirit. As I continued to mature in my walk with Christ, my hope transformed into an assurance of God's promises in many areas of my life.

One by one, my questions were answered, and with each answer my faith increased until I developed the confidence to surrender complete control in all areas of my life to God (including my spiritual battles). The proclamation in Hebrews 11:1 became a reality in my life. "Now faith is confidence in what we hope for and assurance about what we do not see." Paul addresses this reality in his letter to the Ephesians. The letter begins with this greeting.

> *To the saints in Ephesus, the faithful in Christ Jesus.* (Ephesians 1:1)

Paul addresses the believers as faithful and goes on to describe the spiritual blessings available to them in Christ Jesus, including this promise in Verses 13—14.

> *And you also were included in Christ when you heard the message of truth, the gospel of your salvation. When you believed, you were marked in him with a seal, the promised Holy Spirit, who is a deposit guaranteeing our inheritance.* (Ephesians 1:13-14)

Of great interest to me were the similarities in the Old Testament proverb (24:14), Paul's New Testament greeting to the church in Ephesus, and the promises uncovered in the first chapter of John's Gospel. Take notice below of how they align with each other.

Proverbs: *Know also that wisdom is like honey for you*
Paul: *You were included in Christ when you heard the message of truth, the gospel of your salvation*
John: **His light is our hope!**

Proverbs: *If you find it (wisdom), there is a future hope for you*
Paul: *When you believed, you were marked in Him with a seal*
John: **His light is our victory!**

Proverbs: *And your hope will not be cut off*

Paul: *The promised Holy Spirit is a deposit guaranteeing our inheritance*

John: **His light is our inheritance!**

Are you beginning to see the consistent pattern in these messages that were written hundreds of years apart? The process begins with hearing the gospel message. As you continue to seek God's wisdom, you begin to develop hope in God's promises. That glimmer of hope keeps you engaged until head knowledge transforms into heart knowledge, and belief sets in. As belief matures into faith, we develop a "confidence in what we hope for and assurance about what we do not see" as the Holy Spirit enlightens us day by day.

As we revisit the first chapter of Ephesians, Paul attests to the early stages of this pattern, identified in the believers in Ephesus.

> *For this reason, ever since I heard about your faith in the Lord Jesus and your love for all God's people, I have not stopped giving thanks for you, remembering you in my prayers.* (Ephesians 1:15-16)

He then encourages them to continuing seeking a deeper relationship with the Lord and prays on their behalf that the Holy Spirit would make known to them the hope for which God has called them.

> *I keep asking that the God of our Lord Jesus Christ, the glorious Father, may give you the Spirit of **wisdom** and revelation, so that you may know him better. I pray that the eyes of your heart may be enlightened in order that you may know the **hope** to which he has called you, the riches of his glorious **inheritance** in his holy people.* (Ephesians 1:17-18)

But there is more! Relevant to our study, Paul's prayer transitions to a request for all believers to know the incomparable power available to us through Jesus Christ to defeat the enemy.

> [18a] *I pray that the eyes of your heart may be enlightened in order that you may know...* [19]*his incomparably great power for us who believe. That power is the same as the mighty strength he exerted when he raised Christ from the dead and seated him at his right hand in the heavenly realms, far above all rule and authority, power and dominion, and every name that is invoked, not only in the present age but also in the one to come. And God placed all things under his feet and appointed him to be head over everything for the church, which is his body, the fullness of him who fills everything in every way.* (Ephesians 1:19-23)

Borrowing from a verse previously highlighted in our study, Paul, in the next set of verses, leaves no room to misinterpret the identity of that over which we may take authority.

> *As for you, you were dead in your transgressions and sins, in which you used to live when you followed the ways of this world and of the ruler of the kingdom of the air, the spirit who is now at work in those who are disobedient. All of us also lived among them at one time, gratifying the cravings of our flesh and following its desires and thoughts.* (Ephesians 2:1-3)

As you near the end of Ephesians Chapter 2, you see the pattern completed. Paul, having begun with thanksgiving for the faith already established by hearing the Word of God, then prays that the Holy Spirit will increase their wisdom and allow them to see clearly the hope that God has called them to and the power available to them through Jesus Christ. As the section concludes below, he builds confidence in that for which they hope for and assurance in what they cannot see.

> But because of his great love for us, God, who is rich in mercy, made us alive with Christ even when we were dead in transgressions—it is by grace you have been saved. And God raised us up with Christ and seated us with him in the heavenly realms in Christ Jesus, in order that in the coming ages he might show the incomparable riches of his grace, expressed in his kindness to us in Christ Jesus. (Ephesians 2:4-7)

There is a similar expression of confidence found in Hebrews.

> [1]Therefore, holy brothers and sisters, who share in the heavenly calling, fix your thoughts on Jesus, whom we acknowledge as our apostle and high priest. [6]But Christ is faithful as the Son over God's house. And we are his house, if indeed we hold firmly to our **confidence** and the **hope** in which we glory. (Hebrews 3:1, 6)

There is so much more we could unpack in the Bible on the topic of hope, faith, and confidence. In fact, I encourage you to do a topical study on the word 'hope' in Scripture. I am quite sure you will find benefit from it. My purpose in sharing this brief framework is to assist in your transition from hoping that you can attain victory in your Christian walk to developing a confidence and an assurance that victory through faith in Jesus Christ is already yours. Remember, we are not fighting *for* victory, but instead, we are fighting from a position *of* victory.

Let me share a few more verses that may help to transition your hope from a verb (expressing hope) to a noun (belief in hope)!

For I know the plans I have for you," declares the LORD, *"plans to prosper you and not to harm you, plans to give you* **hope** *and a future.* (Jeremiah 29:11)

The LORD *is good to those whose* **hope** *is in him, to the one who seeks him.* (Lamentations 3:25)

May the God of hope fill you with all joy and peace as you trust in him, so that you may overflow with **hope** *by the power of the Holy Spirit.* (Romans 15:13)

But those who **hope** *in the* LORD *will renew their strength. They will soar on wings like eagles; they will run and not grow weary, they will walk and not be faint.* (Isaiah 40:31)

For everything that was written in the past was written to teach us, so that through the endurance taught in the Scriptures and the encouragement they provide we might have **hope**. (Romans 15:4)

We are now at a key transition point in this study, but before identifying the specific steps for victory as defined in Scripture, there is value in reviewing the firm foundation already set in place.

1. We have established the clear evidence of a spiritual dominion that, while unseen, has significant influence in determining the direction of our lives.

2. We have identified the opposing forces in this spiritual domain as well as the opposing agendas for our lives.

3. We now know that, like it or not, we are engaged in spiritual warfare and the main battlefield is the mind.

4. We have identified Satan as our enemy along with his lies, schemes, temptations, accusations, and the already defeated and fallen angels that carry out his battle plans.

5. We have established a clear, overarching strategy for victory, which is to take complete control over our thought life.
6. We have taken the time to mentally prepare ourselves through the study of God's Word as our spiritual boot camp and continual combat training.
7. We have transitioned our hope into faith, having established a supreme confidence and assurance of our identity in Christ as our personal Lord and Savior, our authority through Christ, and our position of victory seated with Christ in the heavenly realms.
8. Having fully established our faith and complete confidence in our Chain of Command (Father, Son, and Holy Spirit) and their battle plan for victory, our combat training continues by gaining insight into the weapons we are provided to attain the victory that was prepared for us in advance.

As we enter into this part of the study, our primary reference will be the Book of Ephesians, with a purposeful and extensive focus on Chapter 6—"The Armor of God." There is so much to unpack in these eight verses, and we will spend the next several chapters taking an in-depth look at Paul's message to the believers in Ephesus and more importantly God's message to us. As we move forward, the verses below will be repeated in whole or in part to emphasize specific spiritual truths, but we will begin with a full review of this exceedingly powerful passage.

> Finally, be strong in the Lord and in his mighty power.
> [11] Put on the full armor of God, so that you can take your stand against the devil's schemes. [12] For our struggle is not against flesh and blood, but against the rulers, against the authorities, against the powers of this dark world and against the spiritual forces of evil in the heavenly realms.
> [13] Therefore put on the full armor of God, so that when the day of evil comes, you may be able to stand your ground,

and after you have done everything, to stand. **¹⁴** *Stand firm then, with the belt of truth buckled around your waist, with the breastplate of righteousness in place,* **¹⁵** *and with your feet fitted with the readiness that comes from the gospel of peace.* **¹⁶** *In addition to all this, take up the shield of faith, with which you can extinguish all the flaming arrows of the evil one.* **¹⁷** *Take the helmet of salvation and the sword of the Spirit, which is the word of God.* **¹⁸** *And pray in the Spirit on all occasions with all kinds of prayers and requests. With this in mind, be alert and always keep on praying for all the Lord's people.* (Ephesians 6:10-18)

Paul's entire letter to the Ephesians carried with it several major themes, including the following.

1. We are saved by grace and made alive in Christ by our profession of faith in Him.
2. Everyone is now invited to partake in God's grace (Jews and Gentiles).
3. Acceptance of grace carries with it the riches and fullness of God's blessings to believers.
4. The church is represented as Christ's current spiritual and earthly body, functioning through the faithful service of its members and by application of their various spiritual gifts.
5. We are to put off our old self, abandon our former sinful desires, and put on our new identities in Christ as we begin to walk as children of light.
6. Walking in the love of Christ brings with it a call to peace, unity, humility, and patience with one another.
7. We are strongly cautioned to be on guard against the devil's schemes, and we have instructions to always remain faithful in God's promises.

Of course, the focus of our study is directed toward the last theme mentioned above, for it is the devil's schemes that are always in contradiction to the will of God and the plans He has for us. We will spend a great deal of time exploring the full meaning of Verses 11-17; however, Verse 10 serves as a great introduction, and Verse 18 is a vital reminder that our communication with God and our attempts to serve Him should always begin and end in prayer.

The first thing I want to point out is the encouragement we find in Verse 10. "Finally, be strong in the Lord and in his mighty power." This is in direct correlation with the topic we just discussed from Hebrews 11:1, "Now faith is confidence in what we hope for and assurance about what we do not see." After all of Paul's instruction and inspiration to the church in Ephesus, he strongly encourages them to transition their hope into a faith that stands strong in the Lord and His mighty power. It is the same power he referenced earlier in his letter.

I pray that you will begin to understand the incredible greatness of His power for us who believe Him. This is the same mighty power that raised Christ from the dead and seated Him in the place of honor at God's right hand in the heavenly realms. (Ephesians 1:19-20)

This is also the same power that meets Saul on the road to Damascus and radically changes a 'Pharisee of Pharisees' into an outspoken apostle of Jesus Christ (Acts 9:1-19). As Paul continues in describing the full armor of God, his call to stand firm in the confidence and assurance of what was once only hope for these new believers is repeated three times. God Almighty is now their Commander-in-Chief and Jesus sits at His right hand. The good news of the gospel is that we too can stand in the assurance of God's mighty power. In addition, you may remember from our earlier discussion in "Press on Toward the Goal" that as Christians, we too are already seated with Christ in heaven.

⁴ But because of his great love for us, God, who is rich in mercy, ⁵ made us alive with Christ even when we were dead in transgressions - it is by grace you have been saved. ⁶ And God raised us up with Christ and seated us with him in the heavenly realms in Christ Jesus. (Ephesians 2:4-6)

The same power that physically raised Jesus from the dead made us alive with Christ even when we were spiritually dead in following the ways of this world. No matter how radical it may seem to Paul, our justification is equally assured. God gives us His word to build our faith into an unwavering confidence of that assurance. My friend, you can be strong in the Lord and in his mighty power. That may not be how you feel at all times, but it is to be believed at all times. This study is but one of countless resources available to help you to tap into that assurance through a dedicated focus on God's influence in your life.

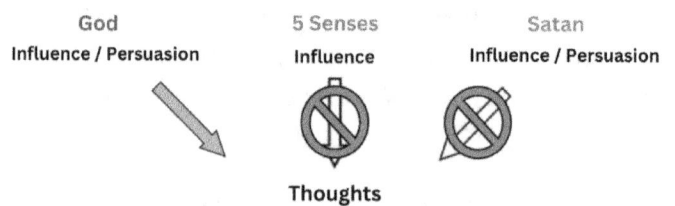

You can block out Satan's influence, and by allowing the wisdom of the Holy Spirit to guide you, you can discern between the right and wrong influences of this world. Remember, God has given you the path to victory. **Take captive every thought to make it obedient to Christ!**

Chapter 8: The Power and Privilege of Prayer

Among the many methods available for building our faith into the utmost confidence in God, the power and privilege of prayer carries a unique importance. Later in our study, we divide the armor of God into defensive and offensive weapons with which to battle Satan in the spiritual realm. Prayer and praise are among the offensive weapons mentioned in Paul's letter to the Ephesians. We will begin by exploring what the Bible has to say about prayer.

Earlier in our study, I asked these two questions.
1. When you want to talk with God, what do you do?
2. When God wants to talk with you, what does He do?

The obvious answer to question number one is—pray. As stated previously, Ephesians 6:18 is a vital reminder that our communication with God and our attempts to serve Him should always begin and end in prayer.

> *And pray in the Spirit on all occasions with all kinds of prayers and requests. With this in mind, be alert and always keep on praying for all the Lord's people.* (Ephesians 6:18)

I hope through the course of this study I have helped you come to the realization that God has always desired to be in a personal and intimate relationship with you. The Bible tells us that God is omniscient and knows our every thought, need, and desire. Nevertheless, He gives us free will to determine the course and depth of that relationship. So, the obvious question for many is how important is prayer and what role does it play in establishing and/or maintaining that relationship?

I cannot think of a better way to answer that question than to begin with what Christians call the Sinner's Prayer. If you are not familiar with that term, I borrowed and slightly revised the following explanation from Wikipedia. Find it at this online address: (https://en.wikipedia.org/wiki/Sinner%27sprayer).

> *This is an evangelical Christian term referring to a prayer of repentance by anyone who feels convicted of sin in their lives and has the desire to begin a personal relationship with God through his son, Jesus Christ. While some Christians see reciting the sinner's prayer as the moment defining one's salvation, others see it as a beginning step of one's lifelong faith journey.*
>
> *Since it is considered a matter of one's personal will, it can be prayed silently or aloud, read from a suggested text, or repeated after someone. There are no specific words considered essential, although it usually contains an admission of sin and a petition asking that Jesus enter into the person's heart and become the center of their life.*
>
> *As an example, Billy Graham would frequently lead those that were willing in this simple prayer; "Dear Lord Jesus, I know that I am a sinner, and I ask for Your forgiveness. I believe You died for my sins and rose from the dead. I turn from my sins and invite You to come into my heart and life. I want to trust and follow You as my Lord and Savior. I ask this in Your Name."* [1]

That simple act of prayer opens the door to eternal salvation through Jesus Christ, and if sincere and heartfelt, lays the initial foundation for the relationship God intended for all his children. Most evangelical Christians will reference Paul's statement in Romans to illustrate the importance of this specific prayer.

> *If you declare with your mouth, "Jesus is Lord," and believe in your heart that God raised him from the dead, you will be saved.* [10] *For it is with your heart that you*

believe and are justified, and it is with your mouth that you profess your faith and are saved. (Romans 10:9-10)

So, there is our first answer. A simple and humble prayer of repentance begins your true faith journey with the one true God of the universe and assures your eternal destiny. I don't know about you, but I would call that a pretty good start. However, before we go any further in this discussion, may I ask if you have ever prayed this simple prayer and asked Jesus Christ for the forgiveness of your sins and invited Him to be your personal Lord and Savior?

If not, may I encourage you to take a moment, whether you are in a group or all alone, to follow the leading of the Holy Spirit and invite Jesus into your heart right now? If you are uncertain how to proceed, feel free to use the prayer offered by Billy Graham as your guide. Remember, it is not the words that are important, it is the attitude of your heart.

If you are among other Christians, I trust you will receive nothing but joy, affirmation, and acceptance from them. If you are alone, God still hears you, but do not keep your decision to yourself. Please share your decision with another brother or sister in Christ at your earliest convenience. Your decision to accept Jesus Christ as your Savior needs to be followed up with encouragement, training, and discipleship—for we know that Satan is on the prowl and will be diametrically opposed to the choice you have made for new leadership and influence in your life. Fellowship with other believers that have a firm foundation in their faith will be a vital next step if you are to walk victoriously as a new Christian.

If today is the day that you chose to accept victory over defeat through Jesus Christ, then let me be the first to congratulate you! You have taken the first step in a marvelous journey, and all of heaven is rejoicing, including a loving Father who longs to share his goodness and grace with you. I encourage you to pursue Him with passion and get plugged into a body of believers who can help you grow in your faith. There is so much to learn and enjoy. After all, the Gospel is good news to all who hear and apply its wisdom. And to think, it all started with a simple prayer.

There are, of course, additional factors that will help us to evaluate the importance of prayer. One such topic, the doctrine of justification by faith, was quoted early in our study by Dr. Albert Mohler from his book *The Disappearance of God*. He states, "Without this doctrine, we are left with a denial of the Gospel itself, and salvation is transformed into some structure of human righteousness." [2]

There are many world religions, and even within Christianity, many denominations that profess the existence of God and endorse the concept of prayer. However, the Bible clearly teaches that justification (redemption from sin—past, present, and future) and the gateway to eternal salvation is available only through the profession of faith in Jesus Christ as our personal Lord and Savior. You can believe in God and you can pray, but belief in God is not enough, and prayer falls short without Jesus as our intermediary.

> *It is by the name of Jesus Christ of Nazareth, whom you crucified but whom God raised from the dead, that this man stands before you healed. [11] Jesus is "the stone you builders rejected, which has become the cornerstone." [12] Salvation is found in no one else, for there is no other name under heaven given to mankind by which we must be saved.* (Acts 4:10-12)

> *Therefore, my friends, I want you to know that through Jesus the forgiveness of sins is proclaimed to you. [39] Through him everyone who believes is set free from every sin,* **a justification** *you were not able to obtain under the law of Moses.* (Acts 13:38-39)

Therefore, the relationship that God intended to have with each one of us is first dependent upon our humble request for forgiveness (in prayer) and subsequent acceptance of Jesus Christ as our Savior. We are also taught to address our prayers to God through Jesus and in His name. Jesus himself proclaimed this to be true as recorded in John's gospel.

> *Jesus answered, "I am the way and the truth and the life. No one comes to the Father except through me." (John 14:6)*

Justification carries with it the righteousness of Jesus and by our faith (confidence/assurance) in Him, we are clothed in His righteousness. The apostle Paul addressed this in many of his letters, even pointing back to the Old Testament as a reference for his Jewish audience at the time of his writing.

> *Yet he (Abraham) did not waver through unbelief regarding the promise of God, but was strengthened in his faith and gave glory to God,* **21** *being fully persuaded that God had power to do what he had promised.* **22** *This is why "it was credited to him as righteousness."* **23** *The words "it was credited to him" were written not for him alone,* **24** *but also for us, to whom God will credit righteousness - for us who believe in him who raised Jesus our Lord from the dead.* **25** *He was delivered over to death for our sins and was raised to life for our **justification.*** (Romans 4:20-25)

> *It is because of God that you are in Christ Jesus, who has become for us wisdom from God - that is, our **righteousness**, holiness, and redemption.* (1 Corinthians 1:30)

Without His righteousness, we are left to build our relationship with God through the works of our flesh. Scripture tells us that we cannot attain justification or eternal salvation through our own efforts, therefore, with that mindset, we are blocked from the relationship that God longs to have with us.

All of us have become like one who is unclean, and all our righteous acts are like filthy rags; we all shrivel up like a leaf, and like the wind our sins sweep us away. (Isaiah 64:6)

For it is by grace you have been saved, through faith—and this is not from yourselves, it is the gift of God— ⁹ not by works, so that no one can boast. (Ephesians 2:8-9)

There is a third aspect affiliated with this initial prayer and our decision to accept Jesus Christ as our Savior. To help illustrate this resulting truth we need to look back at one of the other first level theological statements from our introduction—Affirmation of The Trinity. Dr. Mohler writes, "The early church clarified and codified its understanding of the one true and living God by affirming the full deity of the Father, the Son, and the Holy Spirit—while insisting that the Bible reveals one God in three persons." **³**

As Christians, we are taught to believe in the Trinity. When we are invited to partake of the kingdom of God, we are called into fellowship with the Father, Son, and Holy Spirit. The relationship that God intended to have with His children included the righteousness of Jesus and the indwelling of the Holy Spirit. However, accepting Christ as our Savior is the prerequisite for receiving the Holy Spirit.

Whoever believes in me, as Scripture has said, rivers of living water will flow from within them." ³⁹ By this he meant the Spirit, whom those who believed in him were later to receive. Up to that time the Spirit had not been given, since Jesus had not yet been glorified. (John 7:38-39)

But the Advocate, the Holy Spirit, whom the Father will send in my name, will teach you all things and will remind you of everything I have said to you. (John 14:26)

13 But now in Christ Jesus you who once were far away have been brought near by the blood of Christ. 22 And in him you too are being built together to become a dwelling in which God lives by his Spirit. (Ephesians 2:13, 22)

The Holy Spirit is vital to maturing in our faith and strengthening our relationship with God. It is the Holy Spirit who grants wisdom and discernment, knowledge and understanding. He is our interpreter as we read the Bible and makes possible the application of God's Word to our everyday lives. He guides our thoughts and our decision-making processes as we pursue the righteousness of God's calling. The Holy Spirit is the third person of the Trinity necessary in forming the relationship that God intended to have with each one of us. Without Him, the effectiveness of Scripture is vastly diminished in our lives.

The person without the Spirit does not accept the things that come from the Spirit of God but considers them foolishness and cannot understand them because they are discerned only through the Spirit. (1 Corinthians 2:14)

Are you starting to get the picture? At its earliest application, calling out to Jesus Christ through the power of prayer, and with a heartfelt desire, accomplishes the following.

- ➤ Our justification (redemption from sin—past, present, and future)
- ➤ Opens the gateway to our assurance of eternal salvation
- ➤ Clothes us in the righteousness of Jesus
- ➤ Provides a direct line of communication with our Heavenly Father
- ➤ Allows the indwelling of the Holy Spirit

➢ Calls us into a full fellowship with Father, Son, and Holy Spirit (as God originally intended)

With that in mind, might it be a good idea to make prayer a daily activity and a permanent part of your life? If you have determined that the answer is yes, then let me offer another bit of encouragement. Don't make prayer complicated—it's just a conversation with God. If I am being honest, this was a challenge for me when I first became a Christian, and I suspect it may seem awkward for many in the early stages of forming their relationship with God. I had so many questions. How do I address the God of the universe? Where should I be when I pray? What are the proper words to use? Should I pray silently or out loud? I have listened to others pray, and I am not that eloquent.

If any of those questions sound familiar, let me remind you of these truths.

➢ God knew you before the beginning of time.
➢ He *knit you together in your mother's womb.*
➢ He created you apart from any other human being and specifically gifted you for His purpose.
➢ He knows your needs, wants, fears, and desires before you can even express them to Him.
➢ He loves you unconditionally and created you to be in fellowship with Him.
➢ He opened a pathway for that relationship through His Son, Jesus Christ.
➢ He longs to be our 'Abba Father' and the number one priority in our lives.
➢ In the battle for our minds, hearts, and souls, **God wants you to be victorious!**

My friend, prayer is not only how we *establish* the proper relationship with God, but it is also how we *maintain* a relationship with God. Because of His unconditional love for us, none of our earlier questions or concerns are relevant. He just wants to hear from us, spend time with us, and be involved in our lives. However, as mentioned previously, God gave us free will to determine the course and depth of that relationship. Remember the last paragraph in the 'Letter from a Friend'?

I want you to meet my Father. He wants to help you too. My Father's that way you know. Just call me. I have so much to share with you. But I won't hassle you. I'll wait because I love you! Your friend, Jesus.

If God is anything, He is patient. When I look through the rear-view mirror of my life, I am continually amazed and grateful for the mercy and grace that God extended to me for thirty-four years until I opened the door of my heart to Him. And even now, that same gratitude is often expressed for the mercy and grace that continue to cover me like an eagle's wings. Over time, the Holy Spirit nurtured a desire in my heart to pursue a deeper relationship with God, and I learned to talk to Him on a regular basis, just like I would a best friend or a loving parent. His answers to my questions and the direction I so desperately needed most often came by reading the love letters and short stories He wrote to me thousands of years ago.

Scripture teaches us that God desires to be preeminent in all we do. Reading the Bible and spending time in prayer are two of the most important pathways in surrendering our lives to His influence and His will. In addition to Paul's motivation in Ephesians 6:18, the Bible tells us to be continually in prayer.

And pray in the Spirit on all occasions with all kinds of prayers and requests. With this in mind, be alert and always keep on praying for all the Lord's people. (Ephesians 6:18)

16 Rejoice always, 17 pray continually, 18 give thanks in all circumstances; for this is God's will for you in Christ Jesus. (1 Thessalonians 5:16-18)

Verse 17 in the King James Bible commands that we *pray without ceasing*. Taken at face value in our western culture, this would seem somewhat daunting if not impossible, but if we first preface Paul's writing in the original Greek language, his message becomes quite clear. The Greek word for "without ceasing" is *adialeiptos*. That word does not mean nonstop, it means *continually recurring*. In other words, we can punctuate moments within our daily activity with intervals of recurring prayer. That might include prayers...

- ✓ for a specific need
- ✓ to aid in making an important decision
- ✓ to express gratitude or thanksgiving
- ✓ to offer praise and worship
- ✓ to intercede for someone else
- ✓ to simply stay connected with our spiritual power source

What you will learn over time is that prayer is like any other function in life where repetition builds confidence. What may have initially felt awkward or unintentional develops into a habit of continually recurring conversation with God. As you mature in your faith and begin to recognize God answering those prayers and orchestrating events in your life, you develop a quiet confidence. Whether the answer is *Yes*, *No*, or *Patience my child*, you will know that God is listening.

> *This is the confidence we have in approaching God: that if we ask anything according to his will, he hears us.* (1 John 5:14)

In light of the above, don't be surprised if Satan attempts to interrupt your prayer life. In addition to the common distractions of life that he will incorporate to dissuade you, he also remains active in the spiritual realm where your prayers are received. Let me sidestep for just a minute to illustrate an important point. There is an interesting passage in the Old Testament Book of Daniel that alludes to this battle between angels and demons (God's messengers and Satan's miscreants) in the spiritual realm.

During the seventy years that the Israelites were held captive in Babylon, the Bible tells us that Daniel was highly regarded by three successive kings: Nebuchadnezzar, Belshazzar, and Cyrus. (Darius is also mentioned as a lesser king who served under Cyrus.) Throughout the Israelite's tribulations and his own personal trials, Daniel remained faithful to Almighty God, prayed diligently, and found favor in God's sight.

The beginning of Chapter 9 tells us that by studying the scriptural writings of Jeremiah the prophet, Daniel understood that the Israelite's captivity would last seventy years. As the promise of Israel's release drew near, Daniel cries out to the Lord for forgiveness, mercy, and restoration. **While he was still praying**, God sent his angel, Gabriel, to assure Daniel that his prayers had been heard.

> He (Gabriel) *instructed me and said to me, "Daniel, I have now come to give you insight and understanding.* **23 As soon as you began to pray,** *a word went out, which I have come to tell you, for you are highly esteemed."* (Daniel 9:22-23)

God heard Daniel's prayer and immediately dispatched his angel, Gabriel, to provide assurance as well as an explanation for Daniel's troubling dream. As Chapter 10 begins, Daniel is once again distraught by a revelation he is given regarding a great war to come. For three weeks he takes no food or wine as he mourns the meaning of this vision. Then Scripture records that on the 24th day of the first month, the angel that God dispatched to comfort Daniel finally arrives. This time, however, the angel's greeting is noticeably different.

> Then he continued, "Do not be afraid, Daniel. Since the first day that you set your mind to gain understanding and to humble yourself before your God, your words were heard, and I have come in response to them. ¹³ But the prince of the Persian kingdom resisted me twenty-one days. Then Michael, one of the chief princes, came to help me, because I was detained there with the king of Persia. ¹⁴ Now I have come to explain to you what will happen to your people in the future, for the vision concerns a time yet to come." (Daniel 10:12-14)

Did you catch that? Once again, God dispatches an angel to answer Daniel's prayer, but the angel is delayed in getting to Daniel because of a battle in the heavenly realms. To help illustrate this point, let me refer to a familiar source, the *Layman's Bible Commentary Set*.

> Daniel has been fasting and praying for three weeks, and the angel had been quickly dispatched to respond to his prayers and desires. Daniel's prayers are heeded because he has set his heart on understanding and because he has humbled himself before God. Yet there has been a long delay between Daniel's petition and the angel's response because the messenger sent to Daniel became involved in a fight with the prince of the Persian kingdom that lasted three weeks.

> Clearly this is a hostile and aggressive spiritual being, perhaps working to affect the kingdom of Persia for evil. Eventually the messenger of God, still struggling against the evil force, summons the help of Michael, the

archangel, the most powerful of the angels, and is able to continue on his way to Daniel.

This passage alerts the reader to some of the truths about the unseen spiritual world. It is evident that angels are real, and both good and bad angels (demons) can influence the affairs of human beings. [4]

I suspect that few Christians have ever considered this dimension to their prayer life. Perhaps, some of the lessons learned from this passage are as follows.

1. Just as was stated in 1 John 5:14, we can have confidence that if we ask anything of God, according to His will, He hears us.
2. Sometimes the answer is yes and sometimes the answer is no. But if the answer to our prayer seems delayed, it may be the result of an unseen battle between good and evil.
3. We have the freedom to pray out loud; however, based on this truth there may be times when our petitions are best offered silently to God. Remember, Scripture tells us that God is omniscient, and he knows our thoughts. Satan does not have that ability, and he relies on the clues we give him through our words and our actions to try to derail us.
4. Perhaps our prayers ought to include intercession for the angels that God dispatches to aid or comfort us.

The beginning of this conversation regarding prayer mentioned the power and privilege of prayer. There is an aspect of privilege that significantly multiplies the power of prayer, and that aspect is praise. The Bible is replete with references to praising God; however, many Christians may not realize that praise can function as an offensive weapon in our spiritual battle. To illustrate this point, let me share from Derek Prince's book *Spiritual Warfare* regarding "The Weapon of Praise" (Page 111).

The next great weapon of attack that follows prayer is praise. In a sense, you could consider praise as one type of prayer. In the Bible, praise is frequently related to God's awesomeness or fearfulness. Praise calls forth God's supernatural intervention—especially against the enemies of God's people.

> LORD, our Lord, how majestic is your name in all the earth! You have set your glory in the heavens. ² Through the praise of children and infants you have established a stronghold against your enemies, to silence the foe and the avenger. (Psalm 8:1-2)

We see here that God has provided strength for His people against their enemies. Praise is a weapon used to silence Satan. This lines up with Revelation 12:10, a vision that has yet to be fulfilled, but it tells us a great deal about Satan's activity at this time.

> Then I heard a loud voice in heaven say: "Now have come the salvation and the power and the kingdom of our God, and the authority of his Messiah. For the accuser of our brothers and sisters, who accuses them before our God, day and night, has been hurled down. (Revelation 12:10)

Satan's primary activity and main weapon against us is accusations. He is accusing us continually before God. You might say, "Well why doesn't God silence Satan?" Simply, because God has given us the means to silence Satan, and He is not going to do it for us. The means to do it is praise.

The mouth is the primary channel for releasing our spiritual weapons against Satan's kingdom. It is praise that ascends through the heavenlies, reaches the throne of God, and silences Satan's accusations against us. If we do not learn to use our mouths, we cannot win the war. [5] (Note: This reference is condensed and revised to align with NIV Bible translations.)

This reference borrowed from Derek Prince ends with a strong statement regarding the power of the spoken word, which is something our study will address in much greater detail as we go forward. Psalm 149 is a declaration of praise to God and affirms the power and victory available to God's people. Verse 6 perfectly aligns these two topics and emphasizes how praise and prayer combine with the Word of God to form a powerful weapon against Satan and his demons.

> *May the praise of God be in their mouths and a double-edged sword in their hands.* (Psalm 149:6)

There is so much more to learn about the power of prayer, but this is not a study on prayer. This is a study on spiritual warfare. I believe we were successful in outlining some important basics regarding prayer; however, before we venture on, it is never a bad idea to look to Jesus as our example. Jesus was in constant prayer with his Father. When He chose to follow the will of God and leave behind the throne of heaven to clear the path for our salvation, His lifeline to the Father was through prayer. It was so important that among the many things Jesus taught his disciples, was how and when to pray.

> *One day Jesus was praying in a certain place. When he finished, one of his disciples said to him, "Lord, teach us to pray, just as John taught his disciples."* (Luke 11:1)

Throughout the New Testament, those who followed Jesus and even some who opposed Him referred to Him as *teacher*, *rabbi*, or *prophet*. People were amazed by His wisdom and the words He spoke as an educator and mentor. However, Jesus also knew the importance of leading by example. The verse above is Him modeling one aspect of how we should live our lives, and in this instance how to interact and communicate with our heavenly Father. Observing Jesus in submission to the Father created a curiosity among the disciples to better understand the power and privilege of prayer.

We've already highlighted the importance of creating and maintaining your relationship with God through consistent communication (allowing God to speak to you through His word and your interaction with Him through prayer). Jesus was carrying out His Father's will and prayer was a vital aspect in staying connected to Almighty God and true to the path laid out for His purpose.

> *I am the true vine, and my Father is the gardener. ⁴ No branch can bear fruit by itself; it must remain in the vine.* (John 15:1, 4)

Scripture records twenty-five specific instances when Jesus prayed. I recommend setting aside some time to explore the list provided below. Studying the prayer life of Jesus will not only shed light on why He prayed but also will assist you in modeling your prayer life. Allow me to share just a few important lessons from among the Scripture references provided.

Jesus prayed on a regular basis. "Jesus often withdrew to lonely places and prayed." (Luke 5:16:) Prayer was integrated into every aspect of His life. Jesus would punctuate moments within His daily activity with intervals of recurring prayer (pray without ceasing).

Jesus often prayed alone. "Jesus often withdrew to lonely places and prayed." (Luke 5:16:) In our hectic culture, it can be important for us to find time to isolate, without any distractions, and focus on

God. Psalm 46:10 tells us, "Be still, and know that I am God." Sometimes, the only way to do this is to do so alone with our heavenly Father.

Jesus prayed for others. "I pray for them. I am not praying for the world, but for those you have given Me, for they are Yours." (John 17:9) Praying for others is referred to as intercessory prayer. We are called to pray for others.

Jesus prayed with others. "[Jesus] took Peter, John, and James with Him and went up onto a mountain to pray." (Luke 9:28) Intercessory prayer may be done in person or from a distance. When given the opportunity to pray with someone in person, don't delay. Intercede with them while they are with you.

Jesus taught us to be persistent in prayer. "Then Jesus told his disciples a parable to show them that they should always pray and not give up." (Luke 18:1) One of the more difficult lessons for Christians to learn is that not all our prayers are answered in the way we hope or expect. Unanswered prayer is a challenge, especially for new believers. However, we can have confidence that if we ask anything of God, according to His will, He hears us. Remember 1 John 5:14. "This is the confidence we have in approaching God: that if we ask anything according to his will, he hears us."

Jesus prayed according to His knowledge of God. Jesus said, "God is spirit, and His worshipers must worship in spirit and in truth." (John 4:24) This entire study is an effort to increase your knowledge of God. As your knowledge of and relationship with your heavenly Father improves, so will your prayer life. May I remind you of the foundational verse for this study? "We demolish arguments and every pretension that sets itself up against **the**

knowledge of God, and we take captive every thought to make it obedient to Christ."

As you review this list, let me close this chapter with a reminder that pertains to our topic of study. There are two specific instances when Jesus prays to rebuke Satan, and twice He warns us to avoid temptation.

Rebuke

> *Simon, Simon, Satan has asked to sift all of you as wheat.* ³² *But I have prayed for you, Simon, that your faith may not fail. And when you have turned back, strengthen your brothers.* (Luke 22:31-32)

> ¹¹ *I will remain in the world no longer, but they are still in the world, and I am coming to you. Holy Father protect them by the power of your name, the name you gave me, so that they may be one as we are one.* ¹⁴ *I have given them your word and the world has hated them, for they are not of the world any more than I am of the world.* ¹⁵ *My prayer is not that you take them out of the world but that you protect them from the evil one.* ²⁰ *My prayer is not for them alone. I pray also for those who will believe in me through their message.* (John 17:11, 14-15, 20)

I cannot help but pause here to highlight the encouragement we find in this message from John's gospel. If you have placed your faith in Jesus Christ as your personal Lord and Savior (by believing in the message originally shared and recorded by the gospel writers), then you can rest in the knowledge that Jesus is interceding on your behalf today and asking Almighty God to protect you from Satan's schemes. Jesus is your advocate today and every day! Give Him praise!

Warnings Against Temptation

39 Jesus went out as usual to the Mount of Olives, and his disciples followed him. 40 On reaching the place, he said to them, "Pray that you will not fall into temptation." 45 When he rose from prayer and went back to the disciples, he found them asleep, exhausted from sorrow. 46 "Why are you sleeping?" he asked them. "Get up and pray so that you will not fall into temptation." (Luke 22:39-40, 45-46)

9 This, then, is how you should pray: "'Our Father in heaven, hallowed be your name, 10 your kingdom come, your will be done, on earth as it is in heaven. 11 Give us today our daily bread. 12 And forgive us our debts, as we also have forgiven our debtors. 13 And lead us not into temptation, but deliver us from the evil one.'" (Matthew 6:9-13)

Twenty-five specific instances when Jesus prayed

The following list was compiled by Steve Shirley. Steve is the administrator for JesusAlive.cc:(https://jesusalive.cc/ques204.htm) [6]

(Luke 3:21-22) At His baptism.

(Mark 1:35-36) In the morning before heading to Galilee.

(Luke 5:16) After healing people.

(Luke 6:12-13) Praying all night before choosing His 12 disciples.

(Matthew 11:25-26) While speaking to the Jewish leaders.

(John 6:11) Giving thanks to the Father before feeding 5000.
(Also see: Matthew 14:19, Mark 6:41, Luke 9:16)

(Matthew 14:23) Before walking on water.
(Also see: Mark 6:46, John 6:15)

(Mark 7:31-37) While healing a deaf and mute man.

(Matthew 15:36) Giving thanks to the Father before feeding 4000.
(Also see: Mark 8:6-7)

(Luke 9:18) Before Peter called Jesus "the Christ."

(Luke 9:28-29) At the Transfiguration.

(Luke 10:21) At the return of the seventy.

(Luke 11:1) Before teaching His disciples the Lord's Prayer.

(John 11:41-42) Before raising Lazarus from the dead.

(Matthew 19:13-15) Laying hands on and praying for little children.
(Also see: Mark 10:13-16, Luke 18:15-17)

(John 12:27-28) Asking the Father to glorify His name.

(Matthew 26:26) At the Lord's Supper.
(Also see: Mark 14:22-23, Luke 22:19)

(Luke 22:31-32) Prayed for Peter's faith when Satan asked to "sift" him.

(John 17:1-26) Prayed for Himself, His disciples, and all believers just before heading to Gethsemane.

(Matthew 26:36-46) In Gethsemane before His betrayal. (He prayed 3 separate prayers.)
(Also see: Luke 22:39-46, Mark 14:32-42)

(Luke 23:34) Right after being nailed to the cross, Jesus prayed, "Father forgive them; for they know not what they do."

(Matthew 27:46) While dying on the cross, Jesus cried out, "My God, My God, why hast thou forsaken me?"
(Also see: Mark 15:34)

(Luke 23:46) In His dying breath, Jesus prayed, "Father, into thy hands I commend my spirit.

(Luke 24:30) Prayed a blessing on the bread before He ate with others after His resurrection.

(Luke 24:50-53) He blessed the disciples before His Ascension.

1. Sinner's Prayer. (n. d.) Retrieved from https://en.wikipedia.org/wiki/Sinner%27sprayer
2. R. Albert Mohler Jr., *The Disappearance of God* (Colorado Springs: Multnomah Books, 2009), 4
3. R. Albert Mohler Jr., *The Disappearance of God* (Colorado Springs: Multnomah Books, 2009), 4
4. *Layman's Bible Commentary Set, Vol. 7—Daniel thru Malachi* (Uhrichsville: Barbour Publishing, 2008) 46
5. Derek Prince, *Spiritual Warfare* (New Kensington, PA: Whitaker House, 1987)
6. How many times did Jesus pray in the Bible? (n. d.) Retrieved from https://jesusalive.cc/ques204.htm

Chapter 9: Our Spiritual Weapons to Defend Against the Enemy

In the previous chapter, I emphasized several key verses from the book of Ephesians to confirm the hope available to those willing to place their trust in Jesus Christ as well as the blessings offered through the confident prayers of faithful Christians. The quote below from the *Layman's Bible Commentary Set* highlights another key aspect regarding Paul's letter to the church in Ephesus and aligns perfectly with the major emphasis of this study.

> Paul's letter to the Ephesians has long been considered a masterwork of doctrine and **critical thinking**. As he transitions from theology to ethics and what God has done on behalf of believers, he addresses practical ways in which believers should respond with **a focus on the Christian walk**. [1]

The city of Ephesus was the capital of the Roman province in Asia. Paul's letter to the believers in Ephesus was written while he was in prison in Rome and many scholars believe the letter was intended to be circulated and read among all the churches in Asia Minor. The first three chapters are theological in nature, emphasizing New Testament doctrine, however, the last three chapters are practical and focus on Christian behavior.

Perhaps more than any of Paul's writings, the book of Ephesians emphasizes that **living a victorious Christian lifestyle begins with our thought process**. What we come to understand is the dual purpose of Paul's writing.

1. This is a letter of encouragement written to remind believers of their immeasurable blessings in Jesus Christ (as quoted earlier from Ephesians 2:4-7), to be thankful for those blessings, and to live in a manner worthy of them.

2. But as we will see, it is also a letter of caution. For despite our personal and intimate relationship with Jesus, and even more so because of that relationship, we as Christians are sure to be tempted by Satan in the carnal things of this world and even into complacency. It was for this reason, that in the last part of his letter, Paul reminds all believers of the full and sufficient spiritual armor supplied to us through God's Word and by His Spirit, and of our need for vigilant and persistent prayer. (Parts of this introduction were adapted from *The MacArthur Bible Handbook—New Testament*—Page 120.)[2]

We see this theme consistently in Paul's letters and throughout the entire Bible. Guarding and controlling our thought processes (our minds) is the preeminent pathway to victorious Christian living. After clearly identifying the challenge, Paul offers a battle plan for victory in Ephesians, Chapter 6, when he advises all believers to employ the full armor of God. The purpose of his message, and the chapter you are now reading, is to transition from the battle for our minds to the need to make proper use of the essential spiritual weapons provided to defeat the enemy.

Whether we realize it or not, as ambassadors of God's kingdom on the earth, we are automatically participating in a spiritual battle with a determined and highly organized dominion of evil ruled by Satan. It is important, however, that we recognize the battle is not limited to Christians but instead plays out in the minds of all humanity. The task assigned to us as believers is to break down any remaining mental strongholds of ignorance, prejudice, or skepticism, thus releasing both believers and nonbelievers from the lies of the enemy and instead sharing the truth, joy, and freedom found in submission and obedience to Jesus Christ.

Success in this God-ordained endeavor will require the acknowledgement and application of two main factors, one of which we've already stated. We are not fighting *for* victory; we are fighting from a position *of* victory. Satan's agenda for all mankind was totally defeated by the death, burial, and resurrection of Jesus Christ. As believers, we've accepted the baton and it is now our responsibility to demonstrate and administer the victory that Jesus has already won.

Next, we must learn how to make proper use of the available and distinctly effective spiritual weapons that God has provided for us. These spiritual weapons fall into two main categories: weapons of defense and weapons of attack.

Please notice from above that Satan's influence is not just present in the minds of Christians. His influence affects all of humanity, however, there is a dedicated and focused intensity on the lives of Christians. We are given not only the ability to discern the attacks and win the battle but also the responsibility of sharing the gospel that we might bring others to the saving knowledge of Jesus Christ. As a reminder, our condition prior to accepting Jesus Christ as our Savior is clearly and succinctly summarized in Paul's letter to the Colossians. Notice where the enmity with God originates.

> *Once you were alienated from God and were enemies **in your minds** because of your evil behavior.* (Colossians 1:21)

By contrast, the next two verses proclaim our new condition and identity when we are reconciled by faith in Jesus and hold fast to the hope presented in the gospel.

> *But now he has reconciled you by Christ's physical body through death to present you holy in his sight, without blemish and free from accusation - if you continue in your faith, established and firm, and do not*

move from the hope held out in the gospel. (Colossians 1:22-23)

There are several points of interest in these two verses.

1. Our new identity in Christ is created when we are clothed in His righteousness and thus found *'holy in his sight, without blemish.'* When we accept Jesus Christ as our Savior, our sins are forgiven—past, present, and future—and our salvation is secured.

2. We are *'free from accusation.'* First, this would encompass accusations from those trying to pervert, dilute, or deny the gospel as was the common persecution directed toward most of the early New Testament churches and which continues to this day.

3. We are *'free from accusation.'* Second, and consistent in all of Paul's letters, this is also a reference to the incessant accusations of the enemy.

    a. *For the accuser of our brothers, who accuses them before God day and night...,* (Revelation 12:10)

4. We are *'free from accusation—if you continue in your faith.'* Here we see another example of the prerequisite principle and the importance of a consistent commitment to the study of God's Word. A continuance in your faith is the prerequisite to avoiding temptation. If we allow ourselves to follow the temptation and fall into sinful behavior, accusation and condemnation from the enemy are sure to follow.

5. We are encouraged to *'continue in your faith, established and firm.'* If you remember, we suggested that the establishment of your faith results from a lifelong quest to study God's Word until it becomes the rock you stand on and the principal point of reference in defeating the enemy

and ultimately glorifying your Heavenly Father. This reference to standing firm is repeated later in our key verses for this chapter.

6. We are encouraged *'do not move from the hope held out in the gospel.'* As stated earlier, the significance of hope is that it keeps us engaged. Continuous engagement in Scripture results in the strengthening of our faith and the ability to stand firm against the enemy's attacks. *Now faith is confidence in what we hope for and assurance about what we do not see.* (Hebrews 11:1)

7. We are encouraged *'do not move from the hope held out in the gospel.'* There are a million things in this life that can cause us to drift away from our relationship with God through the study of His word. One day missed leads to a week, a week missed leads to continued drifting away from our firm foundation. The longer you drift away from God's Word, the harder it is to return, and/or, to defend yourself. I once heard a wise man say, "no one drifts in the right direction." The lack of influence from God's Word only leaves open the potential for Satan's influence to penetrate and take hold.

> *We must pay more careful attention therefore, to do what we have heard, so that we do not drift away.* (Hebrews 2:1)

Notice the progression on either side as we introduce additional Scripture references into our diagram.

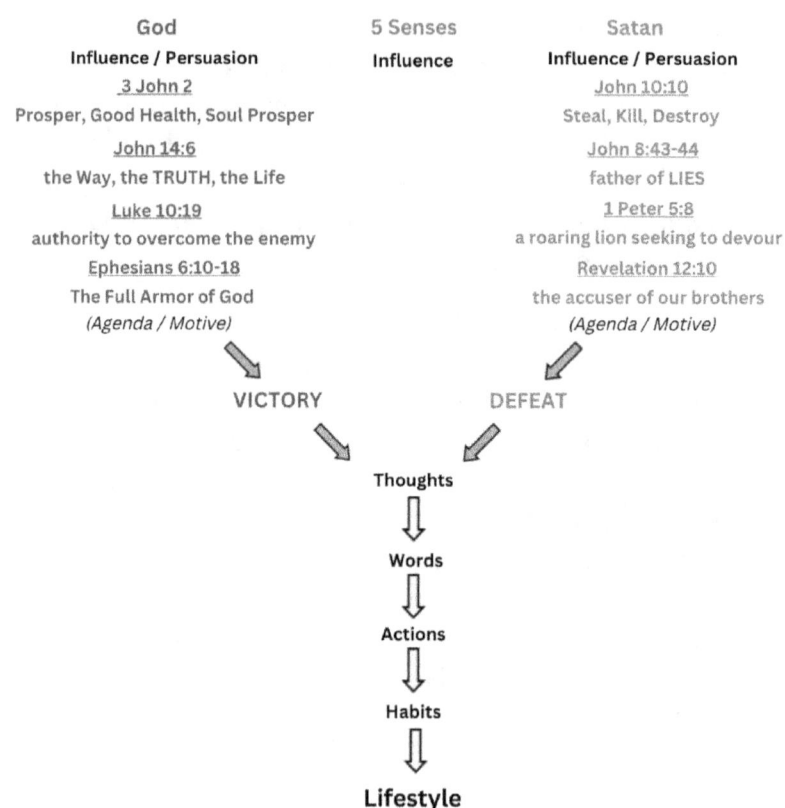

Throughout the course of this study, we have clearly established Satan's agenda for our lives. We know he is the father of lies and roams the earth in enmity toward God and His children. In addition, we see in Revelation that he is our accuser.

> *For the accuser of our brothers, who accuses them before God day and night.* (Revelation 12:10)

Satan's pattern throughout the ages has been consistent. The pattern begins with his lies and temptations, a subsequent fall into sin, and then persistent accusation and condemnation. Once the sin has been committed, he will continue to torment you with thoughts of guilt, insecurity, inferiority, and separation. Unfortunately, the statements below and similar thoughts are familiar to many.

- ✓ *How can I call myself a Christian when I have sinned by _____ (fill-in-the-blank)?*
- ✓ *I am such a failure; how could God ever love me/forgive me/use me/trust me?*
- ✓ *All those other Christians are so pure, I could never be like them or associate with them.*

Therefore, it is imperative that we understand and make proper use of the spiritual weapons God has provided for us. As we continue into this critical part of our study, might I share with you the same prayer that Paul had for the church in Colossi?

We continually ask God to fill you with the knowledge of his will through all the wisdom and understanding that the Spirit gives, so that you may live a life worthy of the Lord and please him in every way: bearing fruit in every good work, growing in the knowledge of God, being strengthened with all power according to his glorious might so that you may have great endurance and patience, and giving joyful thanks to the Father, who has qualified you to share in the inheritance of his holy people in the kingdom of light. For he has rescued us from the dominion of darkness and brought us into the kingdom of the Son he loves, in whom we have redemption, the forgiveness of sins. (Colossians 1:9-14)

Once again, there are several points of interest in these verses.

1. *We continually ask God to fill you with the knowledge of his will.* We know from our study that God wants you to walk in victory!

   > *Do not conform to the pattern of this world, but be transformed by the renewing of your mind. Then you will be able to test and approve what God's will is—his good, pleasing and perfect will.* (Romans 12:2)

2. *Through all the wisdom and understanding that the Spirit gives.* Remember the words of Solomon.

   > *Get wisdom, get understanding; do not forget my words or turn away from them. Do not forsake wisdom, and she will protect you; love her, and she will watch over you. Wisdom is supreme; therefore, get wisdom. Though it cost all you have, get understanding.* (Proverbs 4:5-7)

3. *Being strengthened with all power according to his glorious might.* Remember, this power is only available to us if we are under the proper spiritual authority, and if so, there is no greater power.

   > *That power is the same as the mighty strength he exerted when he raised Christ from the dead and seated him at his right hand.'* (Ephesians 1:19-20)

4. *For he has rescued us from the dominion of darkness.* Notice the past tense of this statement. The work has already been done. Remember, we are not fighting for victory, we are fighting from a position of victory!

5. *For he has - - - brought us into the kingdom of the Son he loves, in whom we have redemption, the*

forgiveness of sins. Again, this is past tense—we are already a new creation in Christ when we accept Jesus as our Savior.

6. *For he has rescued us from the dominion of darkness.* This reference to a dark and dangerous place of spiritual rebellion is a common theme in Paul's writing. We touched on Paul's unique, God given ability to see and discern this invisible realm in our section on hypocrisy, but a brief review would be beneficial.

In "The Danger of Hypocrisy," we focused on Acts Chapter 26 and the third description by Paul of his encounter with Jesus on the road to Damascus. If you remember, Verses 12 - 18 provide us with special insight into Paul's spiritual discernment. It was Jesus that detailed the specific purpose for Paul's ministry, opened his eyes to the dominion of darkness, and clearly identified Satan as the enemy.

I have appeared to you to appoint you as a servant and as a witness of what you have seen and will see of me. I will rescue you from your own people and from the Gentiles. I am sending you to them to open their eyes and turn them from darkness to light, and from the power of Satan to God. (Acts 26:16-17)

Paul gives us further evidence of this special revelation in two additional letters. First, there were certain people within the church in Galatia that were trying to minimize Paul's authority as an apostle by claiming that he had first been taught by the 'Jerusalem Apostles' but then broke ranks with them and had begun to follow his own path. As a result, his opponents were suggesting that his apostleship should be subordinate to the other apostles. Paul makes it absolutely clear that he received no special training from the other apostles. His gospel and his commission to preach came directly from Jesus.

> *I want you to know, brothers and sisters, that the gospel I preached is not of human origin. I did not receive it from any man, nor was I taught it; rather, I received it by revelation from Jesus Christ.* (Galatians 1:11-12)

In addition to the account above, Paul finds occasion to defend his ministry again in 2 Corinthians as some in the church challenge his authority as an apostle having been swayed by false teachers. Others criticized the contrast between the forcefulness of his letters and his meekness in person. After a rather lengthy defense of his ministry, including the many hardships endured in preaching the gospel, Paul shares an even greater revelation granted him by the Lord.

> *I will go on to visions and revelations from the Lord. I know a man in Christ who fourteen years ago was caught up to the third heaven. Whether it was in the body or out of the body I do not know—God knows. And I know that this man - was caught up to paradise and heard inexpressible things, things that no one is permitted to tell. I will boast about a man like that, but I will not boast about myself, except about my weaknesses. Even if I should choose to boast, I would not be a fool, because I would be speaking the truth. But I refrain, so no one will think more of me than is warranted by what I do or say, or because of these surpassingly great revelations. Therefore, in order to keep me from becoming conceited, I was given a thorn in my flesh, a messenger of Satan, to torment me. Three times I pleaded with the Lord to take it away from me. But he said*

to me, "My grace is sufficient for you, for my power is made perfect in weakness." (2 Corinthians 12:1-9)

NOTE: The NIV Bible titles this passage "Paul's Vision," and the NKJV titles it "The Vision of Paradise."

Although Paul begins to write these verses in the third person, he soon makes it clear that he is referring to himself. He was transported to the third heaven where he heard things that he was not permitted to describe. By first writing in the third person, Paul attempts to understate the event as much as possible but also presents it as indisputable evidence that he was uniquely ordained by Jesus to be an apostle to the Gentiles. Could these "visions and revelations" be a manifestation of what Jesus had prefaced to Saul on the road to Damascus?

*I have appeared to you to appoint you as a servant and as a witness of what you have seen **and will see of me**. (Acts 26:16—Jesus speaking to Saul)*

Paul's direct revelation from his first encounter with Jesus and subsequent look into the heavenly realms explains his keen awareness of the enmity within these spiritual dominions. Referring to our chapter on hypocrisy once again, we note this. It is Paul's unique insight into spiritual warfare that is fervently preached in each of his letters to the new believers as he attempts to open their eyes from darkness to light while exposing Satan as the church's primary adversary. The intensity with which Paul identifies Satan and his dominion seems to grow with each letter. Below are just a few examples.

I pray that the eyes of your heart may be enlightened in order that you may know... ¹⁹his incomparably great power for us who believe. That power is the same as the mighty strength he exerted when he raised Christ from the dead and seated him at his right hand in the heavenly realms, far above all rule and authority, power and dominion, and every name that is invoked, not only in the present age but also in the one to come. (Ephesians 1:18-21)

The Son is the image of the invisible God, the firstborn over all creation. For in him all things were created: things in heaven and on earth, visible and invisible, whether thrones or powers or rulers or authorities; all things have been created through him and for him. (Colossians 1:15-16)

Then the end will come, when he (Jesus) hands over the kingdom to God the Father after he has destroyed all dominion, authority, and power. For he must reign until he has put all his enemies under his feet. (1 Corinthians 15:24-25)

There is perhaps no stronger reference to this opposing spiritual kingdom than in Ephesians, Chapter 6. Verse 10 starts a section titled "The Armor of God," and the subsequent verses will serve as a key reference point in understanding the weapons we are afforded to defeat Satan.

Finally, be strong in the Lord and in his mighty power. Put on the full armor of God, so that you can take your stand against the devil's schemes. For our struggle is not against flesh and blood, but against the rulers, against the authorities, against the powers of this dark world and against the spiritual forces of evil in the heavenly realms. (Ephesians 6:10-12)

Considering Paul's unique insight into spiritual warfare, can you imagine his passion as he tries to prevent the enemy from stealing the truth of the gospel from these new believers? Like many of us, there was so much to learn, so much to absorb, and perhaps some frustration as they attempted to transition their lives to live under the influence of the Holy Spirit. For though their eyes had been opened to the gospel message, the full maturity necessary to see and understand the things that Paul knew to be true would take time and deep spiritual discernment.

The same is true for us and the world we live in. Many of us as new believers, me included, are initially ignorant of this spiritual battle taking place all around us, much less how it affects all of humanity. The importance of Paul's message in Ephesians is just as vital to us and our world today as it was to the church in Ephesus. In fact, we may face a more challenging impediment. As we begin to strengthen our understanding of these critically important verses, I believe this excerpt from the *Layman's Bible Commentary Set* will outline the difficulty we face in a technically advanced culture.

> *Throughout human history people have devised ways to deal with the existence of evil spirits. However, there is a tendency in modern society to dismiss them as superstition and incompatible with scientific and sophisticated views of reality. The devil has become the subject of jokes and cartoons rather than given serious consideration. Even among many Christians there is a reluctance to express belief in Satan as a personal being, thus refuting the truth of Scripture.*

> *However, the Bible is clear about the reality of evil spirits, and weaves that teaching into the totality of its doctrine. It was Satan who engineered the fall of humankind. He did his best to seduce Jesus through various temptations, hoping to prevent God's saving work. It is Satan who, according to Jesus, snatches away the "seed" (the Word of God), attempting to keep people from believing (Matthew 13:19). It is Satan who blinds the eyes of men*

and women to keep them from seeing the truth of God. As a result, hell was created for the devil and his angels.

If one is to dismiss such biblical teachings about the devil, is it not also necessary to do the same for all teachings about the spiritual realm? If there is no devil, why should we believe there are angels? And if we rule out the devil and angels, why should we think there is a heaven or hell? If we question the teachings of Jesus about Satan, do we also question the other things he taught? And how do we explain the foolishness, empty pride, cruelty, and selfishness of human beings that exceed anything else found in the animal kingdom? Like it or not, what the Bible says about Satan is important to a complete understanding of human and spiritual reality. [3]

Stop for a minute and read that last sentence again. The entire purpose of this study has been, and will continue to be, an attempt to offer a "complete understanding of human *and* spiritual reality." (Note that this is reality and not a theory!) After an extensive study of Scripture describing our plight and exposing the enemy's battle plan, we are now at a critical junction as we begin to outline the specific steps towards victory.

At the risk of being repetitive, there is value in drawing attention to the common themes represented in the verses from Ephesians, Chapter 6, and the foundational verses of our study in 2 Corinthians, Chapter 10.

Finally, be strong in the Lord and in his mighty power. Put on the full armor of God, so that you can take your stand against the devil's schemes. For our struggle is not against flesh and blood, but against the rulers, against the authorities, against the powers of this dark world and against the spiritual forces of evil in the heavenly realms.

Therefore, put on the full armor of God, so that when the day of evil comes, you may be able to stand your ground. (Ephesians 6:10-13)

For though we live in the world, we do not wage war as the world does. The weapons we fight with are not the weapons of the world. On the contrary, they have divine power to demolish strongholds. We demolish arguments and every pretension that sets itself up against the knowledge of God, and we take captive every thought to make it obedient to Christ. (2 Corinthians 10:3-5)

Theme 1: We are most definitely engaged in spiritual warfare.
- ➢ *For our struggle is not against flesh and blood*
- ➢ *We do not wage war as the world does*

Theme 2: Satan is our enemy.
- ➢ *So that you can take your stand against the devil's schemes*
- ➢ *Demolish strongholds, arguments and every pretension that sets itself up against the knowledge of God*

Theme 3: We are not immune to spiritual warfare.
- ➢ *So that **when** the day of evil comes*
- ➢ *For though we live in the world, **we** do not **wage war** as the world does*

Theme 4: The battle will be won or lost in the minds of believers.
- ➢ *Put on the full armor of God, so that you can take your stand against the devil's schemes.*
- ➢ *We take captive every thought to make it obedient to Christ*

Theme 5: We cannot and are not expected to fight and win in our own power.
- ➢ *Be strong in the Lord and in his mighty power*
- ➢ *The weapons we fight with have divine power*

In reference to the final theme listed above, there was one last paragraph in the *Layman's Bible Commentary Set* regarding the Full Armor of God that bears noting.

> As Paul introduces the concept of God's armor, he is reinforcing what he has already written about putting on the new self. Whatever people lack that makes them weak, vulnerable, and incomplete, God will supply. They are not strong in themselves but can become strong in God's power. [5]

The last paragraph in the commentary above offers a perfect transition point as we begin to take a closer look at each individual item in Paul's armor analogy. For while it emphasizes the need for our total dependence on God's power to fight and win this spiritual battle, there is also a subtle reference to the importance of fully appropriating our new identity in Jesus Christ.

The challenge for us is to break away from our traditional thinking and how we normally perceive war in a temporal world. For example, in the visible and tangible world that we identify with, most everyone will understand that a helmet is meant to protect your head from physical harm. However, in the spiritual realm, the helmet of salvation takes on a completely different meaning, as do the other articles of God's armor.

To help make this point, we need to take a closer look at two of the recent comments from Scripture and the Layman's Commentary.

1. *We demolish **arguments** and **every pretension** that sets itself up against the knowledge of God.*
    a. These are Satan's lies, schemes, and accusations, and the point of initial influence is your mind.
    b. That is why we are instructed to take captive every thought and make it obedient to Christ.

2. As Paul introduces the concept of God's armor, he is reinforcing what he has already written **about putting on the new self.**

   a. *You were taught, with regard to your former way of life, to put off your old self, which is being corrupted by its deceitful desires; to be made new in the attitude of your minds; and to put on the new self, created to be like God in true righteousness and holiness.* (Ephesians 4:22-24)

   b. We are clothed in His righteousness! When Paul speaks of the armor of God, the same principle applies. These are not just items of protective clothing that we put on and take off as needed. **They are LIFE APPLICATIONS and the characteristics of Christ that we need to understand, embrace, and model in our everyday walk.**

Our temporal, modern-day thinking is once again the main challenge. Returning to the helmet example, we naturally understand that a helmet is worn in times of danger, then when the danger is abated, we take the helmet off. However, when Paul speaks of putting on the full armor of God in accordance with our ongoing spiritual battle against the dominion of darkness, his reference is meant to imply permanency. There are only a few times that I will reference the original Greek in this whole study, but this is important.

Paul's summary statement to the Ephesian believers, as found in Verse 11, is to put on the full armor of God. The Greek word translated "put on" is ἐνδύω (Strong's #1746). The English translation is endýō (pronounced en-doo'-o) which literally means "to sink into or put on" and is used to express putting on a piece of clothing. It is not just the definition of this verb that is important, but also its tense and mood. In this verse, ἐνδύω is in the aorist tense, which means **it is a one-time action**; and it is in the imperative mood, **which makes it a command**. The believer is therefore commanded to put on the full armor of God one time (this happens when a person receives Christ) and is then given the purpose for doing so, "... to be able to stand against the methods of the devil." https://www.studylight.org/language-studies/greek-thoughts.html?article=529) [6]

Putting on the full armor of God is equivalent to putting on the new self. When we are offered a new life through the transformation of salvation, we are called to live differently. God grants that free gift to those who choose to accept it. The gift is not for us to put it on and take it off as we please. Referring to the verse above, we are to "put off our old self" and "put on our new self—created to be like God in true righteousness and holiness." Is there any part of that last verse that implies complacency or permission to vacillate between good and evil as we see fit?

Likewise, Paul's implication is to permanently put on the full armor of God! For if there is a crack in the armor, or should we let down our guard ever so slightly, we can rest assured that the enemy will target whatever area of our life is left exposed and unprotected. Similar to the quote about remaining under the proper authority, a Christian not wearing the full armor of God is an unprotected Christian.

Now, as we have discussed, it is only the disciplined study of God's Word that will result in the wisdom necessary to heed Paul's advice. Sadly, most Christians will never mature to this level of understanding, and as a result, they lead compartmentalized lives, putting on and taking off God's *righteousness and holiness* as they deem appropriate. My friends, we ought not fall prey to this pretension that sets itself up against the knowledge of God.

As Christians, we are taught not to compartmentalize our lives. In other words, do not act like the world Monday through Saturday and then *put on* your Christian veneer on Sundays when you go to church. Try as you might, you won't find that principle anywhere in the Bible. In fact, it is strongly criticized and labeled as hypocrisy, and we know that hypocrisy damages God's reputation and the reputation of all Christians. A compartmentalized faith also exposes the individual to the dangers of sin and temptation. The article below provides an excellent commentary on the danger of living a compartmentalized Christian life. It was adapted from an online editorial and can be found at this web address. http://www.revelation.co/2009/09/18/are-you-a-compartmentalized-christian-judge-yourself/ [7]

Humans tend to compartmentalize things in life. They act a certain way at work, then another way with friends, etc. Their attitudes, beliefs, and language change depending on their environment. It is dangerous to compartmentalize your faith and the Bible teaches NOT to do it. Christianity is NEVER to be compartmentalized. We are called to follow Christ 100% of the time.

Christianity is a daily struggle. As we are confronted with new situations, we must do our best to follow God's will. But struggling against sin can be difficult for the spiritually immature. Some believers think it is okay to sin if you show up on Sundays or profess that you are a Christian. Unfortunately, it doesn't work that way. While Christians do sin, no Christian should live in habitual sin. Now, God does not expect us to be perfect. But we should quickly repent, confess sin, and be cleansed of it.

If we place our spiritual life in a "faith" compartment in our minds, it automatically means we have other compartments which are not bound by that faith and which are open to Satan's influence. **If you compartmentalize your faith, you're sending an invitation to Satan to step into an open doorway.** Instead, we must build all compartments on our faith, so that our faith is exposed in all areas of our lives. Every thought or action should be governed by our faith.

When we continue with a compartmentalized Christianity, it only breeds hypocrisy and tame faith. So how do we protect ourselves? We can avoid creating a Christian compartment in our minds if; 'we capture each thought and make it obedient to Christ.' We should always walk in the light of God. Then we can have confidence in the promises of our Lord.

There are countless reasons why we are called to be consistent in our walks with the Lord, but considering the encouragement just received, let's combine the principle of a non-compartmentalized faith with the spiritual weapons we are afforded according to the Scriptures. Until now, I have referenced only Verses 10–13 from Paul's message to the Ephesians. This is written as a strong reminder of the spiritual forces at work against us, and as the reason we need to ready ourselves for battle ("to be able to stand our ground").

> *Finally, be strong in the Lord and in his mighty power. **Put on** the **full** armor of God, so that you can take your stand against the devil's schemes. For our struggle is not against flesh and blood, but against the rulers, against the authorities, against the powers of this dark world and against the spiritual forces of evil in the heavenly realms. Therefore, **put on** the **full** armor of God, so that when the*

day of evil comes, you may be able to stand your ground.
(Ephesians 6:10-13)

In the next set of verses, as Paul introduces the individual components of God's armor, I would again challenge us to break away from our traditional thinking and ask ourselves, what does it really mean to PUT ON the full armor of God? To answer that question, let me repeat a statement I made earlier. These are not just items of protective clothing, they are life applications and the characteristics of Christ that we need to understand, embrace, and model in our everyday walks.

> *[14] Stand firm then, with the belt of truth buckled around your waist, with the breastplate of righteousness in place, [15] and with your feet fitted with the readiness that comes from the gospel of peace. [16] In addition to all this, take up the shield of faith, with which you can extinguish all the flaming arrows of the evil one. [17] "Take the helmet of salvation and the sword of the Spirit, which is the word of God. [18] And pray in the Spirit on all occasions with all kinds of prayers and requests. With this in mind, be alert and always keep on praying for the saints.* (Ephesians 6:14-18)

There are any number of commentaries written in explanation of "The Full Armor of God." I was particularly drawn to a commentary by Adrian Rogers and how it so closely aligned with the premise of this study. Adrian Rogers was a Southern Baptist Pastor and served three terms as President of the Southern Baptist Convention. He published eighteen books and founded the Adrian Rogers Pastor Training Institute for ministers.

The following descriptions of the armor have been adapted from *The Armor of Christian Warfare* by Pastor Adrian Rogers and can be found online at https://www.crosswalk.com/faith/spiritual-life/the-armor-of-christian-warfare-1149596.html. [8]

What I found fascinating about this commentary is the implication of putting on your new self, or specifically, how clothing yourself in God's righteousness and holiness as part of your everyday life plays such a vital role in winning or losing the battle with Satan. Consistent and enduring application of these truths will allow you to stand your ground against the schemes of the enemy. Inconsistency is an invitation to the devil to temp you with sin, destroy your witness, and keep you separated from God. Remember, we are training for victory and God wants you to win!

The Believer's Integrity - A soldier in Paul's day wore a leather belt to protect his loins and carry his weapons. In Christian armor, it is integrity that holds the big and small things of your life together. **Would people say that you are a person of integrity? If not, then you cannot win the battle.**

The Believer's Purity - The breastplate was used to cover vital organs. For Christians, the breastplate is righteousness. The enemy wants to attack with lies and impurity and have you engage in all temptations of the flesh. He's looking for a crack in your armor and Satan knows where that crack is. **Is your heart pure before God? If not, then you cannot win the battle.**

The Believer's Tranquility - A soldier had hobnails on the soles of his shoes because he needed solid footing when fighting. When Satan comes against your tranquility, he throws out doubt and discouragement to upset you. **Do** you have peace right now? If not, then you cannot win the battle.

The Believer's Certainty - The shield protected a soldier from sharp objects. Satan is going to fire flaming arrows of temptation at you because he knows a spark can ignite a big fire. You need to be firm in your faith. **Are there seeds of doubt in your mind? If so, then you cannot win the battle.**

The Believer's Sanity - The helmet protected a soldier's head because if his head was wounded, he wouldn't be able to think appropriately. Every believer needs to have their mind under the control of Almighty God. The most important thing for you to have, at all times, is an assurance of your salvation. **Do you know that you are saved? If not, then you cannot win the battle.**

I trust these last two commentaries have provided sufficient motivation for us to apply the intended permanency of Paul's message to our attempt to live a victorious Christian lifestyle. Our challenge is to be consistent in all areas of our life as we pursue the holiness and righteousness of God.

*And do this, understanding the present time: The hour has already come for you to wake up from your slumber, because our salvation is nearer now than when we first believed. The night is nearly over; the day is almost here. So, let us put aside the deeds of darkness and **put on** the armor of light. Let us behave decently, as in the daytime, not in carousing and drunkenness, not in sexual immorality and debauchery, not in dissension and jealousy. Rather, clothe yourselves with the Lord Jesus Christ, **and do not think** about how to gratify the desires of the flesh. (Romans 13:11-14)*

As was stated earlier, this is not an easy task, and it cannot be accomplished under our own power. But take encouragement my brothers and sisters, for Paul also gives us great hope in Philippians 4:13 and 2 Timothy 4:18.

- *I can do all things through Christ who strengthens me.* (NKJV)
- *The Lord will rescue me from every evil attack and will bring me safely to his heavenly kingdom. To Him be glory for ever and ever. Amen.* (NIV)

Before we make the transition to the offensive weapons mentioned in the full armor of God, let me share with you several verses of encouragement that Paul wrote to his good friend and fellow missionary, Timothy.

- ***Train yourself*** *to be godly. For physical training is of some value, but godliness has value for all things, holding promise for both the present life and the life to come.* (I Timothy 4:7-8)
- ***Be diligent*** *in these matters; give yourself wholly to them, so that everyone may see your progress. Watch your life and doctrine closely. Persevere in them, because if you do, you will save both yourself and your hearers.* (I Timothy 4:15-16)
- ***Take hold*** *of the eternal life to which you were called when you made your good confession in the presence of many witnesses.* (I Timothy 6:12)
- ***Guard*** *what has been entrusted to your care.* (I Timothy 6:20)

Train yourself, be diligent, take hold, guard. God has given you everything you need to live a victorious Christian lifestyle. Just remember, it all begins by capturing every thought to make it obedient to Christ!

1. *Layman's Bible Commentary Set, Vol. 11—Galatians thru Philemon* (Uhrichsville: Barbour Publishing, 2008) 43, 57
2. John MacArthur, *The MacArthur Bible Handbook—The New Testament* (Nashville: Thomas Nelson, 2003)
3. *Layman's Bible Commentary Set, Vol. 11—Galatians thru Philemon* (Uhrichsville: Barbour Publishing, 2008) 69
4. *Layman's Bible Commentary Set, Vol. 11—Galatians thru Philemon* (Uhrichsville: Barbour Publishing, 2008) 69
5. Studylight.org—Greek Thoughts. (2001-2019) Retrieved from https://www.studylight.org/language-studies/greek-thoughts.html?article=529
6. Revelation. co—Compartmentalized Christian. (n. d.) Retrieved from https://www.revelation.co/2009/09/18/are-you-a-compartmentalized-christian-judge-yourself/
7. Crosswalk.com—The Armor of Christian Warfare. (n. d.) Retrieved from https://www.crosswalk.com/faith/spiritual-life/the-armor-of-christian-warfare-1149596.html

Chapter 10: Our Offensive Weapons—The Power of the Spoken Word by Example

If you have made it to this point in the study, I give you tremendous credit for your diligence and perseverance! We have covered a great deal of biblical and spiritual truth while judiciously exploring some of the most important and relevant Scriptures in the Bible concerning spiritual warfare and the pursuit of a victorious Christian lifestyle.

I hope and pray that your persistence will continue, for everything we have covered so far has led us to what I consider to be the most important part of this study, **The Power of the Spoken Word!** As cited in Chapter 9, I would like to reference a previous comment.

Success in this God-ordained endeavor will require the acknowledgement and application of two main factors, one of which we've already stated. We are not fighting *for* victory; we are fighting from a position *of* victory. Satan's agenda for all mankind was totally defeated by the death, burial, and resurrection of Jesus Christ. As believers, we've accepted the baton and it is now our responsibility to demonstrate and administer the victory that Jesus has already won.

Next, we must learn how to make proper use of the available and distinctly effective spiritual weapons that God has provided for us. These spiritual weapons fall into two main categories: weapons of defense, and weapons of attack.

Chapter 9 was all about the defensive weapons that we are provided and how to fully appropriate them in our everyday battle with the enemy.

Remember, we are to...

- *Be made new in the attitude of our minds* (Ephesians 4:23)
- Be clothed in the *true righteousness and holiness of God* (Ephesians 4:24)
- **Put on** the **full** armor of God, (*one time/permanently*), and stand firm against the devil's schemes (Ephesians 6:11)

This defensive armor is intended to ward off the enemy's attack. But as we continue to read in Ephesians, Chapter 6, Paul now turns to **our** weapons of attack, the offensive weapons provided to all Christians who have placed their hope, trust, and faith in Jesus Christ. The purpose of this chapter and the next is to assure you that you have the power, permission, and authority not only to defend yourself, but also to take the offensive and defeat Satan's schemes. In addition, the instruction provided in Scripture confirms and aligns with the comment above. It is now **our** responsibility to demonstrate and administer the victory that Jesus has already won."

*Take the helmet of salvation and **the sword of the Spirit, which is the word of God**. And pray in the Spirit on all occasions with all kinds of prayers and requests. With this in mind, be alert and always keep on praying for all the saints.* (Ephesians 6:17-18)

Every well-studied military officer and every battle tested soldier knows that you cannot be victorious in warfare without deploying an overwhelming offensive. The Bible teaches us that the Word of God is exactly that—an overwhelming offensive weapon that can and must be used against Satan's lies, temptations, and accusations.

> **For the word of God is alive and active.** *Sharper than any double-edged sword, it penetrates even to dividing soul and spirit, joints and marrow; it judges the thoughts and attitudes of the heart.* (Hebrews 4-12)

In the past, words may have sounded as trivial to you as they did to me. This is often a sign of temporal and/or spiritual immaturity. In fact, there are many like my former self who have never given much thought to this gift that God has provided to every human being. Words are important and powerful, and like any gift, they can be used for good or evil.

> *There exists, for everyone, a sentence - a series of words - that has the power to destroy you. Another sentence exists, another series of words, that could heal you. If you're lucky you will get the second, but you can be certain of getting the first.* —Philip K. Dick

I think this quote is fascinating for two reasons. First, it highlights the potential for words to be used for good or evil. Second, there is truth to the fact that everyone can expect the evil! So, while this chapter is devoted to using the Word of God to defeat Satan's schemes and begin our walk toward a victorious Christian lifestyle, it will benefit us to know what the Bible says about the negative potential of our words as well. To start that discussion, we return to the basics of our diagram.

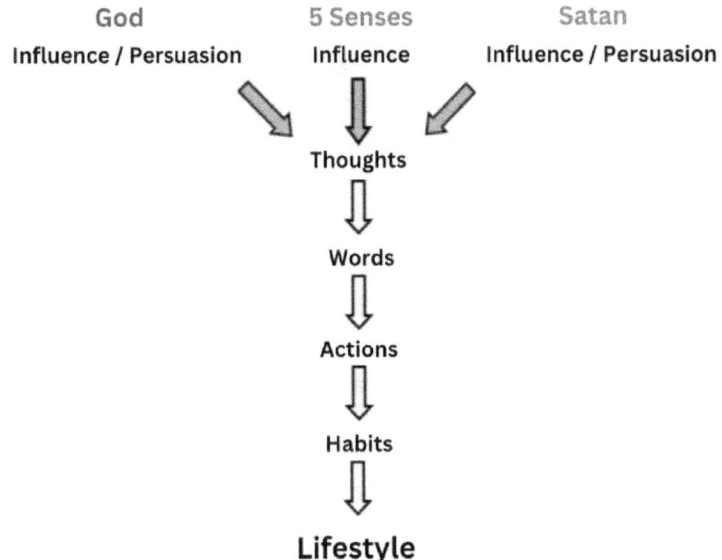

Lifestyle

Remember, this entire study is based on <u>who</u> we allow to be the major spiritual influence in our thought lives. As we review the diagram above, we are reminded that our words originate from our thoughts. If we allow the devil's persuasion to permeate our thoughts, we can rest assured the evidence will be apparent in the words we use to communicate to others and in directing our own actions. Perhaps the strongest warning in Scripture regarding this issue was offered by the apostle James in a portion of his New Testament letter titled "Taming the Tongue."

> [2] *We all stumble in many ways. Anyone who is never at fault in what they say is perfect, able to keep their whole body in check.* [3] *When we put bits into the mouths of horses to make them obey us, we can turn the whole animal.* [4] *Or take ships as an example. Although they are so large and are driven by strong winds, they are steered by a small rudder <u>wherever the pilot wants to go</u>.* [5] *Likewise, the tongue is a small part of the body, but it makes great boasts. Consider what a great forest is set on*

fire by a small spark. ⁶ The tongue also is a fire, a world of evil among the parts of the body. It corrupts the whole body, sets the whole course of one's life on fire, and is itself set on fire by hell. ⁷ All kinds of animals, birds, reptiles and sea creatures are being tamed and have been tamed by mankind, ⁸ but no human being can tame the tongue. It is a restless evil, full of deadly poison. (James 3:2-8)

In this part of his letter, James was issuing a particular caution to those that might consider themselves teachers of the Gospel, but this is a message that all Christians need to understand and apply to their daily walks. As you read his warning, the reference to Satan's potential influence upon our words is hard to miss or ignore, and his mention of the devil in subsequent Verses 3:15 and 4:7 leaves little doubt that James is confident in identifying the source of this evil.

Verse 6 is highlighted for a reason. Take just a minute to read that verse again, and I think you will notice how closely it aligns with our diagram. The tongue...

- **Is a world of evil among the parts of the body**—just like our thoughts, our words must be held in check until we can discern their origin
- **Is set on fire by hell**—Satan influences our thoughts which then manifest in our words
- **Corrupts the whole body**—our words determine our actions and ultimately our habits
- **Sets the whole course of one's life on fire**—our actions and habits determine our lifestyle

James uses a sequence of word pictures to make his point. Of special interest to me was the quote, "wherever the pilot wants to go" when referring to a large ship. Just as a small rudder determines the direction of a large ship, so too can the tongue set the course for a person's entire life. You are the pilot of your life, and you will determine the authenticity of your Christian lifestyle. A person's words reflect their heart and character. And your heart and character are determined by the primary spiritual influence in your thought life.

The message from this passage of scripture is clear, words are important and powerful! When used incorrectly, they have the potential to negatively affect our lives and the lives of others. Words can harm those who speak them (like a poison in your system) and they can harm those they are spoken to by wounding like a knife. While the tongue would seem an unimpressive part of the body, it is restless and unstable. Without the proper spiritual influence, its ability to do evil can never be fully restrained.

The major emphasis of our study, has been focused on the personal detriment and consequence of allowing Satan to negatively influence our thoughts. However, I would consider myself negligent if I did not underscore the importance of the final statement above. When our thoughts manifest into harsh words directed toward others, the consequences can be just as damaging. I came across a short parable years ago that painted the perfect word picture to illustrate the harmful effects of demeaning others. This seems like the perfect place to share it with you.

> There once was a little boy who had a bad temper. His father gave him a bag of nails and told him that every time he lost his temper, he must hammer a nail into the back of the fence. The first day the boy had driven 37 nails into the fence.
>
> Over the next few weeks, as he learned to control his anger, the number of nails hammered daily gradually dwindled down. He discovered it was easier to hold his temper than to drive those nails into the fence. Finally,

the day came when the boy didn't lose his temper at all. He told his father about it, and the father suggested that the boy now pull out one nail for each day that he was able to hold his temper.

The days passed, and the young boy was finally able to tell his father that all the nails were gone. The father took his son by the hand and led him to the fence. He said, "You have done well, my son, but look at the holes in the fence. The fence will never be the same. When you say things in anger, they leave a scar just like this one. You can put a knife in a man and draw it out. It won't matter how many times you say I'm sorry, the wound is still there." **A verbal wound is as bad as a physical one.** (Author unknown.)

If you are in any kind of position to influence others, whether as a spouse, parent, teacher, pastor, coach, employer, friend, or just a stranger in passing, please keep this parable in mind. You never know when a negative word or series of words will leave permanent psychological scars or have the power to destroy other people or their dreams!

Therefore, may I encourage you to be cautious in the use of careless words aimed at others? As followers of Christ, we are called to encourage and/or gently correct when appropriate. Even though we are all at risk of stumbling, the ability to control one's words is an expression of genuine faith, a mark of maturity for Christians, and really should be nonnegotiable for all believers. Take heed of Jesus' teaching when He said that people will have to give an account for every careless word they speak.

But I tell you that everyone will have to give account on the day of judgment for every empty word they have spoken. 37 For by your words you will be acquitted, and by your words you will be condemned. (Matthew 12:36-37)

In reality, we all stumble and none of us can completely tame our tongues. If we could, we might achieve perfection, but that isn't likely while we occupy this fallen world. Isn't it wonderful to know that our God does not expect us to be perfect nor does He expect us to fight the battle on our own? On the contrary, we can be encouraged that He has given us his Son, his Holy Spirit, and his Word to defeat the devil's schemes. Earlier in his letter, James also writes the following.

> My dear brothers and sisters, take note of this: Everyone should be quick to listen, slow to speak and slow to become angry, [20] because human anger does not produce the righteousness that God desires. [21] Therefore, get rid of all moral filth and the evil that is so prevalent and humbly accept the word planted in you, which can save you. (James 1:19-21)

Did you catch that? Get rid of (rebuke) the negative persuasion of Satan that is so prevalent in this world and humbly accept the positive influence of God in your thought life and in the words you speak, which have the power to save you! This is a message repeated throughout the Old and New Testaments. King David also understood the power of the spoken word as he recorded the following instructions to his son.

> He who guards his mouth and his tongue keeps himself from calamity. (Proverbs 21:23)

> My son, if your heart is wise, then my heart will be glad; my inmost being will rejoice when your lips speak what is right. (Proverbs 23:15-16)

In our pursuit of victory, there will remain an ongoing challenge to control the potential for negative thoughts to manifest into negative words; however, when managed properly, our words have the ability to affect a significantly positive force in our lives and in the lives of others. So, it is time to get started on the offensive!

As Christians, I cannot think of a better place to start a discussion on the power of the spoken word than at the beginning. As such, we begin our conversation in Genesis, Chapter 1.

> *In the beginning God created the heavens and the earth.* (Genesis 1:1)

As we all know, this simple sentence continues to be at the center of one of the most highly contentious debates between those of faith and the secular world. For us as Christians, it is the foundation of our world view.

> *By faith we understand that the universe was formed at God's command, so that what is seen was not made out of what was visible.* (Hebrews 11:3)

God created all things, holds all things together, and is in control of all things. This is an important pillar of our faith and worthy of a separate discussion all its own. However, relevant to our study, I want us to focus on **how** God created the heavens and the earth.

As you read the first chapter of Genesis you can't help but notice the following repetition.

> *³ And God said, "Let there be light," and there was light.*
> *⁶ And God said, "Let there be an expanse between the waters to separate water from water."*
> *⁹And God said, "Let the water under the sky be gathered to one place, and let dry ground appear."*
> *¹¹Then God said, "Let the land produce vegetation..."*
> *¹⁴And God said, "Let there be lights in the expanse of the sky to separate the day from the night..."*

²⁰And God said, "Let the water teem with living creatures, and let birds fly above the earth. . ."
²⁴ And God said, "Let the land produce living creatures according to their kinds..."
²⁶Then God said, "Let us make mankind in our image, in our likeness..."

As I have stated before, there is a special purpose for repetition in the Bible and if you have never done it before, I would ask that you take some time to consider the relevance of *how* God created all that we know and all that we attempt to understand about His creation. God *spoke* the universe into existence, and **the words He spoke became reality**.

It is vital that we understand the significance of that statement. God's power is manifested through His spoken word. Words matter to God, and He wants them to matter to us because our words also have power, as well as the potential to influence both our temporal and spiritual realities. This chapter is all about helping us understand the power of our words, but before we explore further, there is another critically important dynamic introduced in the creation story.

The initial recipients of the story of creation were the Israelites of Moses' day and the word used for God in Genesis is the Hebrew word *Elohim*. This is a plural noun and was meant to imply that *God is plural, even as God in singular*. Read Verse 2 in Genesis (from a New Testament perspective), and see that it provides the first reference to this plurality by referencing the Spirit of God.

Now the earth was formless and empty, darkness was over the surface of the deep, and the Spirit of God was hovering over the waters. (Genesis 1:2)

Because of our New Testament perspective, we understand the plurality of God as Father, Son, and Holy Spirit. However, there is not a specific reference to Jesus in the remainder of the creation story. Genesis 3:15 serves as the first glimpse of Jesus in the Bible. ("And I will put enmity between you and the woman, and between your seed and her Seed.") God's reference to "her Seed" (capitalized) is Jesus prophesied as a descendant of King David. Nevertheless, we are given the strongest representation of Jesus as part of the creation story in the gospel of John.

> *In the beginning was the Word, and the Word was with God, and the Word was God. ² He was with God in the beginning. ³ Through him all things were made; without him nothing was made that has been made. ⁴ In him was life, and that life was the light of all mankind. ⁵ The light shines in the darkness, and the darkness has not overcome it.* (John 1:1-5)

As you study the gospel of John, you will find he is explicit in stating its purpose—*to present Jesus as God's Son so that we might believe in Him and have eternal life.* (John 20:30-31). These first five verses are emphatic in that declaration and reveal five essential truths about the deity of Christ.

1.) *In the beginning was the Word.* This is meant to describe Christ's eternal presence and points back to the opening lines of Genesis. Before time began, Jesus was there.
2.) *The Word was with God.* Jesus is distinct from God. This points back to the plurality of *Elohim,* plural yet singular.
3.) *The Word was God.* John is not saying that Jesus is simply divine, but that He is God in bodily form and God completely.
4.) *Through Him all things were made.* Jesus was involved in every part of the creation story and we are part of His creation.
5.) *In him was life, and that life was the light of all mankind.* John refers to Jesus as the source of life more than fifty

times in his gospel. The concept of *life* here applies to the spiritual life of a person.

Today, by benefit of the Old and New Testament combined, we have a more vibrant revelation and understanding regarding the fullness of the Trinity than did the Israelites.

- All that God created was spoken into existence by His words.
- All that God created was accomplished through Jesus Christ, His Son (whom John describes as the Word of God).
- The Spirit of God hovers over all that God created.

With that firmly planted in our minds, let's take special notice of Genesis, Chapter 1, Verses 26 and 27.

> **And God said, "Let us make man in our image, after our likeness**: and let them have dominion over the fish of the sea, and over the fowl of the air, and over the cattle, and over all the earth, and over every creeping thing that creepeth upon the earth."* **27** *So God created man in his own image, in the image of God created he him; male and female created he them.* (Genesis 1:26-27 KJV)

We are created in the image and likeness of God! Let that sink in for a minute. The idea that humanity is created in God's image has far-reaching implications. It means a relationship can exist between God and humanity, and men and women can reflect God's nature. In fact, we were created with an expectation to copy our Creator, and as His reflection, given the opportunity to responsibly manage our portion of His creation (both the earth and our own lives).

So, what does it mean to reflect God's nature, and/or, copy our Creator? As would be expected, there are a multitude of commentaries that attempt an explanation. Just a partial list would suggest some of the following.

- ✓ Our ability to reason, choose, and make rational decisions reflects God's supreme intelligence and free will.
- ✓ Our conscience, or moral compass, reflects God's character and holiness.
- ✓ Our desire for fellowship and community reflects God's triune nature. Father, Son, and Holy Spirit exist in perfect love and unity.
- ✓ Our ability to speak and share ideas with each other reflects God's desire to communicate with His creation.
- ✓ Our ability to shape our world with our words reflects God's power as He spoke all that we know (the heavens and the earth) into existence.
- ✓ Our God-given authority to rule over all the earth reflects God's ultimate authority to rule and reign over all creation.

The list could obviously continue for quite some time, but since we are still commenting on verses from Genesis, I thought it would be appropriate to quote Ken Ham from "Answers in Genesis" as part of our discussion. Ken offered this from an article dated August 15, 2015.

> *When Scripture describes all of God's attributes, it is in the context of God being the perfection of such attributes. Humanity shares many of God's attributes, and we were originally created to reflect God's perfect character in righteousness and holiness. Paul's discussions of the new man and old man give us great insight into what it means to be created in the image and likeness of God (Ephesians 4:24; Colossians 3:10). It is an image that bears the righteousness and holiness of God. [2]*

To borrow from Ken Ham's quote, when we go back to the creation story, we realize that "we were originally created to reflect God's perfect character in righteousness and holiness." After being dispelled from his place among the heavens, Satan could not stand the idea that man could reflect God's image and live in perfect unity with their Creator. Thus, the temptation that led to the original sin was purposely intended to disrupt that perfection and create a divide in the relationship between God and man.

From the moment of Adam and Eve's original sin, Satan has been determined to keep mankind from re-establishing that relationship. However, God's intent from the beginning of time was to provide a way back into perfect fellowship with Him through his Son, Jesus Christ. And while we may not attain that perfection this side of heaven (due to the inherent imperfection of our flesh), we know from Scripture that having accepted Jesus Christ as our Lord and Savior, God's grace has already restored that relationship in spirit. As a result, we have been promised a return to perfect fellowship with Him when we are called to our heavenly home.

So, we can celebrate that God has provided the means for us to thwart the schemes of the devil and walk in victory over our flesh. We know now to capture each thought and make it obedient to Christ. However, in the two categories provided to us in Ephesians, Chapter 6, that is a defensive tactic. We need to know that we have been given the means and the authority to take the offensive when necessary and win the war! Moreover, we have been given a command and the responsibility to take hold of that which we have received. (Remember, in the original Greek, "put on the full armor of God" is in the imperative mood, which makes it a command.) Our primary offensive weapon in that effort is the Word of God.

Just as the last chapter helped us to fully appropriate, adopt, and implement our defensive posture, this chapter will help us fully appropriate and put into action the offensive weapons that have been provided to us. While lengthy, our introduction to this chapter was meant to lay the foundation for that truth and application. Just as we have done before, notice the progression on either side of our diagram as we introduce the truth of Scripture into our diagram and now focus on the perfect example set for us by Jesus.

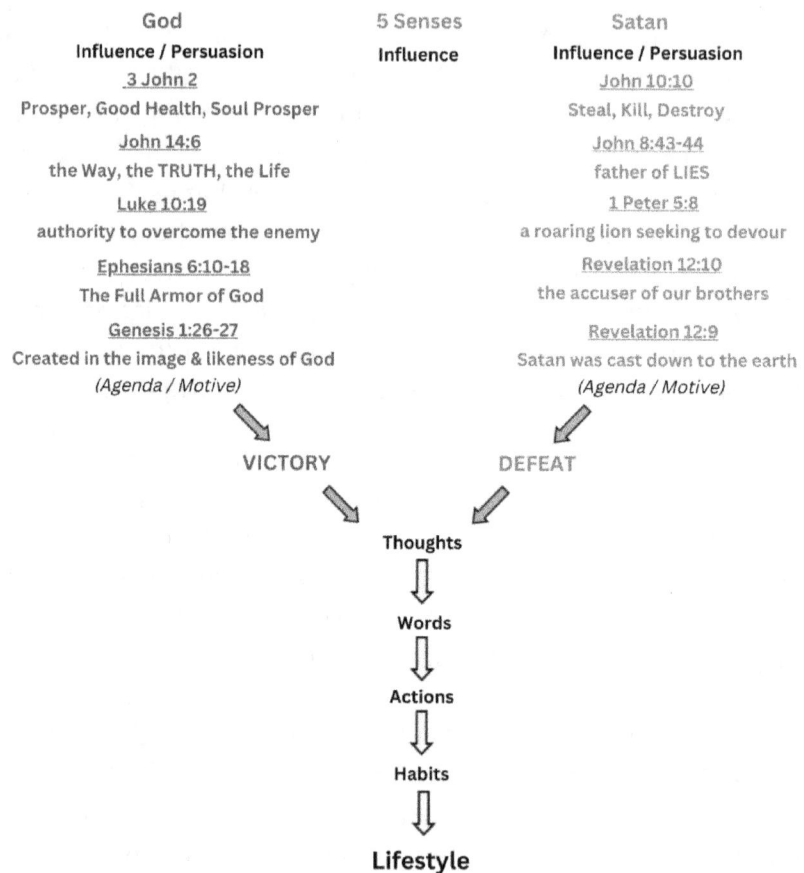

Note first that we have added the verses from Genesis 1:26-27 to the revised diagram. There was great intention in developing the understanding that we were created to reflect the same characteristics as our Creator.

Of the few insights mentioned in the introduction to this chapter, and all the possible ways in which that could be perceived, we are going to focus on the major theme presented by a few of our previous statements.

1. God said, "Let us make man in our image, after our likeness."
2. Words matter to God, and He wants them to matter to us because our words have power to influence our spiritual reality.
3. We were created with an expectation to copy our Creator.
4. God said, "And let them have dominion over...all the earth."

As born-again Christians, the assurance of our faith is found in the fact that our words most definitely have the power to create our spiritual reality. How do we know this? That basic truth of the gospel message is referenced throughout the Bible, but most famously in Paul's letter to the church in Rome.

If you declare with your mouth, "Jesus is Lord," and believe in your heart that God raised him from the dead, you will be saved. [10] For it is with your heart that you believe and are justified, and it is with your mouth that you profess your faith and are saved. (Romans 10:9-10)

When you say those words, "Jesus is Lord of my life," and accept Him into your heart, you have changed your spiritual reality and your eternal destiny forever. You have gone from enmity and condemnation to full acceptance into God's family and your name is written in the Lamb's book of life.

Yes, and I ask you, my true companion, help these women since they have contended at my side in the cause of the gospel, along with Clement and the rest of my co-workers, whose names are in the book of life. (Philippians 4:3)

You have transitioned from being defeated to being victorious. Take special notice of Jesus' words in Revelation as he speaks to the Church in Sardis.

> *They will walk with me, dressed in white, for they are worthy. The one who is victorious will, like them, be dressed in white. I will never blot out the name of that person from the book of life but will acknowledge that name before my Father and his angels.* (Revelation 3:4ᵇ-5)

WOW! BY YOUR WORDS, my dear brothers and sisters in Christ, you are already victorious, and your heavenly Father will never blot out your name from his personal journal of those who are saved through faith in Jesus Christ. What a marvelous truth to hold on to!

We know from this Scripture verse and many others that our eternal destiny has been secured, but we must still fight the spiritual battle. For those who are not mature in their faith, it can be difficult to reconcile that wonderful assurance with the frustration and anguish that accompany Satan's assaults. However, as we mature, we come to the realization that God has multiple reasons for allowing our struggles. In his letters, the apostle Paul shares inspiration from the Holy Spirit regarding God's motives, the first being outlined in Romans, Chapter 5.

> *Therefore, since we have been justified through faith, we have peace with God through our Lord Jesus Christ, through whom we have gained access by faith into this grace in which we now stand. And we boast in the hope of the glory of God. Not only so, but we also glory in our sufferings, because we know that suffering produces perseverance; perseverance, character; and character, hope. And hope does not put us to shame, because God's love has been poured out into our hearts through the Holy Spirit, who has been given to us.* (Romans 5:1-5)

Perseverance through spiritual battles produces character. Remember the earlier quote from Ken Ham, "Humanity shares many of God's attributes, and we were originally created to reflect God's perfect character in righteousness and holiness." As character builds from victory through one struggle, so does hope increase to enlist God's help to make it through the next. Our hope continues to strengthen, like stacking one building block upon another, as we overcome additional attacks by the enemy and begin to build faith foundations, ever striving to reflect the righteousness and holiness of God.

> *2 Consider it pure joy, my brothers and sisters, whenever you face trials of many kinds 3 because you know that the testing of your faith produces perseverance. Let perseverance finish its work so that you may be mature and complete, not lacking anything. 12 Blessed is the one who perseveres under trial because, having stood the test, that person will receive the crown of life that the Lord has promised to those who love him.* (James 1:2-4, 12)

This is a wonderful promise, but perseverance is hard! Building character takes time. Life's trials are not easy or pleasant. However, if we hang onto the promise that James outlined above, we can stand firm in our faith that God is in control, and thereby take hold of the promise that the crown of life, our eternal salvation, is being perfected by each victory through Jesus Christ. Through this process, we come to understand Paul's faith in the statement below.

> *And we know that in all things God works for the good of those who love him, who have been called according to his purpose.* (Romans 8:28)

Maturity in our faith in Jesus Christ results in a victorious Christian lifestyle. This victory is attained when we no longer fear what man may do to us, how or why the devil may tempt us, or even the thought of death itself. King David displays this confidence (as he understands it) in the Old Testament and records it in Psalms.

In God, whose word I praise - in God I trust and am not afraid. What can mere mortals do to me? (Psalm 56:4)

Likewise, Paul addresses it in his letter to the Philippians.

12 Now I want you to know, brothers and sisters, that what has happened to me has actually served to advance the gospel. 19 for I know that through your prayers and God's provision of the Spirit of Jesus Christ what has happened to me will turn out for my deliverance. 21 For to me, to live is Christ and to die is gain. (Philippians 1:12, 19, 21)

Paul's faith in Jesus Christ had matured to the full confidence and assurance that there was nothing mankind or Satan could do to him that could tarnish or relinquish the crown of life set aside for him through his suffering and perseverance. Not even death could separate him from his Savior and the promise of eternal life.

As we consider our own faith journey, there is an important point to be made here. Paul's strong assurance did not develop overnight, and neither will ours. In hindsight, Paul realized that each incident since his encounter with Jesus on the road to Damascus contributed to the advancement of the gospel in his life and in the lives of others.

How many of you have heard this quote before, or something similar? "We live our lives looking through the windshield, but we understand our lives looking through the rear-view mirror." For me, it has a greater impact when expressed, "We live our lives moving forward, but we understand our lives looking backward."

When we accept Jesus Christ as our Savior, the indwelling of the Holy Spirit allows us to see things differently. What we perceived previously as chance encounters or coincidence, we can now interpret as the hand of God orchestrating the events of our lives. There are many literal and figurative references to receiving new sight in the Bible; however, most of us would recognize the concept as outlined in the famous hymn "Amazing Grace" written by John Newton.

> *Amazing Grace, how sweet the sound*
> *That saved a wretch like me*
> *I once was lost, but now am found*
> **'Twas blind, but now I see.** [2]

The ability to gaze in the rear-view mirror and piece together the God-ordained purposes for our struggles is just one of the amazing aspects of this new sight we are given. When combined with the understanding of how God also provides the means and a clear pathway through the obstacle(s), we gain a new understanding of His love for us and an increased confidence "that in all things God works for the good of those who love him, who have been called according to his purpose." Just as with Paul, it is this hindsight (understanding that what I have struggled through has made me better and stronger) that provides the encouragement and confidence to move forward in boldness and without fear.

Let me encourage you to stop here and reflect on the last two statements of the paragraph above. First, when you consider the entirety of the Bible, it is the story of God's plan to redeem mankind through his Son Jesus Christ. In all the *things* that Jesus had to endure to complete that plan, God *was working for the good of the Son who loved Him and had been called according to the Father's purpose*. **God presented Jesus as the perfect example**, and now as Christians, we have been called to honor, obey, and likewise place our unwavering trust in our heavenly Father.

Second, God's plan would not have been complete without the death, burial, and resurrection of Jesus Christ. There was a three-day period when Satan thought he had won. However, by His resurrection, Jesus defeated death and demolished the plans of the enemy. From that point forward, all those who would claim Jesus as their personal Lord and Savior are free from sin's curse, and death is transformed from a feared and irrevocable finality into a beautiful and promise-filled eternity. For even death becomes our greatest victory! **Jesus set that example for us**.

Now, as encouraging as that last statement may be, there are still some who are reading this who will say, "Yes, that is all well and good, but Jesus is special, and He is God's Son. And even though we are saved, and our eternal destiny has been secured, didn't you just say that we must still fight the spiritual battle? Adding that perseverance is hard, building character takes time, and life's trials are not easy or pleasant? I don't think Jesus can relate to my struggles, and I have difficultly believing it was this hard for Him."

If that thought has ever crossed your mind, you are not alone. But there are several discrepancies within that statement that contradict a mature faith in God. Remember first that part of Satan's onslaught is a purposeful attempt to isolate you by making you think that you are all alone in your struggle. If you have ever asked that question, look carefully at the end statement (*I don't think...*). May I remind you that the enemy starts his onslaught in your thought life?

Second, as a born-again Christian, you are also God's son or daughter, and His promise applies to you, "In all things God works for the good of those who love him, who have been called according to his purpose." As you begin to appropriate that belief, your perspective changes as you encounter various trials, and maturity in your faith transforms the conversation from, "Lord, why me, why now, why this?" to, "Lord, help me understand your purpose for taking me through this trial."

Third, you are not alone in this fight. As you gain victory over a particular challenge, there is potential to be an encourager to a fellow believer (or non-believer) going through a similar experience and to let that person know that God is involved, and there is light at the end of the tunnel. By God's design, I believe there is great comfort in knowing that someone else has walked in your shoes and can not only empathize with your struggle but also provide the hope of victory no matter the outcome. Scripture tells us that in this too, Jesus was our example.

> *[14] Therefore, since we have a great high priest who has ascended into heaven, Jesus the Son of God, let us hold firmly to the faith we profess. [15] For we do not have a high priest who is unable to empathize with our weaknesses, but we have one who has been tempted in every way, just as we are—yet He did not sin.* (Hebrews 4:14-15)

We must remember that while Jesus never stopped being fully God, He was also fully man while on this earth. As such, He was afflicted by the same temptations as all men and women. And while He did not and could not sin, God's grace exempts us from the pressure to be perfect. There is great hope and encouragement in calling on the name of the One who was tempted and did not sin, so that we might not fall into sin ourselves. In his second letter, the apostle Peter gives us this assurance.

> *His divine power has given us everything we need for a godly life through our knowledge of him who called us by his own glory and goodness. [4] Through these he has given us his great and precious promises, so that through them you may participate in the divine nature, having escaped the corruption in the world caused by evil desires.* (2 Peter 1:3-4)

Take a minute to rejoice my friends, for God's divine power has given us everything we need to live a victorious Christian lifestyle and escape the schemes of the enemy. While that is certainly reason to celebrate, it is important to note once again the pathway to that victory is through our personal knowledge of Jesus and our personal relationship with Jesus. Remember—we must press on toward the goal. Through that effort we shall know the Truth, and the Truth will set us free!

Throughout his ministry, Paul developed several close friendships with those who joined him in sharing the gospel message. Scripture tells us that he was especially fond of Timothy, a young man whose mother and grandmother had schooled him in the Old Testament *(2 Timothy 1:5)*, had accepted Christ at a young age, and had quickly become a leader in the church at Ephesus. Paul references this promise in his first letter to Timothy.

> *The Spirit clearly says that in later times some will abandon the faith and follow deceiving spirits and things taught by demons. ² Such teachings come through hypocritical liars, whose consciences have been seared as with a hot iron. ⁶ If you point these things out to the brothers and sisters, you will be a good minister of Christ Jesus, nourished on the truths of the faith and of the good teaching that you have followed.*
>
> *⁷ Have nothing to do with godless myths and old wives' tales; rather, train yourself to be godly. ⁸ For physical training is of some value,* **but godliness has value for all things, holding promise for both the present life and the life to come.** *⁹ This is a trustworthy saying that deserves full acceptance. ¹⁰ That is why we labor and strive, because we have put our hope in the living God, who is the Savior of all people, and especially of those who believe.* (1 Timothy 4:1-2, 6-10)

There is so much to unpack in these verses relevant to our study.

1. The origin of things that come against the teachings of Jesus Christ and the indwelling of the Holy Spirit are clearly defined (*deceiving spirits and demons*)
2. Where the attack is focused—our thought life (*whose consciences have been seared as with a hot iron*)
3. The danger of associating with the wrong people (*such teachings come through hypocritical liars*)
4. The consistent pursuit of truth (*train yourself to be godly - nourished on the truths of the faith*)
5. The value of pursuing truth (*holding promise for both the present life and the life to come*)
6. The One we should follow (*you will be a good minister of Christ Jesus - who is the Savior of all people - and of the good teaching that you have followed*)

In this letter to Timothy, Paul points directly to the perfect example set for us by Jesus, and it is this example that we are to follow. But remember, having been made in the image of God, we are also called to reflect that image and become living examples of Christ working in and through us. As he finishes Chapter 4, Paul gives further encouragement to Timothy.

> *[11] Command and teach these things. [12] Don't let anyone look down on you because you are young, **but set an example** for the believers in speech, in conduct, in love, in faith and in purity. [15] Be diligent in these matters; give yourself wholly to them, so that everyone may see your progress. [16] Watch your life and doctrine closely. Persevere in them, because if you do, you will save both yourself and your hearers.* (1 Timothy 4:11-12, 15-16)

In relationship to the verses above, I cannot help but refer once again to the earlier quote from Ken Ham, "Humanity shares many of God's attributes, and we were originally created to reflect God's perfect character in righteousness and holiness." That is the exact encouragement from Paul to Timothy. Watch your life and doctrine closely because you have been called to reflect the love and truth of Jesus Christ. Moreover, as you reflect His righteousness and holiness, others are drawn into the kingdom of God even as your faith is perfected.

Before we move away from Paul's letter to Timothy, there is another interesting point to be made. Of the five leadership traits in Verse 12, Paul suggests for Timothy (and us) to first mimic Christ in speech (*but set an example for the believers in speech*). Whether Jesus was filled with compassion, as He was with the woman caught in adultery (John 8:2-11), or filled with contempt, as He was with the Pharisees and the money changers in the temple (Mark 11:15-17), He presented the Word of God as our model and our authority.

Therefore, having been called to reflect that which we believe in, our words can be tempered with compassion or hardened for rebuke, a message Paul shared in his second letter to Timothy.

> *All Scripture is God-breathed and is useful for teaching, rebuking, correcting, and training in righteousness, so that the servant of God may be thoroughly equipped for every good work.* (2 Timothy 3:16-17)

Paul's encouragement to Timothy is in direct correlation to the evil that surrounded him and a warning of terrible times to come. As you read the first part of Chapter 3 and then Chapter 4, it becomes clear that the use of Scripture to rebuke those engulfed in evil desires is the primary focus of his statement.

> *They are the kind who are loaded down with sins and are swayed by all kinds of evil desires, always learning but never able to come to a knowledge of the truth. So also,*

these teachers oppose the truth. They are men of depraved minds, who, as far as the faith is concerned, are **rejected**. (2 Timothy 3:6-8)

In the presence of God and of Christ Jesus, who will judge the living and the dead, and in view of his appearing and his kingdom, I give you this charge: Preach the Word; be prepared in season and out of season; correct, **rebuke** *and encourage—with great patience and careful instruction.* (2 Timothy 4:1-2)

Likewise, we have the ability to use our words as the primary offensive weapon to rebuke the enemy's attacks. We are given the perfect example to follow in Jesus Christ as well as the authority to overcome Satan's temptations with our words, more specifically with the Word of God. So how do we do that? We return to where this chapter began, to first look at Paul's imagery of God's Word as an offensive weapon (a sword), next to affirm Christ as our model for victory in this battle, and finally to broaden our understanding of the authority granted unto us since the creation story.

Take the helmet of salvation and the sword of the Spirit, which is the word of God. (Ephesians 6:17)

First, it is helpful if we understand Paul's imagery and intent when he speaks of God's Word as the sword of the Spirit. Paul was under arrest in Rome when he wrote this letter. As such, he would have been familiar with the uniform of a Roman soldier. The sword that Paul refers to in Verse 17 is not the long broadsword that we see in most movies. Instead, it is a short, sharp, double-edged sword. This was a primary offensive weapon used for close contact. The symbolism is accurate as the battle with Satan will be close and intense at times.

Second, the commentary below was published September 26, 2010, by Ron Latulippe. Ron was a Baptist Pastor at Rosedale

Baptist Church in Welland, Ontario (just across the U. S. /Canadian border from Buffalo, New York), and at the time of this writing, served as a lay leader in international third world missions.

> *Paul uses the Greek word for the short sword. The sword of the Spirit is the Word of God. There are two Greek words for word. One is logos which describes the spoken words, and the recording of those words. **Logos** is also used to describe Jesus the living word. The other Greek word is rhema and means a saying. It describes words spoken at a specific occasion with a specific purpose in mind. **Rhema** is the application of the logos to a real-life situation, a word appropriate and needed for that moment. So, Paul describes the sword of the Spirit as the rhema of God. Like the sword in battle, the soldier of Christ applies the appropriate word of God to the situation to defend, or wound, or kill as needed.* [3]

Both comments are quite instructive and aid us in understanding Paul's message to the church in Ephesus and to current believers. Once again, there are several key points that warrant further review.

1.) As Paul continues in his analogy regarding the full armor of God, the sword is the first item of battle that is not purely defensive. The protective armor previously mentioned may prevent Satan from inflicting a heavy wound, but it cannot drive him away from us. **The appropriate use of God's Word is the only thing that will cause Satan to flee.**

2.) When you take part in God's army, not only can you expect to engage in battle with the enemy, but also the fight with Satan will be personal and intense at times. You must be prepared to take the offensive.

3.) It is important that we understand the difference between the logos and the rhema. Having a Bible on your nightstand (logos/recorded word) does not scare or repel the devil. However, when you quote Scripture directly from your mouth, and use Scripture appropriate to the attack, it becomes a sharp, double-edge sword that will drive the enemy away from you.

4.) Notice Paul refers to the Word of God as the "sword of the *Spirit*." We are not expected to engage Satan in our power alone. Yes, *we* must wield the sword, but it is the wisdom and power of the Holy Spirit that generates victory on our behalf.

Now, with a better understanding of Paul's imagery, we return to Christ as our model in this battle with the enemy. We find the best example of gaining victory through the Word of God in Luke's gospel. After Jesus was baptized by John the Baptist, the Holy Spirit descended upon Him and led Jesus out into the desert. As Chapter 4 begins, we find this account.

> *Jesus, full of the Holy Spirit, left the Jordan and was led by the Spirit into the wilderness, ² where for forty days he was tempted by the devil. He ate nothing during those days, and at the end of them he was hungry. ³ The devil said to him, "If you are the Son of God, tell this stone to become bread." ⁴ Jesus answered, "**It is written**: 'Man shall not live on bread alone.'"*

> *⁵ The devil led him up to a high place and showed him in an instant all the kingdoms of the world. ⁶ And he said to him, "I will give you all their authority and splendor; it has been given to me, and I can give it to anyone I want to. ⁷ If you worship me, it will all be yours." ⁸ Jesus answered, "**It is written**: 'Worship the Lord your God and serve him only.'"*

*⁹ The devil led him to Jerusalem and had him stand on the highest point of the temple. "If you are the Son of God," he said, "throw yourself down from here. ¹⁰ For it is written: "'He will command his angels concerning you to guard you carefully; ¹¹ they will lift you up in their hands, so that you will not strike your foot against a stone.'" ¹² Jesus answered, "**It is said**: 'Do not put the Lord your God to the test.'" ¹³ When the devil had finished all this tempting, he left him until an opportune time.* (Luke 4:1-13)

Similar to the previous commentary from Adrian Rogers regarding our defensive weapons, Debbie McDaniel wrote about how Jesus modeled the use of our offensive weapon—the Word of God. Debbie is a writer and pastor's wife, and this quote can be found in her online blog. https://www.crosswalk.com/blogs/debbie-mcdaniel/praying-on-the-armor-of-god.html

Sword of the Spirit

The Word of God - When we are tempted, the most effective weapon that God has given to us as believers is the sword of the Spirit, which is the Word of God. Jesus modeled this so beautifully during His temptation in the wilderness. When the devil tried temptation after temptation against Him, Jesus used the sword of the Spirit. Jesus spoke the Word of God to Satan. In Luke 4:1-13, Jesus responded, "It is written, 'You shall worship the Lord God only. Him only you shall serve." and again brought the Scripture back into context, "It has been said, 'You shall not tempt the Lord your God.'" [4]

As you read this account in Luke's gospel and then consider the content of these commentaries, it is interesting to note the following:

- The Holy Spirit was with Jesus in the wilderness.
    > *Jesus, full of the Holy Spirit, left the Jordan and was led by the Spirit into the wilderness.*
- The encounter with Satan was close and intense.
    > *The devil said to him/The devil led him...*
- Jesus quoted the appropriate Scripture for each temptation.
    > *Jesus answered, it is written.../it is written.../it is said....*
- God's Word from the mouth of Jesus caused the devil to flee.
    > *When the devil had finished all this tempting, he left him until an opportune time.*
- We were created with an expectation to copy our Creator and given the authority to take the offensive.
    > *I give you this charge: Preach the Word; be prepared in season and out of season; correct, rebuke and encourage...* (2 Timothy 4:1-2)

We have studied Paul's imagery of God's Word as an offensive weapon (a short, double-edged sword), and we now understand its application. We have affirmed Christ as our model for victory and the necessary presence of the Holy Spirit as we engage in battle. Now it is time to broaden our understanding of the authority granted unto us since the creation story.

If you remember, the focus in Chapter 6 was establishing the vertical authority structure as outlined in Scripture and how it is passed downward from God the Father to His Son, Jesus Christ, and then to those who claim Jesus as Lord and Savior. We referenced multiple Scripture verses to solidify that point, culminating in this quote from Jesus.

> *I have given you authority to trample on snakes and scorpions and to overcome **all** the power of the enemy; nothing will harm you.* (Luke 10:19)

There is yet another significant reference to our God given authority over Satan. The first hint is embedded in the creation narrative, and the glorious affirmation of this truth is pronounced in the Book of Revelation. God uses the bookends of Scripture to bring this marvelous promise to the attention of the mature believer, while the entire historical record of the Old and New Testament point to the victory available through our Savior Jesus Christ and attest to its truth. To help us visualize this promise, we revisit our diagram.

While we have already devoted significant time to Genesis 1:26-27, there is more to discover in these verses relevant to our discussion and the opposing verse offered above from the Book of Revelation.

> *And God said, "Let us make man in our image, after our likeness: and **let them have dominion** over the fish of the sea, and over the fowl of the air, and over the cattle, and **over all the earth**, and over every creeping thing that creepeth upon the earth.* (Genesis 1:26-27 KJV)

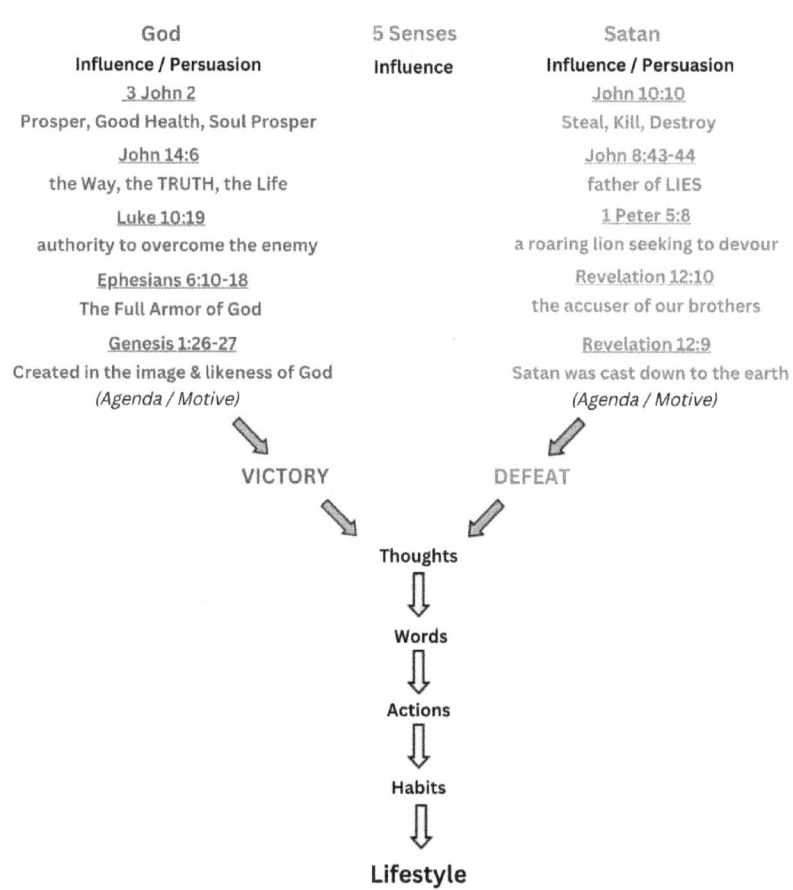

God	5 Senses	Satan
Influence / Persuasion	Influence	Influence / Persuasion
3 John 2		John 10:10
Prosper, Good Health, Soul Prosper		Steal, Kill, Destroy
John 14:6		John 8:43-44
the Way, the TRUTH, the Life		father of LIES
Luke 10:19		1 Peter 5:8
authority to overcome the enemy		a roaring lion seeking to devour
Ephesians 6:10-18		Revelation 12:10
The Full Armor of God		the accuser of our brothers
Genesis 1:26-27		Revelation 12:9
Created in the image & likeness of God		Satan was cast down to the earth
(Agenda / Motive)		(Agenda / Motive)

VICTORY   DEFEAT

Thoughts

⇩

Words

⇩

Actions

⇩

Habits

⇩

Lifestyle

Our previous review of these verses focused on God's creation of mankind in His image and likeness, with just a beginner's glimpse of the significance of that truth. We now shift our attention to another truth found in these verses—the promise of authority granted to us by our Creator at the moment of our creation. Allow me to paraphrase from the above. God said, **"Let them have dominion over ... all the earth."**

As you look at our diagram, this is the first bookend that sets the foundation for our victory through Jesus Christ. The opposite bookend is found in Revelation, Chapter 12.

*The great dragon was hurled down—that ancient serpent called the devil, or Satan, who leads the whole world astray. **He was hurled to the earth**, and his angels with him.* (Revelation 12:9)

When you study the book of revelation, this verse refers to Satan's final expulsion from heaven. From this point on, he is prevented from ever entering heaven again to interrupt the plans of God. While we understand this to be a future event, the Bible tells us that because of his rebellion, Satan and his angels were previously evicted from heaven and given dominion over the earth, that Satan was present in the Garden of Eden, and that he has been leading the whole world astray ever since.

From the original temptation of Adam and Eve and the subsequent fall of man, all of creation has been tainted by sin, and Satan's full-time passion has been to create and maintain that separation between God and His creation. Regarding mankind, we can reference the following as just a sampling of this reality.

Be alert and of sober mind. Your enemy the devil prowls around like a roaring lion looking for someone to devour. (1 Peter 5:8)

For the accuser of our brothers and sisters, who accuses them before our God day and night. (Revelation 12:10[b])

But take comfort my friends and reflect on the bookends. Satan was cast down to earth and continues to take residence here (for now). However, since the creation story, God has given us dominion over **all the earth**, including over every creeping thing that creepeth (or prowls) upon the earth. That includes dominion over Satan and his fallen angels, if we have accepted Jesus Christ as our Lord and Savior, and if we take authority in His name, and if we operate in the wisdom and power of the Holy Spirit. (By the way, isn't it interesting that the first reference to Satan in the Bible is as a serpent or snake?)

> *¹ Now the serpent was more crafty than any of the wild animals the LORD God had made. He said to the woman, "Did God really say, 'You must not eat from any tree in the garden'?" ¹⁴ So the LORD God said to the serpent, "Because you have done this, cursed are you above all livestock and all wild animals! You will crawl on your belly and you will eat dust all the days of your life."* (Genesis 3:1, 14) (Sounds like a creeping thing to me.)

Earlier in our discussion, there was one other significant reference found in the creation story. Remember, John was specific in stating the purpose for his entire gospel—*to present Jesus as God's Son so that we might believe in Him and have eternal life* (John 20:30-31). As we look at these verses again, notice the promise in Chapter 1, Verse 5.

> *In the beginning was the Word, and the Word was with God, and the Word was God. ² He was with God in the beginning. ³ Through Him all things were made; without him nothing was made that has been made. ⁴ In him was life, and that life was the light of all mankind. ⁵ **The light shines in the darkness, and the darkness has not overcome it.*** (John 1:1-2, 4-5)

Darkness is often used in Scripture as a symbol of sin and its effects. It is often contrasted with light, as light is a symbol of forgiveness and the presence of God. John is defining Jesus as the shining light that breaks through the gloom of mortal darkness and rebellion against God. Jesus is the antidote for Satan's grip on this temporal world and the only lasting remedy for the bondage of sin.

Of special interest is the dramatic shift in John's writing from past tense to the present continuous tense. The first four verses are written in past tense as John describes Jesus as being present at the beginning of creation as we know it. The word *was* (past tense) is used seven times in these verses. However, in Verse 5 John alerts his readers that he is not merely describing a past phenomenon, but a present reality and a future promise. "The light shines in the darkness, and the darkness has not overcome it."

This is a reminder that the nature of Jesus is past, present, and future. *(Jesus Christ is the same yesterday and today and forever. Hebrews 13:8).* There has never been a time, nor will there ever be a time, when the light of Christ does not overcome the darkness of this world. Yes, Jesus came to seek and save the lost, and yes, He came to fulfill prophecy and the will of his Father, but He also came to defeat sin and death and the ruler of this dark world.

> *The one who does what is sinful is of the devil, because the devil has been sinning from the beginning.* **The reason the Son of God appeared was to destroy the devil's work**. (1 John 3:8)

You can defeat the lies, temptations, and accusations of the enemy. You can live a victorious Christian lifestyle. You have been given not only the perfect example of victory in Jesus Christ, but also the power and authority of the Word of God as our primary offensive weapon. It is the sword of the Spirit, and it rests armed and ready in the arsenal of the mature believer.

As we continue our walk toward spiritual maturity, the first goal of this chapter is to provide a conceptual understanding of the authority of Scripture when we are engaged in spiritual warfare. The study has taken us from one end of the Bible to the other to build a foundation on which we can stand firm when battling the enemy. There is more to come on the practical application of God's Word when we are in the heat of battle, but before we move on, the Book of Revelation offers us one more glance at the promise of victory.

> *9 The great dragon was hurled down—that ancient serpent called the devil, or Satan, who leads the whole world astray. He was hurled to the earth, and his angels with him. 10 Then I heard a loud voice in heaven say: "Now have come the salvation and the power and the kingdom of our God, and the authority of his Messiah. For the accuser of our brothers and sisters, who accuses them before our God day and night, has been hurled down. 11 They triumphed over him by the blood of the Lamb and by the word of their testimony; they did not love their lives so much as to shrink from death.* (Revelation 12:9-11)

In case you did not catch that, let me reiterate; the proclamation of the gospel is the power that will see Satan defeated! If I could paraphrase Verse 11, it might read, "They won the war over Satan and his demons by the blood of the Lamb and by the word of their testimony."

Under the authority of our Messiah, we can triumph over Satan by the word of our testimony and the proclamation of the gospel (the sword of the Spirit) in direct response to his lies, temptations, and accusations. We need not fear the devil, for the gospel provides us victory, even to the point of death. For the release from this life leads to eternal glory for all those who are followers of Jesus Christ.

THE SWORD OF THE SPIRIT WORKS! We have the option to study the Bible, memorize Scripture, and use the Word of God to defeat the enemy's attacks. With that fact firmly established, it is time to reveal the practical application of this truth as I introduce a topic I call Situational Christianity.

1. Answers in Genesis—What is the Image of God? (08/15/2015) Retrieved from https://answersingenesis.org/genesis/what-is-image-of-god/
2. "Amazing Grace"—A Christian hymn published by John Newton (1779)
3. The Full Armor of God (3)—Ron Latulippe. (09/26/2010) Retrieved from https://www.rosedalebaptistwelland.com/2010/09/26-sn-2/
4. Sword of the Spirit—Debbie McDaniel (08/15/2016) Retrieved from https://www.crosswalk.com/blogs/debbie-mcdaniel/praying-on-the-armor-of-god.html

Chapter 11: Our Offensive Weapons—The Power of the Spoken Word by Practical Application

Throughout this entire study, I have drawn upon personal experiences, advice from mentors, and stories that help illustrate important tenets of our faith. While some may find it peculiar, my attempt to illustrate the practical application of the sword of the Spirit comes from watching professional football in America, more specifically, the National Football League or NFL. Once again, this is something I heard years ago that immediately struck me as worth remembering, and even then, found as an interesting parallel to this study on spiritual warfare. With that, let me introduce the topic I call **Situational Christianity.**

As we begin this chapter, I want to return to the previous quote from Ron Latulippe, as he was describing the difference between the *logos* and the *rhema*.

> *Rhema* *is the application of the logos to a* *real-life* *situation,* *a word appropriate and needed for that* *moment*. *So, Paul describes the sword of the Spirit as the* *rhema of God. Like the sword in battle,* *the soldier of* *Christ applies the appropriate word of God to the* *situation* *to defend, or wound, or kill as needed.* [1]

I am sure you will identify this as a huge understatement, but human beings are extremely complicated creatures. By design, God created each one of us as a unique individual with our own gifts, talents, personality, and purpose. Of course, the other side of that coin is that we all have our own shortcomings, pitfalls, and tendencies toward sin. God focuses on the former. Satan focuses on the latter.

What we know now is that all Scripture is God-breathed and is useful for teaching, rebuking, correcting, and training in righteousness (2 Timothy 3:16-17). But what we also find in Scripture is that Satan is adept at directing his temptations and accusations toward our weaknesses and insecurities. The quote above by Ron Latulippe is an encouragement for us to recognize our areas of weakness, identify what our real-life situation may be when it comes to spiritual warfare, and then with the proper understanding of Scripture, apply the *appropriate* Word of God to defend, wound, or defeat the enemy.

But even as we grow in our faith, different levels of spiritual maturity elicit various and sometimes specific attack strategies from the enemy. We find this referenced in the Parable of the Sower as found in the gospels of Matthew, Mark, and Luke. I have borrowed from Luke's gospel below.

> *11 This is the meaning of the parable: The seed is the word of God. 12 Those along the path are the ones who hear, and then the devil comes and takes away the word from their hearts, so that they may not believe and be saved. 13 Those on the rocky ground are the ones who receive the word with joy when they hear it, but they have no root. They believe for a while, but in the time of testing they fall away. 14 The seed that fell among thorns stands for those who hear, but as they go on their way they are choked by life's worries, riches and pleasures, and they do not mature. 15 But the seed on good soil stands for those with a noble and good heart, who hear the word, retain it, and by persevering produce a crop.* (Luke 8:11-15)

The message here is that as we pursue a victorious Christian lifestyle, there will be multiple battles along the way. Yes, there will be triumphs, but as we mature, Satan will adjust his battle plan and attack on different fronts.

In response, we have the option to become 'good soil' with a noble and good heart, among those who hear the word, retain it, and persevere to produce a life that walks in victory and glorifies our heavenly Father. But to accomplish that objective, we must have a battle plan. That is where the concept of Situational Christianity comes in. Solomon understood it when he wrote the following.

Make plans by seeking advice; if you wage war, obtain guidance. (Proverbs 20:18)

That brings me back to the analogy to professional football. Like them or not, in an eighteen-year period (2001-2019), the New England Patriots earned sixteen division titles, thirteen AFC championship appearances, nine Super Bowl appearances, and six Super Bowl wins. In addition, when it comes to the regular season, the Patriots were the most successful team in professional football during the Bill Belichick and Tom Brady era.

Several years ago, I was watching an interview with Bill Belichick after one of their championship games, and the question was asked (and I'm paraphrasing), "What is it that separates you from other NFL teams and has created this level of success for the Patriots?" Without hesitation, Belichick responded that he prepares his teams to play situation football. The commentator then asked him to define that term.

Belichick went on to explain that in addition to the fundamentals of football, he coaches his teams to be prepared for any offensive or defensive situation that might come up in a game. That may sound impossible to the novice football fan, but he is dogmatic about preparation. For example, if there is less than a minute left in the third quarter, the Patriots have the ball on the twenty-yard line, and the opposing team is set in a certain defensive package, his players know exactly what to do. If you think I might be exaggerating, there are others who have documented Belichick's approach.

The following was adopted from an article written by Ben Volin of the Boston Globe on September 6, 2017.
https://www.bostonglobe.com/sports/patriots/2017/09/06/for-bill-belichick-and-patriots-attention-detail-everything/MJ5hau42tG66vDRqQmYdxN/story.html

Not a day goes by where Belichick isn't grilling his players on a multitude of in-game scenarios. Many Patriots are blown away by Belichick's attention to detail, or as Belichick calls it, situational football.

There are thousands of scenarios that come up during a football season. "We have meetings on situations. So imagine how many situations you can hit in an hour of film," Devin McCourty said. "Bill will say, 'It might only come up once in your whole career.' The situations may seem obscure. But inevitably, they come up at some point during the season."

"The amount of detail that we would put in to running these plays just seemed over-the-top ridiculous," Matt Light recalled. "It's one play that hardly ever comes up, and we practiced it every week religiously. We got into a situation in the game where it obviously ended up being the difference-maker and won us the game, or was a big part of it."

'Situational football' is a catch-all terms that just means preparedness. And no team is more prepared than the Patriots. "Every play is a different situation, sometimes they come up once in a career, sometimes they come up 10 times in a season. So, you just got to be ready.

Everything has a purpose. And no detail too small gets past the Patriots. Belichick's methods test the players mentally just to stay on top of everything — things come up, and if you don't have the answer immediately, then it's a very clear signal to the coaching staff and all the guys around you that you're not going to get in the game. Linebacker David Harris said, "It's kind of like a mystic aura about the Patriots throughout the league, and it's just good to see the inside of it." [2]

Even with all this preparation, the plan doesn't always execute perfectly, but his players are rarely surprised by any circumstance on the field or in doubt about the appropriate play to run in that instance. Of course, it is not hard to understand the overall strategy (or see the big picture). **When you prepare to that level, the percentage for victory rises significantly.**

As a leader, Bill Belichick believes in, teaches, and endorses this philosophy better that any other coach in the NFL. His record speaks for itself. When asked about leadership, I found Belichick's quote quite interesting.

> *Leadership means building a team that's exhaustively prepared, but able to adjust in an instant.* The only sign we have in the locker room is from The Art of War. "Every battle is won before it is fought." You have to know what the opponents can do, what their strengths and weaknesses are, and what to do in every situation. [3]

Okay, you may be thinking this is a crazy analogy, but is it really? Could there be some parallel to our study on spiritual warfare? The answer is yes! To begin with, compare the quotes from Ron Latulippe and Bill Belichick.

- "*Rhema* is the application of the logos to a real-life situation - the soldier of Christ applies the appropriate Word of God to the situation."

- "You have to know what the opponents can do, what their strengths and weaknesses are, and what to do in every situation."

If you read between the lines, it becomes obvious that the key to consistent victory is consistent preparation. This is true in any life endeavor, including your walk toward a victorious Christian lifestyle. My hope is that you will discover the same parallels in applying that level of preparation to our battle against the powers of darkness. I will explain the similarities and the appropriate application of this principle as we attach a spiritual perspective to each paragraph from Ben Volin's article.

> "There are thousands of scenarios that come up during a football season. It might only come up once in your whole career. The situations may seem obscure. But inevitably, they come up at some point during the season."

There are thousands of scenarios that will come up over the course of your lifetime that could open the doorway for Satan to attack. Sometimes, the situation may seem too obscure to be real and may come up only once in your walk as a Christian, but inevitably, situations come to pass at some point in your life or in the life of a brother or sister in Christ. Solomon encouraged us to gain wisdom above all else (Proverbs 4:7, 23). Jesus told us to seek the Kingdom of God and His righteousness as our highest priority (Matthew 6:33). In his second letter to Timothy, Paul encouraged his brother in Christ to be prepared at all times to defend against false doctrine (Satan's lies).

> *In the presence of God and of Christ Jesus, who will judge the living and the dead, and in view of his appearing and his kingdom, I give you this charge: [2] Preach the word; be prepared in season and out of season; correct, rebuke and encourage—with great patience and careful instruction.*

⁵ But you, keep your head in all situations, endure hardship, do the work of an evangelist, discharge all the duties of your ministry. (2 Timothy 4:1-2, 5)

Would you consider yourself adequately prepared to defeat any scheme of the enemy that attempts to discourage, defame, or destroy you? If not, then I give you this charge—prioritize preparation as the first duty of your ministry.

> "The amount of detail that **we** would put in to running these plays just seemed over-the-top ridiculous," Matt Light recalled. "It's one play that hardly ever comes up, and **we** practiced it every week religiously. **We** got into a situation in the game where it obviously ended up being the difference-maker and won **us** the game, or was a big part of it."

There are four references to "we" or "us" in the statement above. Every NFL team is allowed fifty-three players on their final roster, plus coaches, trainers, and various support staff. When you look at a gameday sideline, there are over one hundred team personnel involved in the pursuit of victory. Each one plays a part in the preparation for that game and in encouraging one another when things do not go as planned. It is a cliché, but there is value in a team approach.

We can learn and benefit from this team approach as well. As Christians, there are times when the enemy will attack us individually as well as collectively. Some people would say that the amount of time Christians spend in church, in Bible study, in fellowship, in ministry, and in service to one another appears over-the-top ridiculous. I would counter that sentiment and assert that we are practicing religiously every week (as opposed to practicing religion). **The value of information and shared experience gained collectively becomes invaluable when applied individually.**

God's Word is alive and active and able to speak differently into the hearts and minds of every believer. As hard as we might try, there are limits to our personal understanding of Scripture and to lessons learned from personal failure. But collectively, we gain spiritual discernment and battle awareness at a much faster pace and with greater confidence. I have always been fascinated to hear a different interpretation of Scripture from the pulpit or other resource that broadens my understanding of that passage. And that perspective might be the *difference maker* in gaining victory over a specific attack that we may not have identified previously or known how to defeat. Solomon succinctly identified the benefit of this team approach in Proverbs.

As iron sharpens iron, so one person sharpens another.
(Proverbs 27:17)

When you invite the Holy Spirit into your life, I believe He will not only instill a hunger for God's Word in your heart, but also grant you understanding. When that flame was lit inside me, I couldn't wait to get to church and hear the message from the pulpit. And through consistent attendance and fellowship, I learned lessons from the experience of other Christians and avoided many mistakes that I might have made on my own. Perhaps you will find value, as I did, in this quote from Vernon Sanders Law. **"Experience is a hard teacher because she gives the test first, the lesson afterwards."**

'Situational football' is a catch-all terms that just means preparedness. And no team is more prepared than the Patriots. "Every play is a different situation, sometimes they come up once in a career, sometimes they come up 10 times in a season. So, you just got to be ready."

Let me make an important point here. Hidden in all this talk about preparation is the motivation to win. If consistent preparation is the key to victory, there must be an imperative purpose that would cause us to devote a significant amount of time to that effort. For the Patriots, or any sports team for that matter, the goal is to win a championship. They spend hours and hours practicing and studying film to become the best that they can be.

There has been a major emphasis is this study on our motivation to live a victorious Christian lifestyle and to be the best that we can be for Christ. There is nothing wrong with that goal; however, if we are to succeed in our Christian walks, I believe Paul encourages us in his letter to the Ephesians to look beyond that premise alone.

For we are God's handiwork, created in Christ Jesus to do good works, which God prepared in advance for us to do. (Ephesians 2:10)

God created you and me with a purpose and prepared us in advance to carry out that purpose. As we discussed in "Press on Toward the Goal," developing the habit of daily Bible study and prayer and becoming an active member in the body of Christ through church attendance and fellowship is the preparation to living a victorious Christian lifestyle. Living victoriously in and through Christ is the preparation to carry out the good works that God prepared in advance for us to do, thus glorifying Him. That is the greater goal.

Satan will come against you at every opportunity and at every step along the way in an attempt to steal your motivation, kill your enthusiasm, and destroy God's plan for your life. His tactics are not new, but they may seem new to you. Every situation is different. His attempt to derail you may happen only once in your lifetime, or it may happen repeatedly (as in consistent temptation in an area of weakness or constant accusation for past sins). "So, you just got to be ready!"

Everything has a purpose. And no detail too small gets past the Patriots. Belichick's methods test the players mentally just to stay on top of everything — things come up, and if you don't have the answer immediately, then it's a very clear signal to the coaching staff and all the guys around you that you're not going to get in the game. Linebacker David Harris said, "It's kind of like a mystic aura about the Patriots throughout the league, and it's just good to see the inside of it."

Everything in God's Word has a purpose and no detail of your life is too small for Satan to notice. The Bible tests our spiritual awareness and teaches us to stay prepared for the enemy's attacks. Things will come up, and if you don't have the answer immediately, it is a clear signal to the devil that your head is not in the game. And just like in sports, when that happens, momentum shifts, and the enemy intensifies his attack.

For many like me, there was a mystic aura surrounding the topic of spiritual warfare. I spent the first several years of my Christian walk completely unaware of its existence and even longer not giving the topic serious consideration. Needless to say, it was a real gamechanger when God began to give me ears to hear, eyes to see, and wisdom to discern the enemy's schemes and attacks. I am certainly not an expert in the subject, and there is still much to learn, but from what God has revealed to me, I can honestly say It's "just good to see the inside of it" and know that God has my back.

> *But the Lord stood at my side and gave me strength, so that through me the message might be fully proclaimed and all the Gentiles might hear it. And I was delivered from the lion's mouth. [18] The Lord will rescue me from every evil attack and will bring me safely to his heavenly kingdom. To him be glory for ever and ever. Amen.* (2 Timothy 4:17-18)

Now that we have a generic understanding of Situation Christianity, I would like to get more specific in two areas of application. The first will center around the practical application of the sword of the

Spirit. As you will see, this will follow the model set before us by Jesus in his confrontation with Satan in the desert wilderness. It will also pertain closely to the quote from Ron Latulippe, "Rhema is the application of the logos to a real-life situation - the soldier of Christ applies the appropriate Word of God to the situation."

When you read Luke's gospel account of this confrontation in Chapter 4, Jesus denounces Satan's temptation three times; twice prefaced with, "It is written," and the third time with, "It is said," each time quoting directly from Scripture to correct the purposeful distortion and lies from the devil. Accordingly, we pointed to Jesus as our perfect example in the previous chapter.

A more recent preacher, Billy Graham, devoted his life to preaching the gospel and to worldwide evangelism that followed this same model. What many refer to as the greatest legacy of Billy Graham are these three words; "The Bible Says!" The following was borrowed from an article written by Keith Manuel, and published on baptistmessage.com.

> *The death of Billy Graham is grabbing the headlines in print, on a variety of screens, and over radio waves— avenues he used extensively to spread the gospel. Many are reminiscing on the spiritual counsel he provided Presidents of the United States. Others are remembering his impeccable character, especially during the eighties when ministry failures seemed all too common.*
>
> *While these and many other aspects of his ministry will be discussed, **Graham's use of a simple authoritative phrase, may be his greatest legacy— "The Bible says."** If one reads or listens to the sermons of Billy Graham, a consistent pattern will emerge. He reads the Scripture. He shares what some call "The Big Idea of the Sermon."*

Next, he addresses what famous people say or how people live relative to the subject. Finally, he makes an appeal, not based on the authority of Billy Graham nor based on the ideas of great men and women. He makes his appeal on the only authority any preacher ever has. Graham cries out with a clear, resonate voice, "The Bible says..."

The phrase flowed so freely from Graham that even a secular newspaper, the Chicago Tribune, used it to describe his pulpit presence. The article stated, "A tall figure with swept-back hair, blue eyes and a strong jaw, Graham was a commanding presence in the pulpit with a powerful baritone voice. His catchphrase: "The Bible says ..." [4]

Jesus modeled it, Billy Graham built his entire ministry around it, and we need to know how to unleash its power. When Satan attacks, our best offensive weapon is the Word of God. I referred to the Bible as God's instruction manual for mankind. If you read it with a sincere intent to seek wisdom, the Holy Spirit will begin to unveil its secrets. There are instructions for every aspect of our lives, from the time we are children until we reach old age.

There are countless individuals who misunderstand God's intent for providing this resource. You may have heard people say that the Bible is too restrictive, there are too many rules, or we Christians just are not allowed to have any fun. Now, to be fair, there are some 'religions' that misappropriate God's intent and take His message to those extremes, but the true motivation for all of God's instruction is love.

The 10 commandments and all other instructions in the Bible are not meant to be restrictive. They are meant to be protective of you and the people around you. It may be difficult to comprehend that as a child, but parents know what it is like to try and protect their children. We refer to God as our Heavenly Father, and He refers to us as daughters and sons with a love that we cannot begin to fathom while in this earthly realm.

Think of a few examples of a parent's warnings or rules. When your mom said, "Please don't climb any higher than the second branch," do you think she was trying to prevent you from having fun, or do you think she was trying to protect you from injury? When your dad said, "Don't aim that BB gun at your brother's face," do you think he was trying to prevent you from having fun, or do you think he was trying to protect your brother from injury and you from feeling bad about hurting your brother? I trust you know the answer and hope you see my point.

Remember the main premise of this study—God wants you to be victorious in this spiritual battle. ("Above all things, I wish that you prosper and be in good health, even as your soul prospers.") God's instruction manual is written out of love and offered to keep you out of trouble, to prevent you from being hurt or injuring others, and to open the windows of heaven and allow God to bless you for following in obedience to His word. This is referenced repeatedly in Deuteronomy, Chapters 4—8, but notice the dual promise below from Malachi.

> Bring the whole tithe into the storehouse, that there may be food in my house. Test me in this," says the LORD Almighty, "and see if I will not throw open the floodgates of heaven and pour out so much blessing that there will not be room enough to store it. ¹¹ I will prevent pests from devouring your crops, and the vines in your fields will not drop their fruit before it is ripe," says the LORD Almighty. ¹² "Then all the nations will call you blessed, for yours will be a delightful land," says the LORD Almighty. (Malachi 3:10-12)

Malachi was the last of the Old Testament prophets, and God spoke through Malachi to warn Israel about their disobedience. It had been 100 years since the Jews had escaped enslavement under the Babylonians, and they had grown hard-hearted toward God's love for them. The nation, including its people and priests, had departed from the law of Moses, and had fallen back into their religious rituals. Malachi forcefully rebuked and condemned the people for these abuses and called them into repentance.

Malachi indicted the nation of Israel on at least six counts of willful sin. The verses above pertain specifically to "robbing God" by not honoring the principle of tithing. So, God put forth a challenge to the entire nation to test His promise, to tithe faithfully once again, and to see if God's blessings would not follow. God also promised them protection if they would return to obedience.

For proper context, we must remind ourselves that this was primarily an agricultural economy. The survival of a nation depended on its ability to plant, grow, and harvest crops. So many references from the prophets and even the teachings of Jesus were related to this theme (the Parable of the Sower among them). The floodgates mentioned in Verse 10 are a reference to rain, which the Lord had withheld, resulting in severe damage to Israel's crops. In this culture, rain was a symbol of all manner of blessing.

Likewise, agricultural abundance was a symbol of wealth and prosperity. Even if the Lord had blessed the land with rain, there were any number of pests and/or natural disasters that could ruin a crop before the harvest was completed. The promise of protection from these potential hardships had great meaning to the Israelites.

I venture down this path to add validity to the promises of God's Word and to encourage a disciplined application to its meaning. As we return to our discussion on spiritual warfare, we can have faith that a God given Scripture, spoken with God given authority, and appropriate to the situation, will defeat Satan's attempt to derail us. When this truth first became apparent to me, I was not exactly sure how to apply it in my life.

As mentioned earlier, I had lost everything that was dear to me and almost everything that I had worked twelve years to achieve. Satan was bombarding my mind with thoughts of failure, insecurity, doubt, rejection, and suggesting I give up on life. *You'll never marry again, your children don't love you, you'll never recover financially, God has given up on you, why don't you just disappear—nobody will care.* More frightening were the thoughts of suicide, which had never crossed my mind before. Stubbornly, I kept reading the Bible, desperately searching for answers.

Then one day, as only God can do, he allowed one verse of Scripture to jump off the page and directly into my heart. It was as if I had been given new sight and could instantly identify Satan's strategy to devour me. Satan had already stolen from me and was now trying to kill my ambition to live and destroy my relationship with God the Father, his Son Jesus Christ, and the Holy Spirit. This one verse restored my faith and my will to fight the good fight.

> *I consider that our present sufferings are not worth comparing with the glory that will be revealed in us.* (Romans 8:18)

When Paul wrote his letter to the church in Rome, he titled this section "Life Through the Spirit." It follows the infamous passage in Chapter 7 describing his inner conflict between good and evil, and Chapter 8 begins this way.

> *Therefore, there is now no condemnation for those who are in Christ Jesus, ² because through Christ Jesus the law of the Spirit who gives life has set you free from the law of sin and death.* (Romans 8:1-2)

Then in Verses 16-17, Paul continues.

> *The Spirit himself testifies with our spirit that we are God's children. ¹⁷ Now if we are children, then we are heirs—heirs of God and co-heirs with Christ, if indeed we share in his sufferings in order that we may also share in his glory.* (Romans 8:16-17)

Paul is writing to the collective church body and in doing so uses all plural pronouns. God inspired me to make this passage personal and so this became my victory verse.

> *I consider that [my] present [suffering is] not worth comparing with the glory that will be revealed in [me!]*

You see, I was not fighting against the temptation to sin which leads to failure. I had already failed. Now, the battle in my mind was against blame, accusation, condemnation, and lies about what the future held. But the Word of God, penned by the apostle Paul, became a beacon of hope for me.

- Satan was condemning me, but the Bible says, *There is now no condemnation for those who are in Christ Jesus.*
- Satan was trying to chain me to my failure, but the Bible says, *Through Christ Jesus the law of the Spirit who gives life has set you free from the law of sin and death.*
- Satan was trying to separate me from the God who loved me, but the Bible says, *The Spirit himself testifies with our spirit that we are God's children. Now if we are children, then we are heirs—heirs of God and co-heirs with Christ.*
- I was suffering under the weight and gravity of Satan's schemes, but the Bible says, *We are co-heirs with Christ, if indeed we share in his sufferings in order that we may also share in his glory.*

Look closely at the promise in that last verse and pay special attention to this hidden truth. Jesus suffered under the weight and gravity of Satan's same schemes, but the Bible says, *We are co-heirs with Christ, if indeed we share in his sufferings in order that we may also share in his glory.*

God's plan for His Son (and the plan of salvation) included a time of suffering brought on by Satan's schemes, but that brief period of suffering led to a future glory for the Son of God that we cannot begin to imagine. Listen, if you profess Jesus Christ as your Savior, you will experience periods of spiritual warfare in this lifetime. But as sons and daughters of God, and co-heirs with Christ, find joy in the fact that we share in the same spiritual battle as Christ did, and are therefore promised that we too will share in a future glory to grand for us to envision while occupying these earth suits.

I did not know at the time what *glory* might be revealed in me, but I knew God had a plan for my life, and I knew I could stand firm in that truth and boldly proclaim the promises of Almighty God! My mind had become the battlefield, and God's Word became my primary weapon. Every time a thought of condemnation came into my mind that was contrary to the will of God, I SPOKE OUT LOUD, "I consider that [my] present [suffering is] not worth comparing with the glory that will be revealed in [me!]"

To paraphrase, this was my way of telling Satan, "You may think your fiery arrows and constant mental barrage have me on the verge of defeat, but I know this is temporary and somehow meant for my good. God is my rock and my shield and holds promise for my future. NOW, IN THE NAME OF JESUS CHRIST, GET OUT OF MY HEAD, AND LEAVE ME ALONE!" This was the turning point in my spiritual battle. This was the beginning of an eventual and unavoidable victory celebration. I knew I could win, and God had provided the battle plan.

But notice that I said, *every time* a negative thought came into my head. Very few battles are won with a single shot. We can have complete faith in the Word of God, but Satan will not give up easily. Be prepared to fire your weapon often and until the devil knows you are serious. He will test you, tempt you, and taunt you until he is convinced that you are standing firm on God's promises.

As the heavens are higher than the earth, so are my ways higher than your ways and my thoughts than your thoughts. As the rain and the snow come down from heaven, and do not return to it without watering the earth, so is my word that goes out from my mouth: It will not return to me empty, but will accomplish what I desire and achieve the purpose for which I sent it. (Isaiah 55:9-11)

Remember 2 Timothy 3:16-17, which teaches, "All Scripture is God-breathed and is useful for teaching, rebuking, correcting and training in righteousness, so that the servant of God may be thoroughly equipped for every good work." It is up to us to learn how to use it!

Now, I realize there are many Christians who have never been taught to use the Bible as a resource for defeating an area of Satanic influence in their lives. And even if they believe that is possible, they may not know where to look in the Bible to find reassurance and achieve victory in their personal battle with the enemy. As you will see in the next chapter, the Bible speaks directly to our human frailties and provides us the same remedy used so effectively by Jesus during His temptation in the desert. It is time to be honest with yourself, recognize the vulnerability in your armor, and then **Choose Your Weapon.** Choose a passage of Scripture that is appropriate to the situation and needed for your specific battle. Remember, the soldier of Christ applies the appropriate Word of God to defend, or wound, or defeat the enemy.

1. The Full Armor of God (3)—Ron Latulippe. (09/26/2010) Retrieved from https://www.rosedalebaptistwelland.com/2010/09/26-sn-2/
2. The Patriots and the Art of Situational Football—Ben Volin/Boston Globe. (09/06/2017) Retrieved from https://www.bostonglobe.com/sports/patriots/2017/09/06/for-bill-belichick-and-patriots-attention-detail-everything/MJ5hau42tG66vDRqQmYdxN/story.html
3. Bill Belichick reveals his 5 rules of exceptional leadership—Suzy Welch/CNBC. Make it. (04/13/2017) Retrieved from https://www.cnbc.com/2017/04/13/bill-belichick-leadership-rules.html
4. The Greatest Legacy of Billy Graham: "The Bible Says"—Keith Manuel/baptistmessage.com. (03/02/2018) Retrieved from http://baptistmessage.com/greatest-legacy-billy-graham-Bible-says/

Chapter 12: The Power of the Spoken Word by Practical Application—Choose Your Weapon

For the word of God is alive and active. Sharper than any double-edged sword, it penetrates even to dividing soul and spirit, joints and marrow; it judges the thoughts and attitudes of the heart. (Hebrews 4:12)

In the previous chapter, I mentioned that my spiritual battle was not against the temptation to sin which leads to failure. I had already failed. The battle in my mind was against condemnation, blame, and lies about what the future held. As a result, some might say that the victory verse that I claimed was somewhat generic, and I would agree. But it was the verse that God gave me, and it spoke directly into my spirit for my specific need at that specific time.

I consider that [my] present [suffering is] not worth comparing with the glory that will be revealed in [me!] (Romans 8:18)

You may read that verse, and it may mean nothing to you. I can't explain how the Holy Spirit creates special emphasis in any of our hearts by personalizing what we might consider an otherwise hollow Scripture verse and transforming it into a meaningful and life altering truth, other than to repeat that the Word of God is alive and active. I had probably read that verse a dozen times without stopping to consider its meaning or application. But on that day, it came alive and breathed new life into me.

As we continue in this discussion regarding the practical application of God's Word as the sword of the Spirit, we will consider this battle against blame, condemnation, and lies about the future, but we will also explore the battle against specific temptations to sin. What follows is certainly not meant to be an exhaustive list of all the possible ways that the enemy can attack our minds, nor could we ever attempt to confine Scripture and the abundance of truth that God has provided to defend ourselves and/or take the offensive.

The goal here is to enlighten our hearts and our minds by providing a pathway to understand how truth overcomes lies and how the light of the gospel overcomes the powers of darkness. The illustrations that follow are but a model to stimulate your thinking and accomplish that objective. Of course, when you are engaged in spiritual warfare, it is in the relentless pursuit of Scripture that God allows his Spirit to speak truth into your life and deliver a word appropriate to the situation.

In the first category mentioned above (*blame, condemnation, and lies about what the future holds*), there are a multitude of human emotions influenced by Satan's negative thoughts, some of which include worry, fear, anxiety, unhappiness, hopelessness, despair, depression, etc. Please understand, I don't for a minute discount the clinical factors that can lead to some of these symptoms, but I am suggesting that spiritual warfare can and does contribute to these same emotions.

Look, we are all human, and no matter how grounded we are in our faith, none of us are impervious to these attacks and the subsequent human emotions that follow. Should you find yourself captive to any of the emotions referenced above and below, my hope is that these God-inspired templates might provide a starting point if you have not previously considered the power of Scripture to ward off the lies of the enemy. Let me offer two helpful suggestions as you read through these verses.

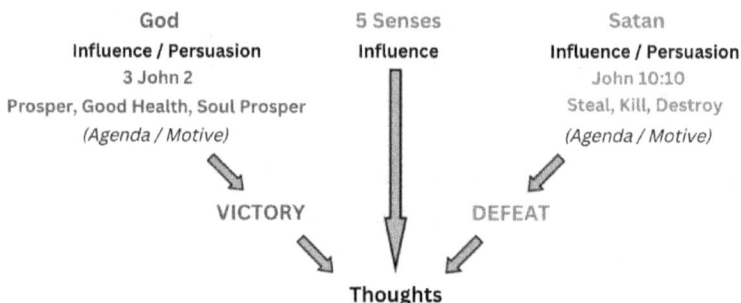

First, consider their application in the context of our diagram. God wants you to prosper—Satan comes to destroy the plans that God has for you.

Second, remember the examples of Jesus in the desert, the apostle Paul as he wrestled with iniquity, and my own struggle with spiritual warfare. In each instance, God provided the appropriate weapon (a verse from Scripture), at the appropriate time, and for the specific need.

> Jesus answered, "It is written: 'Worship the Lord your God and serve him only.'" (Luke 4:8)

> Paul wrote, *I was given a thorn in my flesh, a messenger of Satan, to torment me. Three times I pleaded with the Lord to take it away from me. But he said to me, "My grace is sufficient for you, for my power is made perfect in weakness."* (2 Corinthians 12:7-9)

> *The Holy Spirit inspired me; I consider that [my] present [suffering] is not worth comparing with the glory that will be revealed in [me!]* (Romans 8:18—for personal application)

As you read what God has graciously provided, I encourage you to allow the Holy Spirit to work within you and transform the truth of

Scripture into a double-edged sword powerful and effective for defeating Satan's schemes. Take the necessary action and convert these verses (in whole or in part) into your personal victory statement.

Worry

> *Therefore, I tell you, do not worry about your life, what you will eat or drink; or about your body, what you will wear. Is not life more than food, and the body more than clothes?* ***26*** *Look at the birds of the air; they do not sow or reap or store away in barns, and yet your heavenly Father feeds them. Are you not much more valuable than they?* *27 Can any one of you by worrying add a single hour to your life?* (Matthew 6:24-27)

Some of you reading this may recognize the name, Corrie Ten Boom. Corrie was a Dutch watchmaker and later a writer, who worked with her father and other family members to help many Jews escape the Nazi Holocaust during the second World War by hiding them in her home. They were eventually caught and she was arrested and sent to the Ravensbrück concentration camp. Her most famous book, 'The Hiding Place' is a biography that recounts the story of her family's efforts and how Corrie found hope while imprisoned at the concentration camp.

Note - the Word of God does not need additional support, but I have included some of Corrie's more famous quotes where applicable as they are a direct rebuke of the lies Satan puts in front of us and a temporal reminder to cling to our faith.

> ➤ "Worrying does not empty tomorrow of its troubles. It empties TODAY of its STRENGTH."

Fear

God is our refuge and strength, an ever-present help in trouble. ² Therefore we will not fear, though the earth give way and the mountains fall into the heart of the sea. (Psalm 46:1-2)

Whoever dwells in the shelter of the Most High will rest in the shadow of the Almighty. ² I will say of the LORD, "He is my refuge and my fortress, my God, in whom I trust." ³ Surely he will save you from the fowler's snare and from the deadly pestilence. ⁴ He will cover you with his feathers, and under his wings you will find refuge; his faithfulness will be your shield and rampart. ⁵ You will not fear the terror of night, nor the arrow that flies by day. (Psalm 91:1-5)

I said, 'You are my servant;' I have chosen you and have not rejected you. ¹⁰ So do not fear, for I am with you; do not be dismayed, for I am your God. I will strengthen you and help you; I will uphold you with my righteous right hand. (Isaiah 41:9-10)

But now, this is what the LORD says - he who created you, Jacob, he who formed you, Israel: "Do not fear, for I have redeemed you; I have summoned you by name; you are mine. ² When you pass through the waters, I will be with you; and when you pass through the rivers, they will not sweep over you. When you walk through the fire, you will not be burned; the flames will not set you ablaze. ³ For I am the LORD your God, the Holy One of Israel, your Savior." (Isaiah 43:1-3)

For God hath not given us the spirit of fear; but of power, and of love, and of a sound mind. (2 Timothy 1:7) (KJV)

> "Never be afraid to trust an unknown future to a known God." (Corrie Ten Boom)

Despair/Anxiety

[7] But we have this treasure (Jesus Christ) in jars of clay (ourselves) to show that this all-surpassing power is from God and not from us. [8] We are hard pressed on every side, but not crushed; perplexed, but not in despair; [9] persecuted, but not abandoned; struck down, but not destroyed. [16] Therefore we do not lose heart. [17] For our light and momentary troubles are achieving for us an eternal glory that far outweighs them all. [18] So we fix our eyes not on what is seen, but on what is unseen, since what is seen is temporary, but what is unseen is eternal. (2 Corinthians 4:7-9, 16-18) (Added for emphasis.)

[1] The Spirit of the Sovereign LORD is on me, because the LORD has anointed me to proclaim good news to the poor. He has sent me to bind up the brokenhearted, to proclaim freedom for the captives and release from darkness for the prisoners, [3] to bestow on them the oil of joy instead of mourning, and a garment of praise instead of a spirit of despair. (Isaiah 61: 1, 3)

> "When a train goes through a tunnel and it gets dark, you don't throw away the ticket and jump off. You sit still and trust the engineer. In darkness God's truth shines most clear." (Corrie Ten Boom)

Depression/Unhappiness

Blessed is the one who does not walk in step with the wicked or stand in the way that sinners take or sit in the company of mockers, [2] but whose delight is in the law of the LORD, and who meditates on his law day and night. *3* That person is like a tree planted by streams of water, which yields its fruit in season and whose leaf does not wither - whatever they do prospers. (Psalm 1:1-3)

But let all who take refuge in you be glad; let them ever sing for joy. Spread your protection over them, that those who love your name may rejoice in you. *12* Surely, LORD, you bless the righteous; you surround them with your favor as with a shield. (Psalm 5:11-12)

Blessed is the one whose transgressions are forgiven, whose sins are covered. *2* Blessed is the one whose sin the LORD does not count against them and in whose spirit is no deceit. *3* When I kept silent, my bones wasted away through my groaning all day long. *4* For day and night your hand was heavy on me; my strength was sapped as in the heat of summer. *5* Then I acknowledged my sin to you and did not cover up my iniquity. I said, "I will confess my transgressions to the LORD." And you forgave the guilt of my sin. *11* Rejoice in the LORD and be glad, you righteous; sing, all you who are upright in heart! (Psalm 32:1-5, 11)

I will exalt you, LORD, for you lifted me out of the depths and did not let my enemies gloat over me. *2* LORD my God, I called to you for help, and you healed me. *3* You, LORD, brought me up from the realm of the dead; you spared me from going down to the pit. (Psalm 30:1-3)

Take delight in the LORD, and he will give you the desires of your heart. *5* Commit your way to the LORD; trust in him and he will do this: *6* He will make your righteous reward shine like the dawn, your vindication like the *noonday sun. ²⁵ I was young and now I am old, yet I have never seen the righteous forsaken.* (Psalm 37:4-6, 25)

"Happiness isn't something that depends on our surroundings; it's something we make inside ourselves. There is no pit so deep that God's love is not deeper still." (Corrie Ten Boom)

Suicide

³ The cords of death entangled me, the anguish of the grave came over me; I was overcome by distress and sorrow. ⁴ Then I called on the name of the LORD: "LORD, save me!" ⁵The LORD is gracious and righteous; our God is full of compassion. ⁶ The LORD protects the unwary; when I was brought low, he saved me. ⁷ Return to your rest, my soul, for the LORD has been good to you. ⁸ For you, LORD, have delivered me from death, my eyes from tears, my feet from stumbling, ⁹ that I may walk before the LORD in the land of the living. ¹ I love the LORD, for he heard my voice; he heard my cry for mercy. ² Because he turned his ear to me, I will call on him as long as I live. (Psalm 116:3-9, 1-2)

As I stated earlier, this was not meant to be an exhaustive list of human emotion influenced by the lies of the enemy, nor does it come close to capturing the potential for Scripture to speak against those lies. But what I hope you see in these verses is that God, through his chosen prophets and apostles, has been providing the encouragement and the means necessary to be victorious in this spiritual battle since the beginning of time as we know it.

The Word of God is our primary weapon against Satan's lies. If you or someone you know is struggling in any one of these areas, I would recommend reading the Scripture verses again, take time to meditate on them, and allow the Holy Spirit to speak to your heart and enlighten your mind to the truth of the gospel. Let me also challenge you in the following areas.

1. While generic in nature, each of these verses speaks to an area of our emotions, but also contains a promise. Go back and look for God's promises!

2. Allow yourself the freedom to personalize a verse and begin to speak it aloud against Satan's lies (in the name of Jesus).

3. Go back and read the surrounding verses to gain context and the full measure of God's message to you.

4. Start a topical or word search in a Bible concordance and explore other verses that might provide additional encouragement for you.

5. Engage trusted brothers or sisters in Christ and seek their counsel regarding these verses. You might be surprised that they too have walked in the same shoes and be encouraged by their victory through Jesus.

As we transition into the next category (*temptations that lead to sin*), God's Word remains the primary weapon against Satan's attempt to influence our thoughts and lead us into behavior contrary to the life we are called to as Christians. I have listed relevant Scripture verses to stimulate our thinking and once again demonstrate how the light of the gospel overcomes the powers of darkness. However, before we continue, there are several theological truths that serve as vital precursors to this discussion.

First - God does not tempt us with evil. To suggest otherwise would contrast with everything we have learned so far about our heavenly Father and His will for our lives and it would also be in direct contradiction to basic biblical doctrine. The apostle James was inspired by the Holy Spirit when he wrote the following to his brothers and sisters in Christ as they faced many trials.

When tempted, no one should say, "God is tempting me." For God cannot be tempted by evil, nor does he tempt anyone; ^{14} but each person is tempted when they are dragged away by their own evil desire and enticed. ^{15} Then, after desire has conceived, it gives birth to sin; and sin, when it is full-grown, gives birth to death. ^{16} Don't be deceived, my dear brothers and sisters. ^{17} Every good and perfect gift is from above, coming down from the Father of the heavenly lights, who does not change like shifting shadows. (James 1:13-17)

For some, they confuse this truth with a portion of the Lord's prayer which states, *'and lead us not into temptation.'* Remember, this is how Jesus taught his disciples (and us) to pray and that simple petition is addressed to our heavenly Father. To clear up any confusion, let me share a commentary with you from Albert Barnes. Barnes was an American theologian who graduated from Princeton Theological Seminary in 1823 and served as a Presbyterian minister from 1825–1868. He is best known for his extensive, 14 volume Bible Commentary published in the 1830s.

'And lead us not into temptation' - A petition similar to this is offered by David in Psalm 141:4; *"Incline not my heart to any evil thing, to practice wicked works with the workers of iniquity."* God tempts no man (James 1:13). This phrase, then, must be used in the sense of "permitting." Do not "permit" us to be tempted to sin. In this it is implied that God has such control over the tempter as to save us from his power if we call upon Him. It is not wrong to pray that we may be saved from suffering if it be the will of God (see Luke 22:42). [1]

Second—Satan can only achieve what God has permitted. Our faith is held firm in the fact that God is the Creator of all things spiritual and temporal. Therefore, we believe that God always has been and always will be in complete control over His entire creation, including Satan and the rebellious angels that follow him. Our study of the devil's schemes and the potential consequence of sin has been extensive to this point; however, we have yet to make this point - Satan cannot accomplish a thing without God's permission.

For many, this realty results in an obvious question. If God loves us, why would He grant Satan permission to temp, distract, or harm us in the first place? I would venture the answer to that question has plagued mankind throughout the ages. Scripture would tell us that these trials increase our reliance on God, build our perseverance, and strengthen our faith. Whether meant for discipline or instruction, we are also confident in the truth Paul shared with us in Romans 8:28; *And we know that in all things God works for the good of those who love him, who have been called according to his purpose.*

Satan's reliance on God's permission is probably best illustrated in the first two chapters of Job. Chapter 1 is titled; 'Job's First Test.'

> *¹ In the land of Uz there lived a man whose name was Job. This man was blameless and upright; he feared God and shunned evil. ⁶ One day the angels came to present themselves before the L*ORD*, and Satan also came with them. ⁷ The L*ORD *said to Satan, "Where have you come from?" Satan answered the L*ORD*, "From roaming throughout the earth, going back and forth on it."*

> *⁸ Then the L*ORD *said to Satan, "Have you considered my servant Job? There is no one on earth like him; he is blameless and upright, a man who fears God and shuns evil." ⁹ "Does Job fear God for nothing?" Satan replied. ¹⁰ "Have you not put a hedge around him and his household and everything he has? You have blessed the*

work of his hands, so that his flocks and herds are spread throughout the land.

¹¹ But now stretch out your hand and strike everything he has, and he will surely curse you to your face."
¹² The LORD said to Satan, "Very well, then, everything he has is in your power, but on the man himself do not lay a finger." Then Satan went out from the presence of the LORD. (Job 1:1, 6-12)

In Verse 12 we see God granting His permission for Satan to test Job's righteousness and attempt to destroy Job's confident relationship with his Creator. Also notice that God places a limitation on Satan's evil schemes. Satan may try his best, but God remains in control. We see the same premise in Chapter 2.

On another day, the angels came to present themselves before the LORD, and Satan also came with them to present himself before him. ² And the LORD said to Satan, "Where have you come from?" Satan answered the LORD, "From roaming throughout the earth, going back and forth on it."

³ Then the LORD said to Satan, "Have you considered my servant Job? There is no one on earth like him; he is blameless and upright, a man who fears God and shuns evil. And he still maintains his integrity, though you incited me against him to ruin him without any reason."

⁴ "Skin for skin!" Satan replied. "A man will give all he has for his own life. ⁵ But now stretch out your hand and strike his flesh and bones, and he will surely curse you to your face." ⁶ The LORD said to Satan, "Very well, then, he is in your hands; but you must spare his life." (Job 2:1-6)

The Bible's account of Job is a long and intricate story with many lessons to be learned, but throughout his trials, Job maintains his faith in God and as a result, he is fully restored. When life's trials hit us head on, we too can rely on our Creator to carry us through and redeem us in the end. I point back to the quote from Albert Barnes; 'In this it is implied that God has such control over the tempter as to save us from his power if we call upon Him.'

Third, God will not allow you to be tempted beyond what you can bear and will always provide a way out that will honor Him and strengthen your faith. In his first letter to the church in Corinth, Paul addressed this topic. As the tenth chapter begins, Paul points back to the many temptations the Israelites experienced in the desert after their release from slavery in Egypt. The entire nation wandered in the desert for 40 years and many lost out on God's promised land due to this spiritual battle. Paul's message in 1 Corinthians 10:1-12 has a dual purpose for us today.

(1) We are not the first ones to face the lies of the enemy, no matter the severity or weight of the attack.

(2) More importantly, with the proper relationship in place, our God is faithful, and we can rely on His strength not only to carry us through, but to provide a path to victory.

No temptation has overtaken you except what is common to mankind. And God is faithful; he will not let you be tempted beyond what you can bear. But when you are tempted, he will also provide a way out so that you can endure it. (1 Corinthians 10:13)

The *'way out'* of temptation includes three vital components.

(1) Faith in Almighty God. (This requires a personal relationship with Father, Son, and Holy Spirit.)

(2) Prayer. Borrowing again from Albert Barnes; 'It is not wrong to pray that we may be saved from suffering if it be the will of God.' (Prayer and praise are extremely effective offensive

weapons, as well as our primary means of petitioning God for assistance. (In reference to Barnes' quote, we can look upon Jesus as he prayed in the garden of Gethsemane.)

   a. *Going a little farther, he fell with his face to the ground and prayed, "My Father, if it is possible, may this cup be taken from me. Yet not as I will, but as you will."* (Matthew 26:39)

(3) Rebuke the lies of the enemy with the truth of Scripture. Remember 2 Timothy 3:16-17.

   a. *All Scripture is God-breathed and is useful for teaching, rebuking, correcting, and training in righteousness, so that the servant of God may be thoroughly equipped for every good work."*

Now, as we bring light to these specific areas of temptation, I feel compelled to remind you of the following.

(1) Remember the example Jesus set for us, and/or, the words of Billy Graham. When Satan temps you with a lie, you might find it helpful to start your rebuke with; "It is written..." or "The Bible says..."

(2) Your response to Satan's attack is to be spoken out loud. Satan is not omniscient—he cannot read your mind and does not know your thoughts. God's Word, spoken out loud with your confident voice will rebuke the enemy.

(3) "Dealing with Satan is not a power encounter; it's a truth encounter." This is a quote from Neil Anderson of Freedom in Christ Ministries. Neil continues; "When you expose Satan's lie with God's truth, his power is broken. That's why Jesus said: "You shall know the truth, and the truth shall make you free" (John 8:32). That's why He prayed: "My prayer is not that you take them out of the world but that you protect them from the evil one... Sanctify them by the truth; your word is truth" (John

17:15, 17). That's why the first piece of armor Paul mentions for standing against the schemes of the devil is the belt of truth (Ephesians 6:14). Satan's lie cannot withstand the truth any more than darkness of night can withstand the light of the rising sun." [2]

Alcohol/Drunkenness

Be careful, then, how you live - not as unwise but as wise, [16] making the most of every opportunity, because the days are evil. [17] Therefore do not be foolish, but understand what the Lord's will is. [18] Do not get drunk on wine, which leads to debauchery. Instead, be filled with the Spirit. (Ephesians 5:15-18)

Since an overseer manages God's household, he must be blameless—not overbearing, not quick-tempered, not given to drunkenness, not violent, not pursuing dishonest gain. (Titus 1:7)

Wine is a mocker and beer a brawler; whoever is led astray by them is not wise. (Proverbs 20:1)

Addiction

I have the right to do anything," you say—but not everything is beneficial. "I have the right to do anything"—but I will not be mastered by anything. (1 Corinthians 6:12) (In reference to sexual immorality, but applicable to addiction as well.)

For the grace of God has appeared that offers salvation to all people. [12] It teaches us to say "No" to ungodliness and worldly passions, and to live self-controlled, upright and godly lives in this present age. (Titus 2:11-12)

Offer to God a sacrifice of thanksgiving, and perform your vows to the Most High, ¹⁵ and call upon me in the day of trouble; I will deliver you, and you shall glorify me. (Psalm 50:14-15) (ESV)

And the God of all grace, who called you to his eternal glory in Christ, after you have suffered a little while, will himself restore you and make you strong, firm and steadfast. (1 Peter 5:10)

Infidelity/Adultery

You have heard it said of old, 'You shall not commit adultery.' But I say to you that whoever looks at a woman to lust for her has already committed adultery with her in his heart. If your right eye causes you to sin, pluck it out and cast it from you; for it is more profitable for you that one of your members perish, than for your whole body to be cast into hell. (Matthew 5:27-29)

You shall not commit adultery. (Exodus 20:14) (The Ten Commandments)

Sexual Immorality

But among you there must not be even a hint of sexual immorality, or of any kind of impurity, or of greed, because these are improper for God's holy people. (Ephesians 5:3)

Flee sexual immorality. Every sin that a man does is outside the body, but he who commits sexual immorality sins against his own body. Or do you not know that your body is a temple of the Holy Spirit who is in you, whom you have from God, and you are not your own? (1 Corinthians 6:18-19)

*Therefore do not let sin reign in your mortal body, that you should obey it in its lusts. And do not present your members as instruments of unrighteousness to sin, but present yourselves to God as being alive from the dead, and your members as instruments of righteousness to God. **For sin shall not have dominion over you**, for you are not under law but under grace.* (Romans 6:12-14)

For this is the will of God, your sanctification, that you should abstain from sexual immorality. (1 Thessalonians 4:3)

Theft/Robbery

Whoever robs their father or mother and says, "It's not wrong," is partner to one who destroys. (Proverbs 28:24)

For I, the LORD, love justice; I hate robbery and wrongdoing. In my faithfulness I will reward my people and make an everlasting covenant with them. (Isaiah 61:8)

You shall not steal. (Exodus 20:15) (The Ten Commandments)

Slander/Gossip/Lying

Above all else, guard your heart, for it is the wellspring of life. Put away perversity from your mouth and keep corrupt talk far from your lips. (Proverbs 4:23-24)

You shall not give false testimony against your neighbor. (Exodus 20:16) (The Ten Commandments)

Keep your tongue from evil and your lips from speaking deceit. Turn away from evil and do good; seek peace and pursue it. (Psalm 34:13-14)

Swearing/Foul Language

With the tongue we praise our Lord and Father, and with it we curse human beings, who have been made in God's likeness. Out of the same mouth come praise and cursing. My brothers and sisters, this should not be. (James 3:10)

You shall not take the name of the LORD your God in vain, for the LORD will not hold him guiltless who takes His name in vain. (Exodus 20:7) (The Ten Commandments)

Do not let any unwholesome talk come out of your mouths, but only what is helpful for building others up according to their needs, that it may benefit those who listen. (Ephesians 4:29)

But now you must put them all away: anger, wrath, malice, slander, and obscene talk from your mouth. (Colossians 3:8)

Set a guard, O LORD, over my mouth; keep watch over the door of my lips! (Psalm 141:3)

Pride/Arrogance

Pride goes before destruction, a haughty spirit before a fall. (Proverbs 16:18)

For everything in the world—the lust of the flesh, the lust of the eyes, and the pride of life - comes not from the Father but from the world. (1 John 2:16)

I, wisdom, dwell together with prudence; I possess knowledge and discretion. To fear the LORD is to hate evil; I hate pride and arrogance, evil behavior and perverse speech. (Proverbs 8:12-13)

The fear of the LORD is hatred of evil. Pride and arrogance and the way of evil and perverted speech I hate. (Proverbs 8:13)

Do not keep talking so proudly or let your mouth speak such arrogance, for the LORD is a God who knows, and by him deeds are weighed. (1 Samuel 2:3)

He does not answer when people cry out because of the arrogance of the wicked. (Job 35:12)

The arrogance of man will be brought low and human pride humbled; the LORD alone will be exalted in that day. (Isaiah 2:17)

Proper Parenting

Fathers, do not exasperate your children; instead, bring them up in the training and instruction of the Lord. (Ephesians 6:4)

Fathers, do not embitter your children, or they will become discouraged. (Colossians 3:21)

Start children off on the way they should go, and even when they are old they will not turn from it. (Proverbs 22:6)

Whoever spares the rod hates their children, but the one who loves their children is careful to discipline them. (Proverbs 13:24)

No discipline seems pleasant at the time, but painful. Later on, however, it produces a harvest of righteousness and peace for those who have been trained by it. (Hebrews 12:11)

Discipline your children, and they will give you peace; they will bring you the delights you desire. (Proverbs 29:17)

These commandments that I give you today are to be on your hearts. ⁷ Impress them on your children. Talk about them when you sit at home and when you walk along the road, when you lie down and when you get up. (Deuteronomy 6:6-7)

Children, Honor Your Parents

Children, obey your parents in the Lord, for this is right. ² Honor your father and mother - which is the first commandment with a promise, ³ so that it may go well with you and that you may enjoy long life on the earth. (Ephesians 6:1-3) (Note: This is the only one of the Ten Commandments that includes a promise if it is obeyed.)

Honor your father and your mother, so that you may live long in the land the LORD your God is giving you. (Exodus 20:12) (The Ten Commandments)

Listen, my son, to your father's instruction and do not forsake your mother's teaching. ⁹They are a garland to grace your head and a chain to adorn your neck. (Proverbs 1:8-9)

A rod and reprimand impart wisdom, but a child left undisciplined disgraces its mother. (Proverbs 29:15)

Favoritism/Prejudice

What causes fights and quarrels among you? Don't they come from your desires that battle within you? (James 4:1)

My brothers and sisters, believers in our glorious Lord Jesus Christ must not show favoritism. ² Suppose a man comes into your meeting wearing a gold ring and fine clothes, and a poor man in filthy old clothes also comes in. ³ If you show special attention to the man wearing fine clothes and say, "Here's a good seat for you," but say to the poor man, "You stand there" or "Sit on the floor by my feet," ⁴ have you not discriminated among yourselves and become judges with evil thoughts? (James 2:1-4)

If you really keep the royal law found in Scripture, "Love your neighbor as yourself," you are doing right. ⁹ But if you show favoritism, you sin and are convicted by the law as lawbreakers. ¹⁰ For whoever keeps the whole law and yet stumbles at just one point is guilty of breaking all of it. (James 2:8-10)

Brothers and sisters, do not slander one another. Anyone who speaks against a brother or sister or judges them speaks against the law and judges it. (James 4:11)

Who is wise and understanding among you? Let them show it by their good life, by deeds done in the humility that comes from wisdom. ¹⁴ But if you harbor bitter envy and selfish ambition in your hearts, do not boast about it or deny the truth. ¹⁵ Such "wisdom" does not come down from heaven but is earthly, unspiritual, of the devil. (James 3:13-18)

Stop judging by mere appearances, and make a right judgment. (John 7:24)

Submit yourselves, then, to God. Resist the devil, and he will flee from you. ⁸ Come near to God and he will come near to you. Wash your hands, you sinners, and purify your hearts, you double-minded. (James 4:7-8)

In General

Do not be anxious about anything, but in every situation, by prayer and petition, with thanksgiving, present your requests to God. ⁷ And the peace of God, which transcends all understanding, will guard your hearts and your minds in Christ Jesus. (Philippians 4:6-7)

I know what it is to be in need, and I know what it is to have plenty. I have learned the secret of being content in any and every situation, whether well fed or hungry, whether living in plenty or in want. ¹³ I can do all this through him who gives me strength. (Philippians 4:12-13)

For we do not have a high priest who is unable to empathize with our weaknesses, but we have one who has been tempted in every way, just as we are - yet he did not sin. ¹⁶ Let us then approach God's throne of grace with confidence, so that we may receive mercy and find grace to help us in our time of need. (Hebrews 4:15-16)

*Therefore, since Christ suffered for us in the flesh, arm yourselves also with the same **mind**, for he who has suffered in the flesh has ceased from sin, that he no longer should live the rest of his time in the flesh for the lusts of men, but for the will of God.* (1 Peter 4:1-2)

So then, just as you received Christ Jesus as Lord, continue to live your lives in him, rooted and built up in him, strengthened in the faith as you were taught, and overflowing with thankfulness. (Colossians 2:6-7)

Fear not, for I am with you; be not dismayed, for I am your God; I will strengthen you, I will help you, I will uphold you with my righteous right hand. (Isaiah 41:10)

When you pass through the waters, I will be with you; and through the rivers, they shall not overwhelm you; when you walk through fire you shall not be burned, and the flame shall not consume you. (Isaiah 43:2)

The LORD is my shepherd, I shall not be in want. ² He makes me lie down in green pastures, he leads me beside quiet waters, ³ he refreshes my soul. He guides me in paths of righteousness for his name's sake. ⁴ Even though I walk through the valley of the shadow of death, I will fear no evil, for you are with me; your rod and your staff, they comfort me. ⁵ You prepare a table before me in the presence of my enemies. You anoint my head with oil; my cup overflows. ⁶ Surely your goodness and love will follow me all the days of my life, and I will dwell in the house of the LORD forever. (Psalm 23)

My friends, this is but a small representation of the truth found in God's Word. By providing these Scripture verses, I trust you have come to the realization of the following.

(1) God provided His love letters and short stories as an instruction manual for His greatest creation—mankind. Unfortunately, many still do not know this human handbook exists, refuse to read it, or treat it as a first aid kit and only open the cover in an emergency.

(2) The Bible provides instruction, direction, and correction for every aspect of our lives. We did not and could not cover every challenge that presents itself to humanity, but no matter the circumstance, if your heart truly seeks God's wisdom, you will find the answer in His word.

    a. *But if from there you seek the LORD your God, you will find him if you seek him with all your heart and with all your soul.* (Deuteronomy 4:29)

    b. *So I say to you: Ask and it will be given to you; seek and you will find; knock and the door will be opened to you.* (Luke 11:9)

(3) Scripture can be used to both refute and rebuke the lies of the enemy. If any of the verses offered above align with your current struggle or should the Holy Spirit offer enlightenment from a verse found on your own, write it down, memorize it, and personalize it if necessary. Then meditate on it to refute Satan's lies, and/or, speak it out loud as your double edge sword to rebuke his direct assaults, and he will be forced to flee from you.

(4) **God is immanent.** If you have not heard that term before, it means that God is personable and relatable to those made in His image, while remaining completely distinct and unique from all His creation. He is not a distant deity who sits on a heavenly throne and surveys all of creation with no intent to interact in the affairs of mankind. He is a personal God who created us in His image to be in personal relationship with Him. And remember, God wants you to be victorious!

Before we venture on, I want to introduce one more aspect of "Situational Christianity" that is important for all Christians to understand. To help make my point, I need to return to the previous quotes from Ron Latulippe and Bill Belichick.

Rhema is the application of the logos to a real-life situation, a word appropriate and needed for that moment. So, Paul describes the sword of the Spirit as the *rhema* of God. Like the sword in battle, the soldier of Christ applies the appropriate Word of God to the situation to defend, or wound, or kill as needed. (Ron Latulippe)

"Leadership means building a team that's exhaustively prepared, but able to adjust in an instant. The only sign we have in the locker room is from 'The Art of War.' 'Every battle is won before it is fought.' You have to know what the opponents can do, what their strengths and weaknesses are, and what to do in every situation." (Bill Belichick)

So far, in this conversation regarding the power of God's Word (The sword of the Spirit), we have been focused primarily on the rebuke of Satan's assault in our immediate thought life by quoting Scripture. Even in the example of Jesus' confrontation with Satan in the desert, Jesus rebuked the devil immediately after the temptation to sin was issued. When you look at the first sentence from each of the quotes above, (even though the subject matter is vastly different), you'll notice that the call to preparation is an attempt to equip the individual to act immediately upon being confronted. Take a closer look....

- *Rhema* is the application of the logos to a real-life situation, a word appropriate and needed **for that moment**.
- Leadership means building a team that's exhaustively prepared, but able to adjust **in an instant.**

The supplementary premise of Situational Christianity that I would like to introduce to you was born out of personal experience and then deferred revelation by the Holy Spirit. I did not recognize the confrontation as spiritual warfare during the extended battle, but in hindsight, it became quite clear that the spiritual forces of evil had positioned themselves against God's calling to His people. I won't share all the details here, but the story involves the transition of our small Baptist church in northeast Atlanta.

We averaged about 250 in attendance each Sunday and our metal church building sat on a prime piece of real estate in a fast-growing area. After years of prayer, discussion, and due diligence, we made the decision to sell our property, purchase a new site, and move into a temporary facility as we built a larger church. During the ensuing and complicated multi-year process, Satan threw every possible obstacle in our way including construction delays, financing entanglements, complications with county approvals, and eventually the poison pill of accusation and mistrust among church members and finger pointing toward our pastoral staff.

In the end, the new church was completed, but the sweet spirit of fellowship had been badly tarnished, and attendance was half of what it had been in the old building. The pastoral staff felt betrayed and without spiritually charged leadership, financial difficulty quickly followed. My wife and I moved to Knoxville, TN as the church was struggling to survive and searching for a new pastor.

The moral of the story is this; with much prayer and the sincere desire to be obedient to God's calling, we felt unified and Spirit-led as a congregation when we embarked on this mission. But what we had not done was anticipate the opposing plans of the enemy and prepare ourselves for the spiritual opposition that was sure to confront what God had called us to do. Remember Solomon's quote in Proverbs 20:18? *Make plans by seeking advice; if you wage war, obtain guidance.*

As my personal awareness of spiritual warfare sharpened, I was able to look through the rear-view mirror at this event with a fresh set of spiritual lenses and apply the second principle of Situational Christianity. It is the premise that we can seek wise biblical counsel and prepare ourselves for spiritual confrontations *before* they happen. Look again at the second half of these quotes from Ron Latulippe and Bill Belichick.

- Like the sword in battle, the soldier of Christ applies the appropriate Word of God to the situation to defend..., as needed.

- The only sign we have in the locker room is from *The Art of War*. 'Every battle is won before it is fought.' You have to know what the opponents can do, what their strengths and weaknesses are, and what to do in every situation."

Did you catch that? Every battle is won before it is fought, and as we endeavor to follow God's leading, we can appropriate the Word of God, as needed, to defend against the certain onslaught from Satan - before it happens. Okay Jeff, once again, this sounds great in theory, but what does the practical application of this premise look like? Well, I'm glad you asked.

There are countless examples that we could choose from as we attempt to follow God's individual plans for our lives but let me use marriage as an illustration. We know that God ordained marriage between a man and a woman as a holy sacrament, meant to honor and glorify Him. There are boundaries within that sacrament that include a lifelong commitment among the marriage partners without divorce, a promise to refrain from sexual activity outside the marriage, a commitment to honor and cherish your spouse and to put their needs before your own, and the expectation that your love will prevail during good times and bad.

Relevant to our study, this is God's will for your marriage, and if God ordained your marriage, He wants your marriage to prosper. With that in mind, what do you suppose Satan's agenda might be toward your marriage—or do I even need to ask? If you already know the answer to that question, let me apply the concept of Situational Christianity to win the battle before it is fought. Look again at the quote from 'The Art of War.'

> ➤ You have to know what the opponents can do, what their strengths and weaknesses are, and what to do in every situation.

Therefore, might it be a good idea to seek wise biblical counsel, sit down with your spouse prior to your wedding and begin to make a list of all the possible ways Satan might attack or come against God's plan for your marriage? When you think about it, the enemy's tactics have not changed for thousands of years and really are quite predictable. I would imagine the list of things to avoid might look something like this.

- ✓ Any temptation that opens the path to adultery
    - ➤ Continuing or renewing a relationship with a previous boyfriend/girlfriend
    - ➤ Flirting with a neighbor, coworker, church member, etc.
    - ➤ Withholding sexual relations from your spouse
- ✓ Any temptation that opens the door to financial difficulty
    - ➤ Failure to discuss marital finances
    - ➤ Needless spending and/or accumulating too much debt
    - ➤ Gambling, sports betting, etc.
- ✓ Any activity that draws undue time and attention away from your spouse
    - ➤ Excessive girls/boys' night out activities
    - ➤ Hobbies (sports, yoga, card games, music groups, etc.)

- ➢ Excessive dedication to career advancement
- ➢ Improper vertical alignment—placing children before your spouse
- ✓ Any activity that has the potential for addictive behavior
  - ➢ Alcohol, drugs, pornography
  - ➢ Excessive collecting, hoarding
- ✓ Any temptation or activity that causes you to lie to your spouse
- ✓ Any temptation that causes you to be lazy, unproductive, slothful, unkempt, etc.
- ✓ Any temptation to dwell on negative thoughts regarding your spouse.
  - ➢ Holding a grudge
  - ➢ Unforgiveness
  - ➢ Unfair comparisons to someone else
- ✓ Any temptation that leads to a lack of communication (the silent treatment)

Now trust me, I am not trying to teach a marriage seminar here, however, if we really set our minds to it, we could probably add to the list (which by the way is not a bad idea for any engaged or married couple). What I do hope you see and understand in this example is that by taking a few precautionary steps, we have in essence created a list of what our opponents (Satan and his demons) might do in opposition to God's plan for your marriage.

Creating the list in advance should sharpen our awareness of potential attacks and increase our ability to discern the early stages of temptation. It also provides an opportunity to develop a battle plan for how to defend ourselves in every situation. And by doing so, we have an opportunity to win the battle before it is fought.

This is a strategy that has been used by the world's military powers for centuries. The more you know about your enemy the better you can anticipate their battle plan. As Christians, we have enlisted in

God's army, and He has given each of us an individual assignment and unique abilities to carry out that mission. Now think about applying this principle to your specific calling. Could you develop a similar list of potential temptations for the following?

- ✓ Serving as a member of a church staff (pastor, deacon, operations, administrative)
- ✓ Serving as a full time or part time missionary
- ✓ Serving as an evangelist
- ✓ Serving in a charitable organization
- ✓ Serving as a Christian business leader
- ✓ Serving as a Christian entertainer
- ✓ Serving as a Christian parent
- ✓ Serving as a Christian student
- ✓ Organizing any Christian event (large or small)

Again, the list could go on, but the principle of Situational Christianity can be applied in any mission calling from the Lord. If you have never considered this principle before, I strongly encourage you to incorporate this simple strategy and prepare yourself to win the spiritual battle before it is fought. Let me close this section with the words of Jesus as recorded in Matthew, Chapter 7.

> *"Therefore everyone who hears these words of mine and puts them into practice is like a wise man who built his house on the rock."* *25 The rain came down, the streams rose, and the winds blew and beat against that house; yet it did not fall, because it had its foundation on the rock. 26 But everyone who hears these words of mine and does not put them into practice is like a foolish man who built his house on sand. 27 The rain came down, the streams rose, and the winds blew and beat against that house, and it fell with a great crash. "* (Matthew 7:24)

The decision is quite simple. Prepare yourself in advance for the spiritual storm that is sure to come. Build a rock-solid foundation under the mission God has called you to fulfill. Otherwise, fail to prepare and when the spiritual storm hits, watch your work fall with a great crash. I pray you will choose the former.

Our study surrounding the power of the spoken word from a spiritual perspective has been extensive and I trust it will provide immediate and future benefit as you continue your walk with the Lord. As we continue in this area of study, our final section on 'How to Fight—How to Win' will include the scientific reasons why repetitive speech is effective in spiritual warfare as well as how it works in directing (or re-directing) your lifestyle. I hope you will join me as we contemplate; **The Power of the Spoken Word—Faith Supported by Science.**

1. Notes on the Bible—Albert Barnes/Matthew 6:13. (1834) Retrieved from https://www.sacred-texts.com/bib/cmt/barnes/mat006.htm
2. Neil Anderson, *Daily in Christ/Our Defense Against Satan* (Eugene: Harvest House Publishers, 1993) May 21

Chapter 13: The Power of the Spoken Word —Faith Supported by Science

As we explore the scientific reasons why repetitive speech is effective and how it works in directing (or re-directing) our lives, we are not about to abandon our basis in Scripture. The debate over scientific evidence and biblical faith started hundreds of years ago and continues today. While many would argue the two are incompatible, those with an open mind to biblical truth find that the majority of scientific, geological, and archeological discoveries support and/or reinforce the God of the Bible (Almighty God) as the Creator and Sustainer of all we know about our existence.

There was a simple saying in the early church that proclaimed, 'All truth is God's truth.' Properly interpreted it means that if we understand the Bible correctly, and if we understand scientific data correctly, they will not contradict each other. God is the author of both scriptural truth and scientific truth. (Note: This text was revised from an article in the series: 'Bible vs. Science' by Marshall Shelley.) (https://www.christianitytoday.com/iyf/advice/faithqa/Bible-vs-science.html) [1]

While the Bible has been proven over and over again as a historical record of God's interaction with His creation, as Christians we do not preface the Bible as a scientific resource, but instead as our instruction manual for living a victorious Christian lifestyle. However, as we continue to study the power of the spoken word, there is a sound scientific principle that absolutely supports what the Bible teaches us about employing the spoken word as an effective offensive weapon in the battle for controlling our thoughts. Earlier in our discussion of the creation story, we highlighted the fact that God *spoke* the universe into existence and the words He spoke became reality.

It is vital that we understand the significance of that statement. God's power was manifested through His spoken word, and we were created with an expectation to imitate our Creator. Words matter to God, and He wants them to matter to us because our words also have power to influence (direct or redirect) our spiritual and temporal reality. Remember, the simple expression of heartfelt repentance when voiced through the sinner's prayer has the power to alter your *eternal* destiny. Likewise, our ability to shape our *temporal* reality with our words is also a reflection of God's power in us. Notice the contrasting verses below as penned by Solomon.

> *From the fruit of their mouth a person's stomach is filled; with the harvest of their lips they are satisfied. The tongue has the power of life and death, and those who love it will eat its fruit.* (Proverbs 18:20-21)

> [4] *The words of a man's mouth are deep waters.* [6] *The lips of fools bring them strife, and their mouths invite a beating.* [7] *The mouths of fools are their undoing, and their lips are a snare to their lives.* (Proverbs 18:4, 6, 7)

Now, before we go any further, we need to set the appropriate parameters for our conversation. I do not want our discussion to be interpreted in any way as a 'name-it-and-claim-it' proposition.

1. We were created in the *likeness* of God, and while we should reflect His characteristics, there are limitations to what our words can accomplish in this life.

2. Our words have power to *influence* our temporal reality. We have the ability to dream, invent, and develop portions of our reality through the reasoning skills provided to us by God, but we do not have the

ability to create something out of nothing by simply speaking it into existence.

3. Our ability to shape our world with our words *reflects* God's power in us. That is a marvelous truth, but we are not God! He is the Potter, and we are the clay. We remain within the boundaries of God's will for our lives. I once heard a wise counselor say if you could resurrect every famous inventor and scientist from the past and put them in a room with all the best-known inventors and scientists of today and give them one task—create a single blade of grass without using any of earth's existing elements or chemicals—they would not be able to do it. (Ponder on that for a minute.)

For the purpose of this chapter, we need to make a significant revision to our diagram. Prior to this, our discussion concerning the power of the spoken word has been centered around rebuking the lies of the enemy. But Scripture would also indicate, and science will confirm, that our words can and do influence our thoughts. Notice the progression of influence below now includes an additional step.

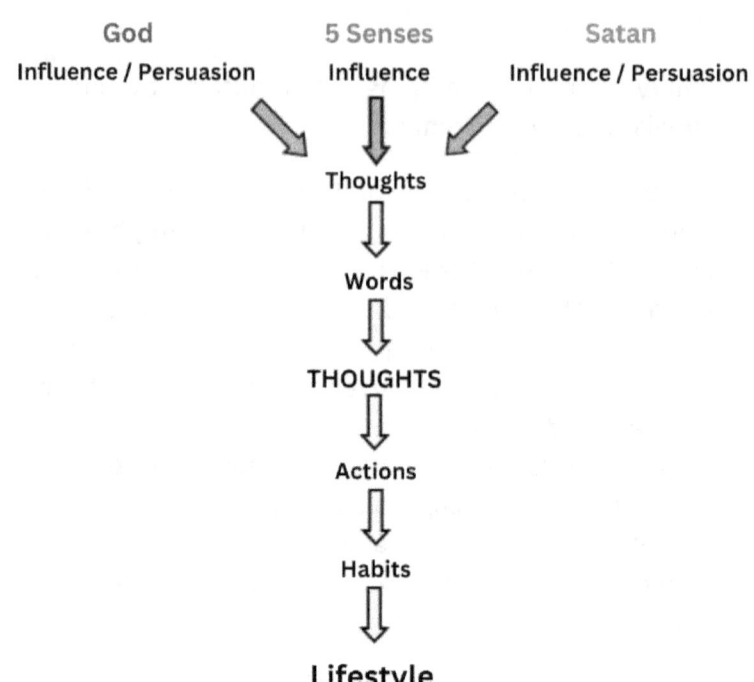

God   5 Senses   Satan
Influence / Persuasion   Influence   Influence / Persuasion

Thoughts

Words

THOUGHTS

Actions

Habits

Lifestyle

For a scriptural reference, we return to the previous verse highlighted in Hebrews. This time, however, we will focus our attention on the later part of the verse.

> *For the word of God is alive and active. Sharper than any double-edged sword, it penetrates even to dividing soul and spirit, joints, and marrow; it judges the thoughts and attitudes of the heart* (mind). *(Hebrews 4-12) (Emphasis added.)*

The *Layman's Bible Commentary Set* shares the following regarding this verse. "The phrase 'soul and spirit, joints, and marrow' is a simple way to refer to the inner life of a human being in all its aspects." [2] In this conversation, our mind is the 'aspect' we need to focus on. The spoken word has the ability to judge (change) our thoughts and affect, alter, or renew the attitude of our heart. How do we do that?

Let me explain once again by referencing my personal struggle. Earlier I stated that my mind had become the battlefield and God's Word became my primary weapon. Every time a thought of condemnation would come into my mind that was contrary to the will of God, I would speak out loud, "I consider that my present suffering is not worth comparing with the glory that will be revealed in me!"

That personalized Scripture verse, spoken out loud from my mouth, had a dual purpose as well as a dual consequence. First, it adamantly and forcibly rebuked the assault coming from the enemy and caused Satan to flee. By repeating this verse each time the enemy attacked, his evil influence and condemnation were completely obliterated and only the *attitude* of the Lord remained, which is joy. The continued study of God's Word only strengthened my resolve that the Word of God is alive and active, and that learning how to use it to rebuke Satan's lies is essential for every Christian who endeavors to live victoriously in Christ Jesus. You may remember this previous quote from Derek Prince as referenced in 'The Power and Privilege of Prayer.'

> The mouth is the primary channel for releasing our spiritual weapons against Satan's kingdom. It is praise that ascends through the heavenlies, reaches the throne of God, and silences Satan's accusations against us. **If we do not learn to use our mouths, we cannot win the war.**[3]

Second, but just as important, hearing my own voice boldly proclaiming victory altered my thought process from my present suffering and caused my mind to focus on the future glory promised to me through Jesus Christ (whatever that might be). For a scientific reference, let me point back to a portion of "Press on Toward the Goal" and an excerpt from "A Walk Through the Human Mind" as copied from *The Mind Unleashed*.

The ability of your conscious mind to direct your attention and awareness is one of the *most important powers you have.* To create change in your life you must learn to control what you consciously focus on. *Deciding* how you will think and what thoughts you will *allow* into your mind will determine your destiny. It can literally be used for good or evil, for constructive or destructive means. [4]

Once again, the question presents itself. How do we do that? Here, the spiritual and the scientific once again align themselves to provide the answer. In the revised order of our diagram, **our words can be used to change our thought patterns**. Think about it. Have you ever tried to think two thoughts at the same time? Take a minute or two and try it now. If you are like me, you will not be able to do it. As soon as I try to entertain a new thought, the original thought is displaced by the new one.

Here is another simple question—has your thought pattern or conversation ever been disrupted by a loud noise, perhaps a clap of thunder or an unexpected shout? In my current daytime profession, my first-floor office window looks out onto a major intersection. There have been several occasions when the unmistakable sound of screeching tires and crunching metal have immediately altered my thought process.

We have not focused on this component of our diagram, but remember, our five senses do have the ability to influence our thinking. With that said, spoken words are sound, and the words that come out of your mouth go into your own ears. Words are the vehicle for change (good or evil), and as stated above, we can decide how and what we will think about. **The simplest way to influence our thoughts is to speak positive words into our own lives.** Zig Ziglar used to famously say, "There is power in words. What you say is what you get." There is a reason why motivational speakers promote this practice, but only recently have we really been able to understand why it works.

Like it or not, the words that come out of your mouth have control of your life. **What comes out of your mouth will determine your future**. Physiologically, psychologically, and scientifically, there is an immense amount of research and material to substantiate this truth. As Christians, it is important we understand that the words proceeding from our mouths should be directed in a way that will always honor and agree with God's Word, but from a temporal perspective, they can also change our thoughts. Therefore, if our words can change our thoughts, we can apply the principles of this study and know that our words are capable of directly influencing our lifestyles (for good or evil).

> *If we understood the power of our thoughts, we would guard them more closely. If we understood the awesome power of our words, we would prefer silence to almost anything negative. In our thoughts and words, we create our own weaknesses and our own strengths.* —Betty Eadie

We see a marvelous example of this in Psalm 42. While a vast majority of the psalms were written by King David, there are ten that were written by the sons of Korah, including Psalm 42. The Sons of Korah were Levites and during David's reign, Scripture indicates that they served in the temple worship as musicians and singers. In this psalm we find a soul lost in thoughts of despair but then transforming the attitude of the heart by outwardly declaring praise to God.

> *⁵Why, my soul, are you downcast? Why so disturbed within me? Put your hope in God, for I will yet praise him, my Savior and my God. ⁸ By day the LORD directs his love, at night his song is with me - a prayer to*

the God of my life. [11] Why, my soul, are you downcast? Why so disturbed within me? Put your hope in God, for I will yet praise him, my Savior and my God. (Psalm 42:5, 8, 11)

As we continue our march toward the assurance of victory, my sincere hope is that this study material has provided sufficient truth from God's Word to validate the fact that we are all capable of controlling our thought processes. The goal going forward is to align what the scientific world has discovered about repetitive speech (commonly referred to as self-talk) and how it supports what Scripture tells us about the power of the spoken word. Remember, we are now focused on the progression of influence as follows:

Thoughts ➡ words ➡ thoughts ➡ actions

Scientific research on the human brain and how it functions has advanced by leaps and bounds over the last twenty years, and there are volumes of recorded data available for self-study. While dated, two books I read years ago contribute to the formation of this entire study. They are *What to Say When You Talk to Your Self* and *Who Are You Really and What Do You Want?* Both were written by Dr. Shad Helmstetter.

Shad Helmstetter, Ph. D., is the best-selling author of more than twenty books in the field of personal growth, including the recent *The Power of Neuroplasticity*. He is the founder of The Self-Talk Institute, which teaches individuals to present self-talk training to groups and organizations, and The Life Coach Institute, which trains and certifies life and business coaches in the U. S. and internationally. Writing in clear, layperson language, Shad introduces the concept of self-talk to the general public. He set the stage for the use of self-talk programming to take its place at the forefront of personal development. For more information on Dr. Helmstetter, visit http://shadhelmstetter.com/.

In full disclosure, these are the only two books that I have read on the topic, and like many of the other books that helped formulate this study, I read them years ago and highlighted what I deemed important at the time. As you read the following, please understand, this is not meant to be a full dissertation on Dr. Helmstetter's life's work nor a comprehensive outline of the research available. However, I do believe that what I understand and share of his writings will corroborate my earlier statement that there is a sound scientific principle that absolutely supports what the Bible teaches us about employing the spoken word as an effective offensive weapon in the battle for controlling our thoughts and ultimately in leading us to walk victoriously as Christians.

The common interpretation of Psalm 23:7 is understood *'as a man thinketh, so is he.'* To many, that would seem an oversimplification. Could our lives possibly be determined simply by what we think? For most, it would seem our thought life is one thing, but our physical life is completely separate. However, as the Bible tends to do, this passage hits the nail squarely on the head. Like many other human discoveries, it would take until the twentieth century for the research of modern-day neuroscientists to unlock the miracle of the human mind and prove how accurate that Biblical passage had been.

In the last two decades, science has discovered more about the function of the human brain than in all previous history combined. By way of a complex physiological process incorporating body, brain, and mind, we become the living consequence of our own thoughts. The relationship between our mental programming and whether we will succeed or fail (whatever those definitions might mean to you, and applied to whatever endeavor you might undertake) is now scientific fact. And you may apply that reality to a long-term goal or simply the objective of the day.

Many of you reading this for the first time may be shocked at this simple statement; **you will become what you think about most**. The reality of human behavior is that your success or failure in any endeavor is heavily influenced by your brain's programming. That temporal programming may be received by others, or it may be developed by what you say when you talk to yourself (consciously or subconsciously). The brain believes whatever consistent programming it receives. And what you allow as testimony about yourself, it will create. Functioning as God designed it, the brain has no choice but to act upon that assertion.

Science has now proven this to be fact and not theory. With our minds, we control most everything in our lives. This includes our health, our personal or professional endeavors, our relationships, and yes, our futures. This truth leads to an interesting question. As we delve deeper into this understanding of the relationship between the influence on our thoughts and the eventual outcome of our lives, could we, in reality, learn how to control our thoughts, override our old programming, and replace it with a specific, word-driven new program? The answer is yes! Simply changing how we receive influence from others, and/or, taking control over our own thoughts and self-talk, will determine our success or failure in this life.

This scientific fact couldn't be more aligned with the truth of Scripture and the foundational premise of this study—'*take captive every thought.*' In his letters, Paul repeats this premise several times, mostly directly in his letter to the Ephesians.

You were taught, with regard to your former way of life, to put off your old self, which is being corrupted by its deceitful desires; [23] *to be made new in the attitude of your minds;* [24] *and to put on the new self, created to be like God in true righteousness and holiness.* (Ephesians 4:22-24)

Before we continue, and to align this text with the premise of our study, there is an important distinction that bears mentioning. As stated earlier, I have not read the complete writings of Dr. Helmstetter, and while his subsequent books may include some spiritual component to his research, the origin of the mind's "influence" and/or "programming" that is referenced in this brief introduction initiates from only one area of our diagram—our five senses.

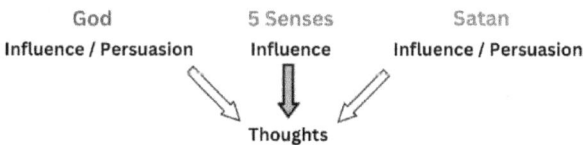

I do not point out this distinction as a discrepancy to the previously stated fact. I believe the science is indisputable and reinforces how our faith is supported by current scientific research. However, prior to the realization of spiritual influence presented in this study, most of the negative programming that we receive comes by way of our five senses. It may have been offered by our parents, our siblings, our co-workers, our spouses, or significant others. Additional sources would include TV shows, news media, social media, and the Internet. Some programming is derogatory or critical and easy to identify. Some programming is suggestive, and you may not perceive it as harmful. Whether intentional or unintentional in its origin, the programming still gets inputted into our brains.

What is important to understand is that your brain is designed to accept whatever you put into it. Remember the analogy from *The Mind Unleashed*. The brain acts like a giant computer hard drive.

Whatever we allow in through our five senses is stored permanently. Whether that information is true or false, positive or negative, good or evil, it is stored at the subconscious or unconscious level. And what your brain receives repeatedly, it automatically accepts as truth.

This incredibly powerful control center is capable of producing any reasonable outcome that you would like it to do, but you have to learn how to program it correctly. If you feed your brain proper information, it will direct you to positive outcomes. If you repeatedly allow false or misleading information, your brain will also act accordingly and respond to that negative programming, most often without you even being aware of it. Sadly, our world is full of bad outcomes for individuals who never understand the power God gives us to control what our minds consume from temporal influence.

I encourage you not to be dissuaded by this brief, one-faceted approach to what has influence over our thought processes. Even though the spiritual component is not considered in this text, it has set the foundation for our discussion on why the spoken word plays such an important part in directing our lives, whether the negative is coming from a temporal or spiritual adversary.

You may be asking, "How does all this work?" Without getting too technical, we'll allow Dr. Helmstetter to give us a brief explanation of how the brain works, then we'll learn how to apply the remedy to negative influence and/or programming.

> Within the brain, a network of tens of billions of neurons, and electrochemical switches called neurotransmitters, telegraph messages to every part of the brain, selecting just the right section of switches, which turn parts of us "on" and parts of us "off."

The brain's microscopic chemical receiving centers respond to almost imperceptible electrochemical signals which deliver nearly unmeasurable but highly potent chemical substances to our brain, our central nervous system, and to our bodies—which in turn control or affect everything we do.

It is the brain's responsibility to take care of us by constantly monitoring our needs and directing the various systems to take the necessary action. The brain automatically responds to every one of our unconscious electrical/chemical, mental and physical commands— those that are principally concerned with keeping us alive.

*But the brain automatically responds to another command—another compelling electrical impulse which also turns the switches in the brain on or off. **Those electrical impulses, those special mental commands which direct and control us, are called thoughts.***

*<u>**Every thought**</u> we think, every conscious or unconscious thought we say to ourselves, is translated into electrical impulses which in turn, direct the control centers in our brains to electrically and chemically affect and control every motion, every feeling, every action we take, every moment of every day. Whatever "thoughts" you have programmed into yourself or have allowed others to program into you, are affecting, directing, or controlling everything about you. Some of the programming is obvious, **but much of it we are never aware of receiving.***
[5] (Condensed from *What to Say When You Talk to Your Self*, Pages 38—40)

Remember, what Dr. Helmstetter just described is not theory; it is a medical, neurological, and scientific fact. With the advancement in medical imaging technology, doctors and scientists can monitor this programming process in the neuron structure of the brain while it's happening. As I've done before, allow me to share an analogy to illustrate what professionals now see in this advanced imaging of the human brain. It is an illustration from my childhood, and I can still picture this in my mind.

Like most neighborhoods, mine included a large field that was vacant, but also included a direct route to places I frequently needed to go. In the spring, when the grass quickly became overgrown, I would cut through the field on my way to a friend's house. The first time I walked through the field it didn't leave much of an impression in the grass. By approximating my previous course, the second and third trip still didn't have much of an impact on the resilient meadow.

As the weeks went by, playing with friends often led me on the same route. Now, there was the beginning of a pathway. When leaving or coming home, I would walk the same trail. Over time, the trail became well defined and the clearest route to follow. I had walked or run over that same pathway so many times, it became a habit, and without thinking about it, I was carving deeper into the grass with each trip.

Now, imagine walking through that field represents the programming in your brain. The first time you receive a new thought or hear a suggestion, it doesn't leave much of an impression in your brain. But if you allow the same programming repeatedly, the pathway becomes clearer, and the program becomes more developed. What scientists discovered is that each time that program (thought) is repeated, you are sending chemical nutrients to specific neural pathways in your brain, and those pathways become more developed over time, just like the path through the field.

This extremely well-documented process of how our brain creates these neuro pathways is called Neuroplasticity. In her book *Brain Matters: How to Help Anyone Learn Anything Using Neuroscience*, author Margie Meacham provides a brief explanation of this term. Also known as "The Brain Lady," Meacham earned her master's degree in learning technologies from Capella University and is currently developing a new master's program in educational technology for American Business and Technology University (ABTU).

She uses brain science to help people learn more efficiently and effectively. Her course designs have been implemented at many Fortune 500 companies and online universities. Meacham also writes a neuroscience blog for the Association of Talent Development (ATD) Science of Learning Community of Practice.

> *Neuroplasticity is the term used to describe how the brain continues to re-invent itself. Older, unused pathways fall away, and new ones, <u>with repetition and focus,</u> emerge. What we think about actually rewires our brains—for better or worse. We now know that **our choice of words** has a direct and immediate effect on our emotional response and makes our brains inclined to respond in specific ways. This is true whether we are reacting to spoken words delivered by someone else, or to the inner self-talk that we hear ourselves "saying" inside our heads.*
> [6] (https://www.td.org/insights/how-words-affect-our-brains)

As mentioned previously, Dr. Helmstetter recently wrote a book on the same topic called *The Power of Neuroplasticity*. At the time I was writing this portion of our study, I had not read either book but did expect that they would both be on my reading list in the near future. Quoting from his second book, Dr. Helmstetter states:

> I learned that although our personal computers are designed to be programmed, they are also designed to let us change those programs. And now we know how to do exactly that. [7] (Who Are You Really and What Do You Want, Page 25)

If you're not experiencing the full fruits of your profession of faith in Jesus Christ, then perhaps it is the negative programs you're allowing from the world, the flesh, or the devil to influence your lifestyle. If you desire to do better in your walk as a Christian, or in any other area of your life, it will only make sense to change your programming. Directly in line with our diagram, your programming affects your beliefs, your words, your actions, your habits, and your results (your lifestyle). So, to make any lasting change, start by making sure you have the proper programs and correct associations that will affect that change.

As I shared about taking my driver's license test, the first step is to become consciously aware of the negative influence in your life and where it is coming from. With repeated effort, overcoming those thoughts will open the door for positive programming to begin. When that positive programming becomes a habit, you will experience significant change in whatever aspect of your life you seek to improve.

As if we didn't already realize it, just this short dissertation confirms what an amazing control center God created in our brains. And because it functions so effortlessly most of the time, it is easy for us to take this miracle for granted. Consider for a minute all the bodily functions that our brain controls without any conscious effort on our parts (those that are principally concerned with keeping us alive). Could you imagine what your day would be like if you had to remind yourself to do the following every few seconds?

- ✓ Okay lungs, take a breath (inhale, now exhale).
- ✓ Okay heart, beat a few times and circulate blood throughout my body.
- ✓ Okay eyes, blink a few times to facilitate my sight.
- ✓ Okay muscles, move in just the right sequence so I can [fill in the blank].
- ✓ Now, repeat!

All these electrical and chemical impulses are going on behind the scenes, yet our brains still have the capacity to respond to another set of directions—our thoughts. Of course, while we instinctively know and understand that a failure in any of these automatic functions can have dire consequences, it is rather amazing that we give such little consideration to the potential positive or negative effects of our thoughts. I suppose it is rather redundant at this point, but I found it quite interesting how Dr. Helmstetter's scientific conclusion aligns itself with the entire spiritual premise of our study.

> *Every thought we think, every conscious or unconscious thought we say to ourselves, is translated into electrical impulses which in turn, direct the control centers In our brains to electrically and chemically affect and control every motion, every feeling, every action we take, every moment of every day. Whatever "thoughts" you have programmed into yourself or have allowed others to program into you are affecting, directing, or controlling everything about you. Some of the programming is obvious, but much of it we are never even aware of receiving.*

Did you happen to notice the number of times 'every' is used in the statement above, starting with 'every thought'? Based on this proven scientific principle, our thoughts will affect *everything* about our lifestyles. Whether we are reflecting on temporal or spiritual persuasion upon our minds, it is frightening to realize that without the proper training, we can find ourselves ignorant of not only its existence, but of its various origins.

Unless we deliberately identify the negative programs we have now and work to eliminate them, we tend to duplicate more of the same. It is only when we become aware of the harmful programs and their source that we can take the first step toward eliminating them.

In either case, we find God's wisdom and instruction in the foundational verse of this study. In this instance, and as a reversal of this chapter's title, science is now supported by our faith.

> *We demolish arguments and every pretension that sets itself up against the knowledge of God, and we take captive **every thought** to make it obedient to Christ.* (2 Corinthians 10:5)

My friends, let me repeat, the entire premise of this study has been focused on capturing and controlling our _every_ thought as the first step toward living a victorious Christian lifestyle. But only now do we begin to fully understand from a spiritual and temporal perspective that our words are the vital second step in directing, redirecting, and controlling both outcomes. While it is important to monitor and control our own internal self-talk, **what we say to ourselves _out_ _loud_ will change our thought processes.** And if we consistently control our thoughts and our words to align with the Word of God, we can walk victoriously in the will of God.

So then, our self-talk not only includes our inner thoughts, but is also made up of the things we say out loud to ourselves, or the words we use to describe ourselves when talking to someone else. What we say about ourselves, be that positive or negative, plays heavily in programming our subconscious minds. It only makes sense that if our words are counterproductive to God's truth, our brain will act on that information to create any number of negative consequences (Satan's lies). Would it not be better to change your attitude by identifying the negative, changing your programming by speaking positively into your life, and creating God-honoring outcomes?

If you stop and think about it, we make dozens of statements about ourselves in a day's time. It may not seem important to direct your words in a positive light until you begin to consider how they accumulate over a week, a month, or a year. Each one of those statements is influencing your subconscious mind and they add up to thousands of self-directives. Over time, they will have a significant impact on who you become, what you accomplish, and how you view yourself and the world.

So, here is the challenge. Begin to listen to everything you say when you speak out loud (to yourself and others). Part of winning this battle should include using your words to create an attitude of continuous victory over the devil's schemes. It doesn't mean that you won't have problems, but a consistent focus on positive self-talk will produce winning results. Eventually, that change in attitude and learning how to control your words will become second nature, just like walking or riding a bike. And when positive self-talk becomes a habit, you will experience tremendous change in your lifestyle. This is one of the greatest gifts you could ever give yourself, and once mastered, it will be a treasure you will not want to give up.

Of course, what we've learned from this study is that habits are created by repetitive actions. Much like repeating your victory verse every time Satan attacks your mind, the secret to self-improvement is also founded in repetition. Once you develop the appropriate words as a counter offensive to the negative patterns in your life, be prepared to repeat them over and over again. Remember, no soldier every won a battle with a single bullet.

For your self-improvement program to be effective, it must be based on the scientific principles we've just uncovered. If it does not align with the premise of neuroplasticity and how the brain works, then it has no basis in science and it will not last. As a child, you learned the alphabet, animal names, numbers, how to walk and talk, and much more, all by repetition. The concept of self-talk works the same way. **The human brain is designed to learn as it goes along—and the secret to doing that is repetition**. The more often you defend against the negative and repeat the positive, the stronger the new programming becomes, until it is permanently documented in the brain. (Just like walking through that vacant field.)

Brothers and sisters, there is so much more that I could share on this topic and from Dr. Helmstetter's books. If time and self-interest allow, I highly recommend adding them to your personal library and sharing them with the ones you love. I have done my best to select specific areas of scientific research that align with the spiritual truth of our study. In that regard, there is one more quote I would like to share from Dr. Helmstetter. I couldn't resist making application of the quote below to our study diagram.

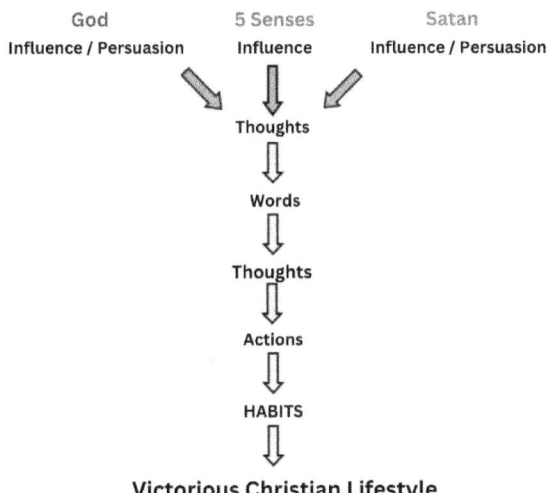

| God | 5 Senses | Satan |
| Influence / Persuasion | Influence | Influence / Persuasion |

Thoughts

Words

Thoughts

Actions

HABITS

Victorious Christian Lifestyle

Most of what you say to yourself is completely without thought. From the moment you wake until you fall asleep, you can have an internal dialogue with yourself without once having to consciously think about what you're saying to yourself; you can go through the entire day with your self-talk on autopilot.

*And yet, during every one of those moments throughout the day, **someone** or something is busy directing, managing, and controlling virtually everything about you. When you get upset at something, or raise your voice at someone, or think you're not up to the task, who do you suppose is in charge?*

At those moments, you're not in charge. Your programs are. When you're not in charge of your programs, your programs are in charge of you. Either you control your self-talk, or it controls you. So, consciously taking control of your own self-talk becomes an incredibly important step. Especially if you want to be in control of your own life, and if you want to have a chance of changing your old programs.

*Making the choice to be aware of every message you give yourself is an important choice. Our unconscious self-talk affects everything we do, from something as seemingly small as getting cross when we're tired, to things as big as which job we apply for. Literally everything in our lives is touched by the influence of our own unconscious self-talk—and thus, by **whomever** or whatever gave that self-talk to us.*

Once we know the truth of that, it shouldn't take a lot of persuasion to convince us to do something about it. [8] (Condensed from *Who Are You Really and What Do You Want*, Pages 47-49)

I don't know about you, but I found the mystery embedded in these last few paragraphs to be quite apparent. Whether by benefit of your previous maturity in understanding biblical truth, or by lessons learned in this study on spiritual warfare, I believe we can eliminate any doubt as to the source of this mysterious *someone* or *whomever* influence.

Our march toward victory in Jesus Christ through the pages of this study has abolished any uncertainty about who stands as our enemy. That "someone" is Satan, and the "unconscious influence" that invades the untrained mind is dispensed by the devil himself and "the spiritual forces of evil in the heavenly realms" (Ephesians 6:12). Knowing that, I couldn't agree more with this author. "Once we know the truth of that, it shouldn't take a lot of persuasion to convince us to do something about it."

I'll finish this chapter with one final quote from Dr. Helmstetter as well as some additional encouragement from God's Word. Let me first repeat the saying from the early church that simply proclaimed, "All truth is God's truth." If we understand the Bible correctly, and if we understand scientific data correctly, they will not contradict each other. God is the author of both scriptural truth and scientific truth.

I have found no contradiction while suggesting that our faith is indeed supported by science in regard to the power of the spoken word. Likewise, and based on the quote below, I find no contradiction that the merging of this scientific fact with a strong spiritual foundation produces a confidence that the enemy can no longer penetrate or defeat. Please take the time to reflect on this truth.

> *Your own Self-Talk to your own inner self is, and always will be, your surest form of inner defense and inner strength.* **Combine that with your personal source of spiritual strength—and no one, nothing can override it.** [9] (Reprinted from *What to Say When You Talk to Your Self*, Page 107)

In the King James Bible, Proverbs 23:7 states, "As (a man) thinketh in his heart, so is he." From the early part of our study, we understood that to control our words, we first needed to control our thoughts. Now, by reinforcing the truth of Scripture with applied science, we have come to understand that our words can play an equally important role in changing our thought processes and as a result, our old programs. Relevant to our study, it is the Word of God that *"judges the thoughts and attitudes of the heart"* (Hebrews 4:12).

> *But what does it say? "The word is near you; it is in your mouth and in your heart, that is, the message concerning faith that we proclaim."* (Romans 10:8)

I encourage you in follow up to this chapter to take some personal study time in the book of Proverbs and pay special attention to every verse that references the mouth, lips, tongue, or words. In fact, if you have never done it before, I suggest you do so with a highlighter in hand. When finished, I believe you will be richly blessed, and I trust you will be inspired to pay close attention to the words that come out of your mouth. I have included a few sample verses below to get you started.

- *The **mouth** of the righteous is a fountain of life.* (Proverbs 10:11)
- *The **tongue** of the righteous is choice silver.* (Proverbs 10:20)
- *From the fruit of his **lips** a man enjoys good things.* (Proverbs 13:2)
- *Pleasant **words** are a honeycomb, sweet to the soul and healing to the bones.* (Proverbs 16:24)

My friends, we have come a long way together. There has been much to learn, and while the application of this knowledge may seem simple, it is not easy. It will take dedication and perseverance to overcome the enemy and begin to realize and take hold of God's calling on your life. But remember the words God spoke to the Israelites, "Now what I am commanding you today is not too difficult for you or beyond your reach." (Deuteronomy 30:11)

In his letter to the church in Corinth, the apostle Paul offered this encouragement.

> *Do you not know that in a race all the runners run, but only one gets the prize? Run in such a way as to get the prize. 25 Everyone who competes in the games goes into strict training. They do it to get a crown that will not last, but we do it to get a crown that will last forever. Therefore, I do not run like someone running aimlessly; I do not fight like a boxer beating the air. 27 No, I strike a blow to my body and make it my slave so that after I have preached*

to others, I myself will not be disqualified for the prize. (1 Corinthians 9:24-27)

We have one chapter remaining and I encourage you to finish strong. For the crown that we pursue is …

The Assurance of Victory!

1. Bible vs. Science—Marshall Shelley. (n. d.) Retrieved from https://www.christianitytoday.com/iyf/advice/faithqa/Bible-vs-science.html
2. *Layman's Bible Commentary Set, Vol. 12—Hebrews thru Revelation* (Uhrichsville: Barbour Publishing, 2008) 24
3. Derek Prince, *Spiritual Warfare* (New Kensington: Whitaker House, 1987), 111
4. The Mind Unleashed - A Walk Through the Human Mind. (n. d.) Retrieved from http://themindunleashed.com/2014/03/conscious-subconscious-unconscious-mind-work.html
5. Shad Helmstetter, *What to Say When You Talk to Your Self* (New York: Pocket Books, 1982) 38-40
6. How Words Affect Our Brains—Margie Meacham. (07/11/2013) Retrieved from https://www.td.org/insights/how-words-affect-our-brains
7. Shad Helmstetter, *Who Are You Really and What Do You Want* (New York: Park Avenue Press, 2003) 25
8. Shad Helmstetter, *Who Are You Really and What Do You Want* (New York: Park Avenue Press, 2003) 47-49
9. Shad Helmstetter, *What to Say When You Talk to Your Self* (New York: Pocket Books, 1982) 107

Chapter 14: Your Assurance of Victory!

Congratulations my friend! It is my sincere hope that through your perseverance in completing this study, you have gained a new level of maturity regarding what may have previously been the *mysterious aura* of spiritual warfare. Even more important, I hope you have increased not only in your personal knowledge of biblical truth, but also in the wisdom and confidence to know that you can defeat Satan's attempts to derail the plans God has in store for your life.

This thorough examination of Scripture was purposely designed to bring you this truth. God wants you to be confident that a Spirit-guided assurance of victory over Satan's schemes is not only available but is also achievable through the power and authority afforded to you in Jesus Christ. The intent of this final chapter is simple yet vital to understand. Just as it has for each of our other topics, God's Word is specific in granting us the assurance of that which we hope for and that which He had destined for us since our profession of faith in Jesus Christ. God wants us to be victorious as Christians!

> *Now faith is confidence in what we hope for and assurance about what we do not see.* (Hebrews 11:1)

By now, the above verse from Hebrews should be quite familiar to you, but one question remains. Specifically, has our diligent study of Scripture increased your faith to a confident assurance that you can, and must, defeat an adversary in a spiritual dimension that you cannot see? The answer to that question lies in the heart of each individual, and its affirmation is imperative. For responding in faith to believe what cannot be seen is essential to the Christian experience. The Bible tells us it is by faith that we believe in Jesus

Christ. If you have taken that first step of faith, can you now believe in the Savior's power to walk victoriously as His disciple? Scripture tells us that you can indeed!

Before we go any further, I would like to offer a simple definition of walking in victory as a child of God and a disciple of Jesus Christ. Relevant to spiritual warfare, victory is the confident assurance that you can get beyond the fiery arrows (the lies, temptations, and accusations of the devil) to pursue all that God has in store for you. Once Satan realizes that you can identify and discern his negative influence, capture each thought to make it obedient to Christ, and consistently stand firm in your faith by quoting Scripture to rebuke his attacks, he will flee from you and shift his attention to those still ill-equipped to defend themselves.

> *Submit yourselves, then, to God. Resist the devil, and he will flee from you.* (James 4:7)

But along with this promise comes a word of caution. We are never invincible in our own power, nor should we become prideful and let our guard down. However, we can walk in the assurance of victory if we remain grafted into the Vine and under the authority of Jesus Christ. This requires that we regularly die to self and the negative influence of our flesh (our old patterns). This means saying **no** to thoughts, attitudes or actions that you know are of demonic or worldly influence. By remaining strong in your faith, you can die to self and let the Spirit of God live through you. By way of humble submission and after every true death to self, there comes a new release of God's presence in your life, like building blocks of confidence.

Now, I'll be the first to admit that dying to self is not an easy process. As creatures of habit, it can be difficult at times to give up comfortable old patterns. If we are being honest, it is quite common for us to assume that God is willing to compromise on one or two behaviors that we hold dear. However, if we continue to negotiate with the Spirit working within us and choose to obey self rather than God, we relinquish the power of Christ available to us and diminish the hope of victory. The author of Hebrews understood this and offers a powerful encouragement to remain faithful in Jesus Christ.

> Therefore, brothers and sisters, since we have confidence to enter the Most Holy Place by the blood of Jesus, **20** by a new and living way opened for us through the curtain, that is, his body, **21** and since we have a great priest over the house of God, **22** let us draw near to God with a sincere heart and with the <u>full</u> <u>assurance</u> that faith brings, having our hearts sprinkled to cleanse us from a guilty conscience and having our bodies washed with pure water. **23** Let us hold unswervingly to the hope we profess, for he who <u>promised</u> is faithful. **35** So do not throw away your confidence; it will be richly rewarded. **36** You need to persevere so that when you have done the will of God, you will receive what he has promised. (Hebrews 10:19-23, 35-36)

Allow me to humbly paraphrase that for you. Since we have the utmost confidence in the saving power of Jesus Christ and in His authority over all of God's creation (including the demonic), we can walk in the full assurance that He who promised us salvation through His Son has cleansed us of all unrighteousness and opened the doorway to a personal relationship with Himself, God the Father. Knowing that He is faithful to walk alongside us, we invite and embody His presence as we pursue victorious Christian life.

In the above example, and throughout the course of this study, I have taken occasion to dissect several passages of Scripture to gain a more complete understanding of how those verses related to our topic of spiritual warfare. As we move forward in our discussion, I would like to apply that same method to the opening paragraph of this section. I believe a momentary review will not only highlight some particularly important aspects of our journey but also add validity to the race we have run and the crown we are now prepared to unveil to a lost and dying world—living a victorious Christian lifestyle. Let me start with the reference to our spiritual maturity.

If you remember from early in our study, we discovered several references in the Bible that speak to the concept of spiritual maturity. As Christians, we each mature at a different pace, and there are many areas of daily Christian life that require guidance from the Holy Spirit to bring us closer to the image of Christ. In his letter to the Corinthians, while Paul addresses unrest in the New Testament church (over leadership preferences), he says the following.

> Brothers and sisters, I could not address you as people who live by the Spirit but as people who are still worldly— mere infants in Christ. I gave you milk, not solid food, for you were not yet ready for it. (1 Corinthians 3:1-2)

This concept is again addressed in Hebrews.

> Anyone who lives on milk, being still an infant, is not acquainted with the teaching about righteousness. (Hebrews 5:13)

In an attempt at relevancy for all Christians, our study began with basic, first level theological priorities and a simple diagram to lay the foundation for our entire thesis. From there, the truth of Scripture began forming the framework for our spiritual shelter. The addition of well thought-out biblical and secular commentary added utility to our structure. Next, the promise of protection came by way of practical instruction from Jesus, the apostles, and the Old Testament patriarchs of the Bible. Finally, wisdom and discernment from the Holy Spirit granted keen insight into the moment-by-moment application of God's Word, appropriate to any situation of temptation or condemnation, and with authority to defeat the devil's schemes. The result of this diligent pursuit and application is that we have built our spiritual foundation (*the teaching about righteousness*) on solid rock.

> The LORD is my rock, my fortress and my deliverer; my God is my rock, in whom I take refuge, my shield and the horn of my salvation, my stronghold. (Psalm 18:2)

Notice the terms David uses to describe God—strength, rock, fortress, deliverer, shield, horn of salvation, stronghold. These are all images of power, yet our God is both accessible and personal. We need to rejoice my friends, as did David, for the power of our God is made available to us through His Son, Jesus Christ, to deliver us from our most aggressive spiritual enemy—Satan. And when we stand firm in the truth of the Gospel, Jesus himself gave us this assurance.

> Everyone then who hears these words of mine and does them will be like a wise man who built his house on the rock. ²⁵ And the rain fell, and the floods came, and the winds blew and beat on that house, but it did not fall, because it had been founded on the rock. (Matthew 7:24-25)

A firm foundation in any aspect of life builds confidence, whether it be in marriage, family, career, or faith. I have often heard that it takes an average of seven years to be fully competent in your career. In the business world, anyone beyond seven years is referred to as a *mature* professional. The consensus by that point is that you have probably experienced most of the good, bad, and ugly that can happen in your line of work, and if you do happen to be caught off guard, you have gained sufficient skills to successfully navigate through that new challenge.

Of course, the goal of this training has been to create *mature* Christians. I doubt it has taken you seven years to complete this study, but what we have learned in our limited time together can produce the same result. Going forward, the time necessary to achieve that result is up to each individual, and the determining factor can be found in the quote we just referenced from Matthew 7:24, "Everyone then who hears these words of mine and **does them** will be like a wise man."

We find a similar encouragement in James 1:22, "Do not merely listen to the word, and so deceive yourselves. **Do what it says."** One does not reach maturity by mere acquisition of knowledge. He or she attains maturity by the recurrent application of that knowledge in daily life. What I hope to convey in the next few Scripture verses is a continuation of the Prerequisite Principle.

> *But whoever looks intently into the perfect law that gives freedom and continues in it - not forgetting what they have heard **but doing it** - they will be blessed in what they do.* (James 1:25)

If you will apply all that you have learned about spiritual warfare and how to defeat the enemy, God's promise to a mature Christian is clear. You can walk in the assurance of victory. Remember, "*Rhema* is the application of the *logos* to a real-life situation." Spiritual maturity is attained by the continual application of knowledge. Notice the verse immediately following Hebrews 5:13.

> *Anyone who lives on milk, being still an infant, is not acquainted with the teaching about righteousness.* **14** *But solid food is for the mature, **who by constant use** have trained themselves to distinguish good from evil.* (Hebrews 5:13-14)

As I read these verses, I couldn't help but draw the parallels found in Paul's letter to the Colossians. Notice how Paul emphasized the same two points in his message to the new believers in Colossi.

Once you were alienated from God and were enemies in your minds because of your evil behavior. But now He has reconciled you by Christ's physical body through death to present you holy in his sight, without blemish and free from accusation - if you continue in your faith, established and firm, and do not move from the hope held out in the gospel. (Colossians 1:21-23)

If it has not become apparent to you yet, the Scripture verses we have quoted so far and those that follow all hold a promise. The promise is the assurance of victory through spiritual maturity, but notice also that the prerequisite of a mature Christian is the *continual* application of your faith. If necessary, take the time to read them again, and then pay close attention as we continue to reveal God's promise of victory to those who have disciplined their minds to accept only the proper influence.

You will keep in perfect peace those whose minds are steadfast because they trust in you. Trust in the LORD forever, for the LORD, the LORD himself, is the Rock eternal. (Isaiah 26:3-4)

The mention of *proper influence* provides an opportunity to reinstate the study diagram back into our discussion. It is a discussion that finds the first introduction of evil in the early chapters of Genesis and the final demise of evil in the closing chapters of Revelation.

*And the LORD God commanded the man, "You are free to eat from any tree in the garden; ¹⁷ but you must not eat from the tree of the knowledge of good and **evil**, for when you eat from it you will certainly die.* (Genesis 2:16-17)

The entire purpose and progression of this diagram is meant to reveal one truth; that if we align ourselves with the proper influence by first disciplining our thought process, the natural sequence of human behavior will result in a victorious Christian lifestyle.

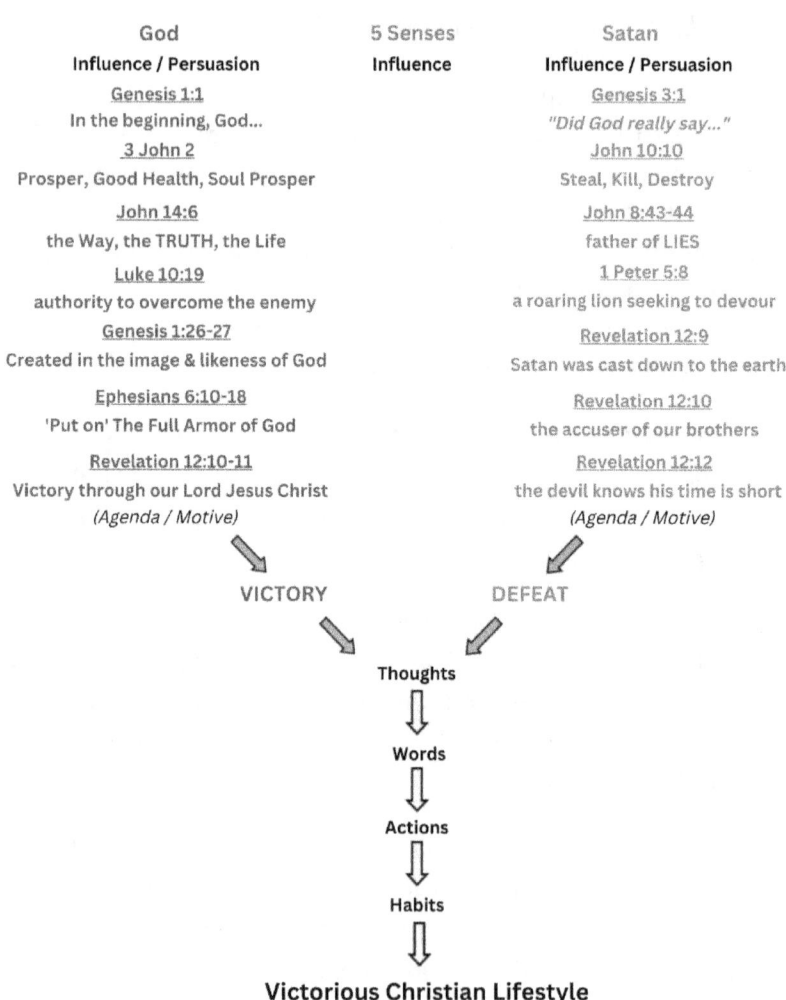

God	5 Senses	Satan
Influence / Persuasion	Influence	Influence / Persuasion
Genesis 1:1		Genesis 3:1
In the beginning, God...		*"Did God really say..."*
3 John 2		John 10:10
Prosper, Good Health, Soul Prosper		Steal, Kill, Destroy
John 14:6		John 8:43-44
the Way, the TRUTH, the Life		father of LIES
Luke 10:19		1 Peter 5:8
authority to overcome the enemy		a roaring lion seeking to devour
Genesis 1:26-27		Revelation 12:9
Created in the image & likeness of God		Satan was cast down to the earth
Ephesians 6:10-18		Revelation 12:10
'Put on' The Full Armor of God		the accuser of our brothers
Revelation 12:10-11		Revelation 12:12
Victory through our Lord Jesus Christ		the devil knows his time is short
(Agenda / Motive)		*(Agenda / Motive)*

VICTORY   DEFEAT

Thoughts
⇩
Words
⇩
Actions
⇩
Habits
⇩
Victorious Christian Lifestyle

Along the way, we have discovered that the battle between good and evil (God vs. Satan) is exhibited throughout the Bible. As we near the end of our study, what we find in Revelation, Chapter 12, is both the promise of eternal victory to those who proclaim Jesus as Lord as well as the promise of Satan's ultimate defeat.

> *Then war broke out in heaven. Michael and his angels fought against the dragon, and the dragon and his angels fought back. ⁸ But he was not strong enough, and they lost their place in heaven. ⁹ The great dragon was hurled down—that ancient serpent called the devil, or Satan, who leads the whole world astray. He was hurled to the earth, and his angels with him.*
>
> *¹⁰ Then I heard a loud voice in heaven say: "Now have come the salvation and the power and the kingdom of our God, and the authority of his Messiah. For the accuser of our brothers and sisters, who accuses them before our God day and night, has been hurled down.*
>
> *¹¹ **They triumphed over him by the blood of the Lamb and by the word of their testimony**; they did not love their lives so much as to shrink from death. ¹² Therefore rejoice, you heavens and you who dwell in them! But woe to the earth and the sea, because the devil has gone down to you! He is filled with fury, because he knows that his time is short."* (Revelation 12:7-12)

Dear friends, as you read these verses, are you able to fully appropriate the truth of Scripture and the personal application to your current and future identity? While we are on this earth, it is the power of the spoken word—God's Word—that assures our temporal victory over Satan. And it is the sacrificial act of Jesus Christ, his death, burial, and resurrection that assures our eternal victory. If you claim Jesus as your Lord and Savior, rejoice my friend, for your sins have been washed clean by the blood of His sacrifice on the cross.

> *This is the message we have heard from him and declare to you: God is light; in him there is no darkness at all. [6] If we claim to have fellowship with him and yet walk in the darkness, we lie and do not live out the truth. [7] But if we walk in the light, as he is in the light, we have fellowship with one another, **and the blood of Jesus, his Son, purifies us from all sin.*** (1 John 1:5-7)

Let me share a closing thought on spiritual maturity. It is not a destination, it is a process. Can we and should we pursue it? Yes, but while we remain in this fallen world, we will never perfect it. Yet, *if we walk in the light*, which to me is a clear reference to the ongoing pursuit of Godly wisdom, we have the promise of sanctification and the ability to share God's glory with others. As our understanding of Scripture deepens and our faith increases, we are called to remain humble and count our blessings, because there are still many who cannot understand this message, for their eyes do not see, nor have their hearts been opened to the truth of the gospel.

> *We do, however, speak a message of wisdom **among the mature**, but not the wisdom of this age or of the rulers of this age, who are coming to nothing. No, **we declare God's wisdom**, a mystery that has been hidden and **that God destined for our glory** before time began. None of the rulers of this age understood it, for if they had, they would not have crucified the Lord of glory. However, as it is written: "What no eye has seen, what no ear has heard, and what no human mind has conceived - the things God has prepared for those who love him - these are the things God has revealed to us by his Spirit."* (1 Corinthians 2:6-10)

You may remember in "Press on Toward the Goal" the suggestion to read the first four chapters of Proverbs and take to heart what the wisest man to ever live, Solomon, had to say about attaining wisdom.

> *Do not forsake wisdom, and she will protect you; love her, and she will watch over you. Wisdom is supreme; therefore, get wisdom. Though it cost all you have, get understanding.* (Proverbs 4:6-7)

I believe God's intent in having me write this book, and the entire premise of this study, has been to reveal a truth *that no human mind has conceived*, but was prepared in advance for those who love God and seek to do His will. It is the result of your diligence and the comprehensive study of Scripture that we can now count ourselves *among the mature*, and can declare God's wisdom to rule our lives and to defeat the enemy. It is the same message that Solomon shared as he began the Book of Proverbs.

> *The proverbs of Solomon, son of David, king of Israel: for gaining wisdom and discipline; for understanding words of insight; ³ for acquiring a disciplined and prudent life. ⁵ Let the wise listen and add to their learning, and let the discerning get guidance. ⁷ **The fear of the LORD is the beginning of knowledge.*** (Proverbs 1:1-3, 5, 7)

Proverbs 1:7 is the perfect verse to highlight another key component of our discussion. In addition to gaining a new level of spiritual maturity, my hope is that your knowledge, understanding, and application of biblical truth will increase significantly. With that in mind, let us talk about the *knowledge of God* and its importance to your spiritual freedom.

Again, before you can identify Satan's lies, you must know God's truth. Winning this war will take a determined and consistent effort to study God's Word until it becomes the rock you stand on and your principle point of reference. I shared the verses below from

Proverbs, with an emphasis on Verse 6, which clearly identifies God as the source of all knowledge and understanding (indeed related to the spiritual realm).

> For the LORD gives wisdom; from his mouth come knowledge and understanding. (Proverbs 2:6)

Our emphasis has now changed to the promises of God that come with the application of that knowledge. As you read the subsequent verses again, I've numbered six distinct references to our assurance of victory.

> (1) He holds success in store for the upright; (2) he is a shield to those whose walk is blameless, (3) for he guards the course of the just (4) and protects the way of his faithful ones. Then you will understand what is right and just and fair - every good path. For wisdom will enter your heart, and knowledge will be pleasant to your soul. (5) Discretion will protect you, (6) and understanding will guard you. (Proverbs 2:7-11)

As you joyfully reflect on these promises, notice how each victory statement is inescapably linked to the application of biblical knowledge (in its various descriptive forms).

- He holds success in store **for the upright.**
- He is a shield **to those whose walk is blameless.**
- He guards the course **of the just.**
- He protects the way of **his faithful ones**.
- **Discretion** will protect you.
- **Understanding** will guard you.

Now, let me try to tie all this together with the foundational verse of our study. As we have just done with the Scripture verses from Proverbs 2:6-11, we need to direct our attention to a specific reference in the passage below. When reading these verses previously, our primary focus has been on the second half of Verse

5, "and we take captive every thought to make it obedient to Christ." That is the most important component of our defensive posture against the enemy. But now the emphasis shifts to the first half of Verse 5. Read these verses again, slowly, and allow the Holy Spirit to bring their full meaning to light.

> *For though we live in the world, we do not wage war as the world does. * ⁴ *The weapons we fight with are not the weapons of the world. On the contrary, they have divine power to demolish strongholds. * ⁵ *We demolish arguments and every pretension that sets itself up* ***against the knowledge of God****, and we take captive every thought to make it obedient to Christ.* (2 Corinthians 10:3-5)

We live in a fallen world that Satan calls home and is heavily influenced by his demonic power. When we claim the title *Christian*, we immediately become combatants in the spiritual war between good and evil. However, the weapons at our disposal to defeat the enemy are not the weapons of this world. Our own spiritual maturity is our primary weapon, and when we hold fast to the truth of Scripture, it is the Spirit of God dwelling within us that has the power to demolish every lie, temptation, and accusation that sets itself up **against the knowledge of God**. But make no mistake, to break the chains of bondage, we must know God's truth and be ready to defend and rebuke the enemy at the point of attack—our thought life! When we do that, the remaining promise in Proverbs 2:9-10 holds true.

> *Then you will understand what is right and just and fair - every good path. For wisdom will enter your heart, and knowledge will be pleasant to your soul.* (Proverbs 2:9-10)

From the beginning of this study, we have clearly charted the two paths available to us as Christians via our diagram. I hope it has become evident that consistently striving toward spiritual maturity and then applying the knowledge of God will result in our lives serving as true reflections of Jesus Christ. If I could paraphrase Proverbs 2:9-10, it might look something like this. Having trained your mind to obey the influence of the Holy Spirit, Godly wisdom will rest in your heart, and the full appropriation of who you are in Christ will bring peace and confidence to living each day as God intends, for you to live in the assurance of victory. The apostle Paul understood this and explains it this way in his first letter to the Corinthians.

> *The Spirit searches all things, even the deep things of God. For who knows a person's thoughts except their own spirit within them? In the same way no one knows the thoughts of God except the Spirit of God. What we have received is not the spirit of the world, but the Spirit who is from God, so that we may understand what God has freely given us. This is what we speak, not in words taught us by human wisdom but in words taught by the Spirit, explaining spiritual realities with Spirit-taught words. The person without the Spirit does not accept the things that come from the Spirit of God but considers them foolishness, and cannot understand them because they are discerned only through the Spirit. The person with the Spirit makes judgments about all things, but such a person is not subject to merely human judgments, for who has known the mind of the Lord so as to instruct him? **But we have the mind of Christ.** (1 Corinthians 2:10^b-16)*

My friend, that is a promise I want you to hold onto. By adoption into God's family, through the saving grace of our Lord, Jesus Christ, and by the purposeful pursuit of Godly wisdom, the Spirit of God has revealed to you the mind of Christ. This is a powerful truth, one powerful enough to defeat sin and death. We must recognize, however, that walking in that truth moment by moment can be interrupted by the distractions of our daily lives. There will be times that our feelings are not aligned with the facts.

In his book, *Returning to Holiness*, Dr. Gregory Frizzell shared a parable related to this topic. Dr. Frizzell pastored the Georgian Hills Baptist Church in Memphis, Tennessee, and served for ten years as Director of Prayer and Spiritual Awakening for the Shelby Baptist Association. He is the author of twelve books on prayer evangelism. The story below was condensed from "The Illustration of the Wooden Stake" (Pages 98-99).

There was a believer who kept having doubts about his salvation. The man thought he had been saved but those terrible doubts just wouldn't leave.

One day God gave him an idea that utterly changed his life. He took a big wooden stake and along with his Bible went behind his barn. He opened the Bible to the promises of John 3:16 and Romans 10:13. He knelt down and prayed a salvation prayer. He told God he was claiming His promise of eternal life. He asked Jesus to be his own Lord and Savior. After this simple heart-felt prayer, he drove the wooden stake deep into the ground with a little of the top left showing.

From that day forward, when he had failures or doubts, he walked right back to that old stake and said these words; "Right there by that stake, I know I called on the name of the Lord. Because God cannot lie, I know He heard me, and I am His child!" He then would say; "Satan you're a liar and in Jesus name, I command you to flee!" It wasn't long until Satan didn't bother to whisper any more doubts about his salvation. The man soon learned to trust God's Word, and not his own feelings or performance.

Do you now see the glorious key? We stand in Jesus' blood and righteousness, not our own. We trust in God's promise, not our feelings or performance. We trust in God's mighty grace to save and keep us, not our ability to *deserve it. We trust in God's unending faithfulness, not in our imperfect faithfulness to Him…. Your security is in a grace that is greater than all your sin. So, go ahead child of God, **rest in Him!** [4] [1]*

<u>For reference purposes</u>:
- *John 3:16 For God so loved the world that he gave his one and only Son, that whoever believes in him shall not perish but have eternal life.*
- *Romans 10:13 For, "Everyone who calls on the name of the Lord will be saved."*

I shared that story to make this statement. A stronger understanding of God's Word and your continued maturity in Christ Jesus form your stake in the ground. Perhaps there is a specific verse from this study that has heightened your awareness of the devil's schemes, or perhaps there is a victory verse from your own personal study of Scripture that allows you to stand your ground when Satan throws his fiery darts at you. In either case, your growing confidence symbolizes the assurance of victory as you willfully rebuke the lies of the enemy and rest in God's truth. King David knew this to be true and spoke of this victory in Psalm 91.

*[1] Whoever dwells in the shelter of the most High **will rest** in the shadow of the Almighty. [2] I will say of the Lord, "He is my refuge and my fortress, my God, in whom I trust." "Because he loves me," says the Lord, "I will rescue him; I will protect him, for he acknowledges my name. [15] He will call on me, and I will answer him; I will be with him in trouble, I will deliver him and honor him. [16] With long life I will satisfy him and show him my salvation." (Psalm 91)*

Did you happen to notice a familiar pattern in these verses? Once again, each victory statement is linked to spiritual maturity and the application of biblical knowledge. Let's take the time to look closer.

1. ***Whoever dwells in the shelter of the most High will rest in the shadow of the Almighty.***
   a. Other words for *dwell* are *live* or *stay.*
   b. God does not provide a physical *shelter* for our protection; He provides a spiritual *shelter.* We are to dwell in the revelation and understanding of His word. Earlier in this section, I outlined the pattern for building a spiritual shelter.
   c. If we live and/or stay within the boundaries of that shelter, God will grant us rest by shadowing us in His truth.

A comparison of this same verse in the original King James Version helps to deepen its meaning.

2. ***He that dwelleth in the secret place of the most High shall abide under the shadow of the Almighty.***
   a. Notice that this translation advises us to dwell in "the secret place."
   b. If you remember the parable of the sower from Mark's gospel, Jesus tells his disciples; "The secret of the kingdom of God has been given to you." (Mark 4:11)
   c. To "abide under God's shadow" indicates that He is ever present in the lives of the righteous.
   d. If we faithfully and consistently apply the wisdom of God, revealed to us by the Holy Spirit, we are then privileged to find daily respite in God's presence.

As he continues, the psalmist repeats this pattern in the next set of verses.

3. **"Because he loves me," says the Lord, "I will rescue him; I will protect him, for he acknowledges my name."**
    a. Our love for God is evident in our obedience to His calling on our lives.
    b. "And this is love: that we walk in obedience to His commands. As you have heard from the beginning, His command is that you walk in love." (2 John 1:6)
    c. Because we love the Lord, there is victory in our obedience!
        i. God will *rescue us* from Satan's grasp and the penalty of sin.
        ii. God will *protect us* from Satan's attempts to draw us back into sin.
    d. *Jesus said, "If you hold to my teaching, you are really my disciples. Then you will know the truth, and the truth will set you free."* (John 8:31-32)

Brothers and sisters, are you beginning to see your spiritual freedom in a new light? We have now made the transition from a conceptual probability (hope) that some control over the attacks of the enemy might be possible, to the absolute confirmation that we can be victorious in this war against Satan and the battle for our souls. While God's promises and the assurance of victory are proclaimed throughout the Bible, the intent of this final chapter is to highlight specific verses preordained to secure your confidence in the power of Almighty God working through you to overcome the evil one. With this awareness firmly in place, I feel certain the Holy Spirit will open your eyes to new revelations of this truth as you continue to study God's Word.

If it is not already apparent, my sincere desire for you is to live the victorious Christian lifestyle. A consistent theme throughout this study has been that God wants you to win in that effort! While these are promises to be believed, let me temper all this good news with a repeat of a previous caution. It is vitally important for us to guard against an attitude of self-confidence and pride as we triumph over Satan's schemes.

I touched on this inherent danger briefly after defining the assurance of victory, but it is critical that we guard against anything that would blur or dull the sense of dependence upon God. We cannot rely on an academic background, spiritual gifts, years in Christian service, any worldly asset, or past achievement. Our success in this endeavor (sometimes the most difficult test of all) is and will remain dependent on God's mercy and grace. Listen to Paul's words in 1 Corinthians 7:25. "I give my judgment, as one that hath obtained mercy of the Lord to be faithful." (KJV)

Based on this caution and the advice garnered from Scripture, I would like to revisit Dr. Frizzell's illustration of the wooden stake. The original premise of the story centered around one man establishing a visual reminder of his salvation and returning to that symbol of God's truth each time Satan launched a fiery arrow of doubt. This was wise counsel, as God often directed the nation of Israel to erect a memorial as a reminder of His power and His promises. As an example, you may remember the story of Joshua as he led the Israelites in crossing the Jordan river.

So Joshua called together the twelve men he had appointed from the Israelites, one from each tribe, ⁵ and said to them, "Go over before the ark of the LORD your God into the middle of the Jordan. Each of you is to take up a stone on his shoulder, according to the number of the tribes of the Israelites, ⁶ to serve as a sign among you. In the future, when your children ask you, 'What do these stones mean?' ⁷ tell them that the flow of the Jordan was cut off before the ark of the covenant of the LORD. When it crossed the Jordan, the waters of the Jordan were cut off. **These stones are to be a memorial** *to the people of Israel forever."* (Joshua 4:4-7)

My original purpose in sharing Dr. Frizzell's story was to offer a parallel to your personal spiritual battle. We know that total victory over Satan's lies is now attainable through the power of Jesus Christ. Might it be a good idea to establish your own visual symbol of victory to help you stand firm when doubt invades your thoughts? If so, might it also be used as a symbol to defend against a spirit of self-confidence or pride and help you build a character of true success?

What will be your stake in the ground? Not too many years ago, the Christian community was enamored with colorful bracelets and other paraphernalia that simply said, "What Would Jesus Do?" Do you remember the WWJD symbolism? When Satan invades your mind and whispers his lies, perhaps your stake in the ground can be similar. Instead of listening to the father of lies and giving credence to what the devil has to say about you, why not ask yourself, "What would Jesus say about me?" Perhaps the apostle Paul captured it best in this succinct quote to the believers in Corinth.

> *Therefore, if anyone is in Christ, the new creation has come: The old is gone,* **the new is here!** (2 Corinthians 5:17)

Can you make that claim? Have you accepted Jesus Christ as your personal Lord and Savior? If the answer is yes, then it is time to fully appropriate the truth that accompanies your profession of faith. **YOU ARE A NEW CREATION IN CHRIST!** And God is no respecter of persons.

Paul assures us that anyone who's heart has been surrendered to Jesus is a new creation in God's eyes. No matter your past, your previous life's history is gone in God's eyes. When God looks at you, He sees only that you are now clothed in the righteousness of Jesus, having been washed clean by the blood of His sacrifice on the cross. You are now part of God's family and an heir to His promises.

> How much more, then, will the blood of Christ, who through the eternal Spirit offered himself unblemished to God, cleanse our consciences from acts that lead to death, so that we may serve the living God! **15** For this reason Christ is the mediator of a new covenant, **that those who are called may receive the promised eternal inheritance**—now that he has died as a ransom to set them free from the sins committed under the first covenant. (Hebrews 9:14-15)

Without doubt, the most glorious truth regarding our new identity is the confidence we have in our eternal inheritance to the kingdom of heaven. However, as we have discussed previously, we are still participants in a spiritual battle while on this earth. In this battle, one of our greatest struggles is to let go of our old selves and the memories that accompany past sins, especially when we realize that Satan's goal is to keep us chained to those memories and prevent us from serving as God has gifted us to serve.

When you fully appropriate your new identity in Christ, the verses above hold a promise for this earthly struggle as well. For the sacrificial blood of Jesus will "cleanse our consciences from acts that lead to death, and, set us free from the sins committed under the first covenant." This falls right in line with the major premise of our study and our ability to control what we think about. What we may *not* have thought about is that God not only offers but also promises to help us with this if we call upon Him.

*Rejoice in the Lord always. Do not be anxious about anything, but in every situation, by prayer and petition, with thanksgiving, present your requests to God. And the peace of God, which transcends all understanding, will guard your hearts and **your minds** in Christ Jesus. Finally, brothers and sisters, whatever is true, whatever is noble, whatever is right, whatever is pure, whatever is lovely, whatever is admirable—if anything is excellent or praiseworthy—**think about such things**. Whatever you have learned or received or heard from me or seen in me - put it into practice. And the God of peace will be with you.* (Philippians 4: 4, 6-9)

When Satan tries to revive those old memories, we call upon God by prayer and petition, with thanksgiving, and we present our request to overcome the enemy's fiery darts of temptation, accusation, and condemnation. "And the peace of God, which transcends all understanding, will guard your hearts and your minds in Christ Jesus." Friends, we might not fully understand it, but if we adhere to the advice of Scripture and focus our thoughts on whatever is admirable, excellent, or praiseworthy, God not only promises to give us a mind that is at peace with Him, but He also promises to be by our side in the good times and the bad.

Isn't it wonderful and comforting to know that victory over the evil one is attainable, but even more glorious that it is not all up to you? Father, Son, and Holy Spirit are at your side, ready to do battle, ready to help you defeat the enemy, and committed to your permanent triumph over Satan's determination to lead you astray. Take a few minutes to meditate on the verses below as a confirmation of this truth.

The path of the righteous is level; you, the Upright One, make the way of the righteous smooth. (Isaiah 26:7)

His divine power has given us everything we need for a godly life through our knowledge of him who called us by his own glory and goodness. Through these he has given us his great and precious promises, so that through them you may participate in the divine nature, having escaped the corruption in the world caused by evil desires. (2 Peter 1:3-4)

I don't know about you, but I find it fascinating when New Testament passages illuminate and confirm Old Testament Scripture. We see this throughout the Bible, and here we have an excellent example of God's purposeful literary design. My current pastor, John Mark Harrison, shared a visual with our church family that was passed on to him by his father (also a pastor). He described the Old Testament as a beautiful stained-glass window placed prominently in a grand and glorious old cathedral. At night, or during a cloudy day, it is often difficult to grasp its full beauty. However, when the sun shines through that mosaic of color, the full majesty and intent of the glass mural comes alive.

Likewise, when the glory of God's Son shines through the mosaic of the Old Testament, its full intent comes alive in our hearts. After all, the entire Old Testament is the story leading up to God's ultimate plan of salvation for mankind through His Son, Jesus Christ. If you have never read the Old Testament with the determination to see the coming Messiah referenced in its historic books, I encourage you to do so. It is fascinating to note how everything in these ancient texts ultimately points to our Lord and Savior.

As you will see, the above verses, written hundreds of years apart from each other, confirm that the best way to interpret Scripture is with additional Scripture references.

Continuing with our theme of God's promises to His righteous believers and the assurance of victory, allow me to highlight three truths from Isaiah that are illuminated in Peter's second letter.

- ***The path of the righteous is level.***
- *(He) has given us everything we need for **a godly life** through our knowledge of him who called us by his own glory and goodness.*

To help us understand the meaning behind these two references, I would like to take us back to our discussion about the full armor of God. In that conversation, we borrowed from Dr. Adrian Rogers regarding his interpretation of the defensive armor. If you remember, he put forth that the articles of protective clothing described by Paul were representative of lifestyle applications to be adhered to by those who call themselves Christians.

If we pattern our lives accordingly, we maintain two key benefits. First, we eliminate any cracks in our armor, otherwise known as areas of sin or stained conscience by which Satan can torment us. Second, when we experience upheaval or times of uncertainty, we are able to maintain a level of composure available only through our faith in Jesus Christ. Isaiah doesn't suggest that the path of the righteous is without problems, but he does offer that the path of the righteous is "level." Peter offers us further hope when he boldly claims that God has given us everything we need to live that "godly life" through our knowledge of Him and application of His truth in our lives. We can live in that confidence!

- *You, the Upright One*
- *His divine power*

Both statements above confirm that we are not in this fight alone, nor should we try to fight in our own power. God, the Upright One, in His divine power has given us everything we need to be victorious through our knowledge and dependence upon Father, Son, and Holy Spirit.

- *You, the Upright One,* **make the way of the righteous smooth.**
- *Through these he has given us his great and precious promises, so that through them you may participate in the divine nature,* **having escaped the corruption in the world caused by evil desires.**

It is here that Isaiah and Peter offer their strongest reference to the assurance of victory. And while the Old Testament reference is subtle and open to interpretation, the New Testament profession by Peter shines its light on the prophet's claim and illuminates its full intent and meaning. Not only has God given us everything we need to live according to His calling on our lives, but also those who choose to participate in His divine nature may confidently claim His promise to escape the corruption in the world caused by evil desires (thoughts). Can I get an Amen?

Brothers and sisters in Christ, from the beginning of this study, my goal has been to present a comprehensive presentation of what the Bible teaches us about spiritual warfare, hopefully in a way that is fresh, new, easy to understand, and simple in practice. We have turned the pages from Genesis to Revelation and discussed a broad range of topics, but it all amounts to nothing if we cannot confidently and consistently exercise the freedom that we hoped for when we accepted Jesus Christ as our personal Lord and Savior and when we participate in God's calling upon our lives.

The promises in these final pages leave no room for doubt. You can live in the assurance of victory! You can walk victoriously as a Christian! You can reflect God's holiness to a lost and dying world. Scripture tells us so.

*Blessed is the one who perseveres under trial because, having stood the test, **that person will receive the crown of life** that the Lord has promised to those who love him.* (James 1:12)

*¹For we know that if the earthly tent we live in is destroyed, we have a building from God, an eternal house in heaven, not built by human hands. ⁵ Now the one who has fashioned us for this purpose is God, who has given us the Spirit as a deposit, **guaranteeing what is to come**.* (2 Corinthians 5:1, 5)

*In fact, this is love for God: to keep his commands. And his commands are not burdensome, ⁴ for everyone born of God overcomes the world. **This is the victory that has overcome the world**, even our faith. ⁵ Who is it that overcomes the world? Only the one who believes that Jesus is the Son of God.* (2 John 5:3-5)

*He who was seated on the throne said, "I am making everything new!" Then he said, "Write this down, for these words are trustworthy and true." ⁶ He said to me: "It is done. I am the Alpha and the Omega, the Beginning and the End. To the thirsty I will give water without cost from the spring of the water of life. ⁷ **Those who are victorious will inherit all this**, and I will be their God and they will be my children.* (Revelation 21:5-7)

*Therefore, **since we have these promises**, dear friends, let us purify ourselves from everything that contaminates body and spirit, perfecting holiness out of reverence for God.* (2 Corinthians 7:1)

How do we go about perfecting holiness? I hope the answer comes to you without hesitation.

We demolish arguments and every pretension that sets itself up against the knowledge of God, and we take captive every thought to make it obedient to Christ. (2 Corinthians 10:5)

As we near the end of our study, I will offer a few significant reminders from God's Word and then close with a prayer for every dear soul who has taken the time to embolden his or her faith by digging deep into His truth with me.

*As I have observed, those who plow evil and those who sow trouble reap it. ⁹ At the breath of God they perish; at the blast of his anger, they are no more. ¹⁰ The lions may roar and growl, yet the teeth of the great lions are broken. ¹¹ **The lion perishes for lack of prey**, and the cubs of the lioness are scattered.* (Job 4:8-11)

The verse <u>1 Peter 5:8</u> tells us: *Be alert and of sober mind. Your enemy the devil prowls around like a **roaring lion** looking for someone to devour.* It is unfortunate and regrettable that Satan may never lack access to an abundance of prey as he roams this earth, however, we rejoice that we no longer have to count ourselves among the quarry. We are now equipped to break free of his lies, schemes, and accusations and share this truth with all who will listen and obey the Word of God.

*¹¹Now what I am commanding you today is not too difficult for you or beyond your reach. ¹⁹This day I call the heavens and the earth as witnesses against you that I have set before you life and death, blessings and curses. **Now choose life**, so that you and your children may live ²⁰ and that you may love the LORD your God, listen to his voice, and hold fast to him. For the LORD is your life.* (Deuteronomy 30:11, 19-20)

You can do this! No matter where you find yourself right now, no matter your current level of spiritual maturity as a Christian, you can apply these truths to your life and begin to claim God's promise of victory. You may be a pastor leading a church, a missionary following God's calling on your life, an ordinary citizen trying to do the best you can for your family, or so down and out that you think there is no way up. What God's Word offers is not too difficult for you or beyond your reach.

Remember, God is no respecter of persons. You can find victory through his Son, Jesus Christ. Choose life! Choose wisdom! Choose to study the Bible. Count your blessings. Take inventory of your assets. Make a conscious effort to think about what you are thinking about—begin to capture every thought and make it obedient to Christ. Then prayerfully and patiently watch as God begins to transform your hope into confidence. Finally, give praise to Father, Son, and Holy Spirit as they come along side you to win the battle between good and evil.

Just remember, Satan is no respecter of persons either. Your position in life is not too lofty to be impenetrable by the enemy's temptation to sin. Likewise, your failures are not too far in the past for Satan to stop throwing the fiery arrows of accusation, condemnation, and doubt. We must never forget, however, that even through the assaults of the devil, we can take great joy in the following.

No temptation has overtaken you except what is common to mankind. And God is faithful; he will not let you be tempted beyond what you can bear. But when you are tempted, he will also provide a way out so that you can endure it. (1 Corinthians 10:13)

My friends, listen to God's voice and hold fast to His teaching. **The Lord is your life!** If this statement is true of you as a Christian, then cast off your doubts and fears and learn to walk victoriously in the confidence of His power and grace. It all starts in your mind.

> For God hath not given us the spirit of fear; but of power, and of love, and of a <u>sound</u> <u>mind</u>. (2 Timothy 1:7 KJV)

Stand Firm in God's power and love! Remember—you win or lose the battle in your thought life. *Capture <u>every</u> thought and make it obedient to Christ.* **This is the definition of a sound mind.**

In the first three chapters of Ephesians, the apostle Paul reminds the predominantly Gentile believers of the spiritual blessings that had been provided for them by their faith in Jesus Christ, the same 'mystery' that transformed his own life. In closing, please allow me to offer this prayer for you just as Paul did for his brothers and sisters in Ephesus.

> [6] *This mystery is that through the gospel the Gentiles are heirs together with Israel, members together of one body, and sharers together in the promise in Christ Jesus.* [14] *For this reason I kneel before the Father,* [15] *from whom every family in heaven and on earth derives its name.* [16] *I pray that out of his glorious riches he may strengthen you with power through his Spirit in your inner being,* [17] *so that Christ may dwell in your hearts through faith.*

> *And I pray that you, being rooted and established in love,* [18] *may have power, together with all the Lord's holy people, to grasp how wide and long and high and deep is the love of Christ,* [19] **and to know** *this love that surpasses knowledge - that you may be filled to the measure of all the fullness of God.* [20] *Now to him who is able to do immeasurably more than all we ask or imagine, according to his power that is at work within us,* [21] *to him be glory in*

the church and in Christ Jesus throughout all generations,
for ever and ever! Amen. (Ephesians 3:6, 14-21)

Beloved, I wish above all things that thou mayest prosper and be in health, even as thy soul prospereth. (3 John 2) (KJV)

1. Dr. Gregory Frizzell, *Returning to Holiness* (Memphis: The Master Design, 2000) 98-99

Epilogue

My friends, I cannot begin to tell you what a humbling experience this has been for me. To say I was reluctant and thought myself unworthy to start this project would be an understatement. Having never done anything like this before, the idea of writing a book was like a bucket list item you don't expect to accomplish. I certainly never expected to be prompted by the Holy Spirit to write about one of the most serious, misunderstood, and neglected topics in all of Christianity—spiritual warfare. To be used by God and consistently amazed at how the Holy Spirit led me to the proper resource time after time and choreographed my simple notes into a powerful symposium of truth was beyond anything I could have imagined.

Yet, with all that God had revealed to me in the course of this study, I still felt as though something was missing. The project felt incomplete—like there was still something that I wanted to say but didn't know what it was or how to express my feeling of inadequacy. Then, as I was reviewing some of my source material one more time, trying desperately to make sure this final prompting didn't go unanswered, the Holy Spirit did it again. He led me to a previous resource whose authors had expressed the same sentiment at the end of their book, and it perfectly articulated what was on my heart.

I am not an expert on this topic. God is. This is not a complete compendium, or the final say on spiritual warfare, but merely a starting point to illustrate a basic truth often overlooked in studies of the Bible. As much as we have uncovered, we have only scratched the surface. There is so much more to learn and apply to our daily lives. Since God allows for deepening levels of interpretation by those who truly seek Him, together we can combine individual lessons learned, build on this foundation, and perhaps make learning these principles easier for those who follow in our footsteps. I welcome your collaboration in that effort and perhaps, if warranted, future reprints of this material would be better than the original version. In conclusion, I find value in repeating a quote in the Bible from James, the half-brother of Jesus. In his letter to the twelve tribes of Israel scattered among the nations, he wrote the following.

> Do not merely listen to the word, and so deceive yourselves. **Do what it says**. [25] Whoever looks intently into the perfect law that gives freedom, and continues in it—not forgetting what they have heard, but doing it—they will be blessed in what they do. (James 1:22, 25)

Realizing that advice to be true in my life, I thought it only appropriate to leave you with a call to action. My invitation to you is to join those who have already made the decision to become victorious warriors in the temporal battle for their souls, and in doing so, have secured their eternal destiny. Utilizing the lessons learned throughout this study (which is my attempt to summarize 'the perfect law that gives freedom'), the following recommendations are intended so that you do not forget what you have heard but instead make daily application of these truths so that God may bless you in all that you do for His kingdom.

My recommendations for a victorious Christian lifestyle:
- Read the Bible consistently. Set aside fifteen to thirty minutes each day to allow God's truth to penetrate your heart and transform your world view. Ask the Holy Spirit for enlightenment.
  - If you've never done this before, the thirty-one chapters of Proverbs is a great place to start.

- o Read one chapter per day to establish the habit. Then transition to the New Testament. I recommend the New King James Version (NKJV) of the Bible.
- Begin or intensify your conversations with God through prayer. He wants to hear from you.
- Keep the Bible and this study close by as ready references. Highlight impactful quotes and make notes in the margins. (It's okay to write in your Bible.)
- Make a conscious decision to think about what you're thinking about and learn to identify the lies and temptations from the enemy.
- Be honest with yourself and identify the sin(s) and/or accusations that Satan is using to defeat you.
- Identify a victory verse and begin to speak it out loud each time you recognize evil influencing your thoughts. Personalize the verse if necessary.
- Be prepared to stand firm. The battle will intensify when you choose to engage in truth.
- Recognize you are not fighting *for* victory; you are fighting from a position *of* victory. The battle has already been won; you just need to fix that fact in your mind.
- When possible, be proactive. Apply the principle of Situational Christianity to your faith-based initiatives.
- Find and attend a church that does not compromise on teaching biblical truth.
- Associate with like-minded Christians. Iron sharpens iron.
- Continue to walk in an attitude of victory and be the light of Christ to a lost and dying world.
- Read this study again. Repetition is how we learn in all areas of our life.
- Share this book and this universal truth with others.

Allow me to offer a bit of encouragement regarding the last bullet point above. A dear bother in Christ once told me that every Christian should have a Paul, a Barnabas, and a Timothy in his or her life. In other words, every Christian should have a spiritual mentor, a partner in ministry, and someone he or she is mentoring.

As you study Paul's life and ministry, you understand that Jesus was his spiritual mentor, followed by the indwelling of the Holy Spirit. During a portion of his ministry, Barnabas traveled with Paul and shared in the responsibilities of preaching the Gospel message. Although Paul was a spiritual mentor to many, Scripture highlights the special relationship with his young apprentice, Timothy.

You may not see yourself as capable of mentoring a fellow brother or sister in Christ; however, having the knowledge of God attained through this study would certainly make you capable of doing just that. The most glaring deficiency in Christianity is discipleship, and the greatest misconception is that you need to be a biblical scholar to mentor someone else. The reality is that if you know just a bit more than the other person, you can begin the role of teacher, and through that effort, discover new truth together.

There are fourteen chapters in this book. Through prayer and discernment, find an individual, or a small group, that would benefit from the knowledge you have obtained. Invite them to read and discuss one chapter per week (men teaching men, women teaching women, or couples teaching couples). When you finish, do it again, encourage your students to do the same, and watch how God will begin to move among His people.

*"Therefore, go and make disciples of all nations, baptizing them in the name of the Father and of the Son and of the Holy Spirit, [20] **and teaching them** to obey everything I have commanded you. And surely, I am with you always, to the very end of the age.* (Matthew 28:19-20)

"Only one life, 'twill soon be past. Only what's done for Christ will last." —From the poem by C.T. Studd

To God be the Glory!

Back to the Beginning

There was a point in my life, perhaps a year or two after accepting Jesus as my personal Lord and Savior, that I earnestly prayed for the Holy Spirit to become the same Counselor to me that Jesus had promised to His disciples. Shortly after sharing that desire with my pastor, Dr. Joe Ford, he and another close spiritual mentor took it upon themselves to pray over me and asked God to release a deeper understanding of Scripture and its application by a renewed indwelling of the Spirit of God. You may remember this verse from the preface to this study.

> But the Advocate, the Holy Spirit, whom the Father will send in my name, will teach you all things and will remind you of everything I have said to you. (John 14:26)

That is a day I will always remember and be grateful for. As a follow up to the request we had just asked of God, both men suggested I read a book by R. A. Torrey titled *The Person and Work of the Holy Spirit* and handed me a copy before I left that intimate encounter. I think I wore out three highlighters as I read that book and scribbled more notes in the margins than any other book other than my Bible. I'm not sure if it is still in print, but if you can find a copy, I'm quite sure you will benefit from reading this introduction to the third person of the Trinity.

That prayer was manifested for me in the following way. What had previously been a vague and uncertain understanding of Scripture transformed into a very practical application of God's Word as it applied to every aspect of my life. Fast forward to my intense battle with the spiritual force of evil and my determination to understand its source, its methods, its agenda, and how to overcome this very destructive enemy. As I searched the Bible for truth regarding spiritual warfare, the Holy Spirit inspired the original diagram below. With this information in hand, I called "Dr. Joe" and asked if I could share my thoughts with him to see if I was on the right track. Not only did he confirm the truth displayed in this simple drawing, but also, I will never forget what he said next. "You could teach this to any member in this church." That confirmation and vote of confidence was the beginning of a ten-year effort to discover what the Bible taught about spiritual warfare and resulted in eight pages

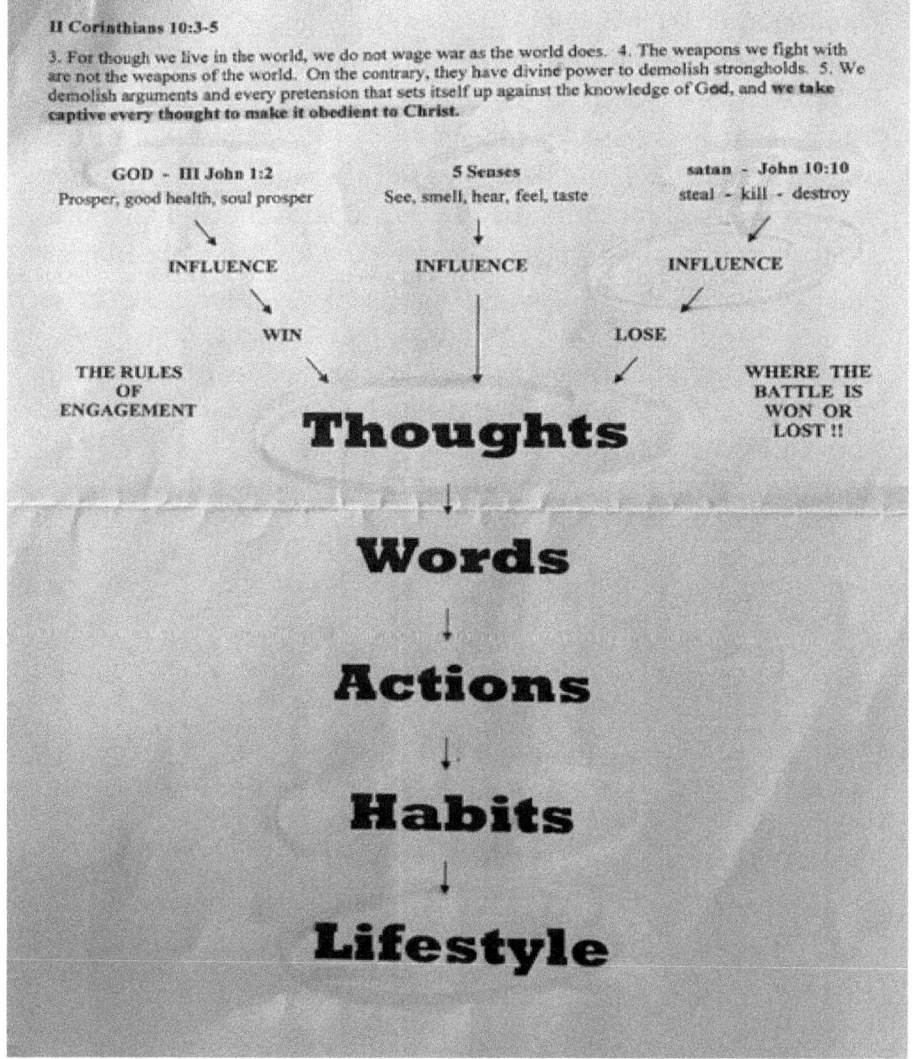

II Corinthians 10:3-5

3. For though we live in the world, we do not wage war as the world does. 4. The weapons we fight with are not the weapons of the world. On the contrary, they have divine power to demolish strongholds. 5. We demolish arguments and every pretension that sets itself up against the knowledge of God, and we take captive every thought to make it obedient to Christ.

GOD - III John 1:2	5 Senses	satan - John 10:10
Prosper, good health, soul prosper	See, smell, hear, feel, taste	steal - kill - destroy

INFLUENCE   INFLUENCE   INFLUENCE

WIN   LOSE

THE RULES
OF
ENGAGEMENT

WHERE THE
BATTLE IS
WON OR
LOST !!

Thoughts

Words

Actions

Habits

Lifestyle

of Scripture verses compiled into five categories of life application. This book, prompted by God's leading and totally inspired by the Holy Spirit, is a result of and in answer to the prayer lifted up to God on my behalf by two dear friends and brothers in Christ over twenty-five years ago.

I've shared two pictures below. The first is of Dr. Joe and his wife Charlotte. Before DeeDee and I moved to Knoxville, Tennessee, this couple poured their lives into us and never stopped encouraging us to mature in our faith. The picture is from our wedding as Dr. Joe officiated over that ceremony. The second picture of Joe and me is a testament to a life-long friendship that developed out of our mutual respect for each other. I was still a practicing agnostic when we first met and for more than twelve months, he and Charlotte set that aside as they prayed diligently for Christ to make Himself apparent in my life. People say God works in mysterious ways. I believe only He could have caused our paths to cross and allowed this minister of the Gospel to soften a hardened heart to the truth of Scripture. I will be eternally grateful, literally, for the day Joe Ford entered my life.

There is another interesting storyline that I couldn't help but share with you at this point. As I began to write this book, I would refer to that long list of Scripture verses and cross them off, one by one, as I incorporated them into the subject matter for each chapter. When I finished the original manuscript, three years later, I had crossed off every single verse, except one. For weeks, I poured over what I had written, looking for just the right place to insert that remaining verse. Unsuccessful in that effort, I surrendered to the thought that it just wasn't part of God's plan.

However, as He had done so many times before, the Holy Spirit assured me He had other intentions. Up to this point, I had not envisioned nor written a proper introduction for the study. And so, the inspiration came as it had before. What was the verse you ask?

> Then David gave his son Solomon the plans for the portico of the temple, its buildings, its storerooms, its upper parts, its inner rooms, and the place of atonement. ¹² He gave him the plans of all that the

Spirit had put in his mind. (1 Chronicles 28:11-12ᵃ)
(NIV)

As it turned out, that remaining verse was undeniably included in 'the plans of all that the Spirit had put in *my* mind. Who was I to cast it aside? With that instruction, I quickly drafted the preface, and the study was complete. If you go back and read it again, the preface also includes the verse below. I could not summarize this completed work more precisely if I tried.

> *All this, I have in writing as a result of the LORD's hand on me, and he enabled me to understand all the details of the plan.* (1 Chronicles 28:19) (NIV)

Next, I want to add a comment about the value of friendship. As I stated earlier, God created us with a desire for relationships—to be in community with others. For whatever reason, I've always cherished deep friendships and have made it an effort to stay connected with people I love and people who have invested in me. I've acknowledged several people who were valuable encouragers to me in this process. If you haven't done so already, please notice that the cover design for this book was created by Bob Gurgul. Bob and I have known each other since we were five years old. He is a talented graphic artist and college professor, and I was thrilled when he agreed to apply his talents to this project.

The first picture sits on the desk in my home office. Bob is the curly headed kid on the left. His twin brother Bill is on the right. And, you guessed it, that's me in the middle. (I have no idea what we're looking at.) The second picture was taken on a recent trip back to the old neighborhood in Brookfield, Wisconsin. Though we may be separated by distance, time has not eroded the friendship we share and the love and respect we have for one another.

I am so grateful for the blessing of friendship. God created each one of us with special talents and a special purpose for our lives. When combined and used for the glory of His kingdom, it is a shining light to a lost and dying world. Cherish your family and friends. Pray that you could begin to see them through God's eyes. Share this inspiration with a good friend, and if you don't have one, be one.

Saving the best for last, the beginning of this story would be incomplete without mention of my incredible wife, Ms. DeeDee. To be honest, I wasn't quite sure what her response would be when I came home from work one day and said, "Darling, I think God wants me to write a book on spiritual warfare." Of course, she knew of my special interest in the subject matter, but this was taking it to a whole new level. We discussed the scope of the project, the commitment required, the sacrifice to be made in other areas of our life, and then we prayed for confirmation and God's leading. From that point on, she was completely supportive and became my biggest cheer leader.

We trusted that we had made the right decision because God had already blessed us with a dynamic ministry. Years earlier, I was asked to co-teach a large Sunday School class and when DeeDee and I united behind that calling, we were both given the opportunity to utilize our primary spiritual gifts. I have the gift of teaching and DeeDee has the gift of administration and organization. Since neither one of us has family in Knoxville, this class has become like family to us, and it has been an honor to serve in this capacity. Not only has she been a blessing in my life, but DeeDee continues to be the hands and feet of Jesus in her service to others.

As I share these final thoughts, the book is finished, and the final editing process is near completion. I could not have gotten this far without my amazing wife, and I couldn't imagine sharing this journey with anyone else. We're not sure where this adventure is going to take us, but we are confident that God has joined us together for His purpose and that He will fully equip us to finish the race.

> Let us not become weary in doing good, for at the proper time we will reap a harvest if we do not give up. [10] Therefore, as we have opportunity, let us do good to all people, especially to those who belong to the family of believers. (Galatians 6:9-10) (NIV)

About the Author

Growing up in the Catholic Church, Jeff never gained any spiritual insight or depth of conviction about his faith, and by age fourteen, he had fallen away from the church and spent the next twenty years as a self-professed agnostic. He learned to rely on himself and developed a quiet confidence in running his own life, proud that he had become a self-made man.

Eventually, the personal and professional success built on self-determination began to collapse and by the grace of God, Jeff was introduced to the Gospel message and accepted Jesus Christ as his personal Lord and Savior when he was thirty-four years old. Once the truth was revealed to him, Jeff quickly developed a sincere hunger and deep fascination for God's word, thus starting his journey to spiritual maturity.

Now, more than thirty years later, Jeff's done nothing special except strive to be consistent. He states, "I'm not formally trained in any denomination of the church, I haven't attended seminary, and I don't have a master's degree or doctorate in theology. I've just been consistent in reading my Bible, attending church on Sundays, and regularly enjoying Christian literature."

Through this consistency, and during a time of intense personal struggle, the Holy Spirit began to open Jeff's eyes to an inherent commonality among all Christians—the struggle with Spiritual Warfare. This study is a true testament to God's ability to save the lost, revive the dead in spirit, and use a common sinner to advance His Gospel. That may not be the background you'd expect for such a weighty topic, but it is the exact reason this book is so unique. Jeff is just like most Christians who will read this book.

Jeff lives in Knoxville, Tennessee. He is married to his wife and best friend, Delena Kay (DeeDee), and they continue to mentor believers of all ages in how to live a victorious Christian lifestyle.

www.ingramcontent.com/pod-product-compliance
Lightning Source LLC
Chambersburg PA
CBHW070900120626
46546CB00001B/72